I0084824

After The Second World War, in Soviet occupied Hungary, everyone waited for the dreaded "Knock" in the night. When it finally came to Balazs and his family, he knew he had to act.

Not since the discovery of Anne Frank's autobiography, has there been another first-hand account of a life spent under terror and an oppressive regime, so vivid and captivating as, REFUGEE.

The author's narrative in third person, shares painful and tender anecdotes that makes one laugh or moves one to tears. Balazs was barely thirteen by the time the violence of the Soviet Communist occupation led to the 1956 Hungarian Revolution. After it's bloody defeat, he set out alone to defect from behind the Iron Curtain to the USA.

REFUGEE

#M14543

REFU☭EE
#M14543

BALAZS SZABO

2017

REFUGEE #M14543

© 2017 Balazs Szabo
Refugee Press

All rights reserved. No part of this book may be reproduced in any form whatsoever, whether by graphic, visual, filming, microfilming, tape recording or any other means, without the written permission of the publisher, except in the case of brief passages embodied in critical reviews and articles).

Refugee Press
Hillsborough, North Carolina

www.balazsart.com

ISBN: 978-0-692-95136-1

Printed in the United States of America 2017

Cover painting and book design by Balazs Szabo

To my wonderful sons, Dominik and Sandor.

Acknowledgements

I am indebted to many special people for helping me with this book. I thank the Honorable Mayor Mary V. Mochary for her confidence in me and for her kind support; James Elledge for suffering to interpret my cover design into digital reality.

I am grateful to Mrs. Delores Cecchetti for her encouragement and friendship, and for typing much of the manuscript before it got to my editor's desk; Laszlo Papp for allowing me to use his photos of the Hungarian Revolution.

Special mention to my friend, Frau Dr. Livia Karwath of Vienna, Austria, a survivor of Auschwitz herself and an inspiration for me to tell my story.

Much gratitude to my editors – Mr. Robin Marshall and Mrs. Jane Struble.

To my adopted American family Ann Scott and Robert P. Morningstar-in whose memory I am dedicating this book. Their unconditional love and their generosity made it possible for me and my brother, Barna, to have the finest education in our adopted country. They were the kindest and most caring people I know and I am forever grateful.

A special thanks to The American Hungarian Foundation of New Brunswick, NJ for their archival assistance and overall support.

Foreword

IF YOU ARE reading these lines, most likely you are living in a free society, a democracy. If you are not so fortunate, then you live under a communist-run country or some other terrorist system and this book was smuggled to you via the black market because you have no rights, no freedoms and you are reading this in secret and fear.

This book is not for you; you already know. It is for those who don't know what kind of hopeless life you are living and wondering if the oppression will ever end in your lifetime.

My name is Balazs (pronounced Balage) and, as fate would have it, my spirit came to a physical existence in 1943 in Second World War-torn Hungary. I had no idea that my first 13 years of life would be spent in the snake pit of Soviet Communist occupation, in terror and constant fear without any hope of ever having the freedoms others enjoy on this planet. The Iron Curtain was a reality, not a myth, for me and my people.

I want you to imagine yourself accompanying me through this real journey, not in the privileged life where you were fortunate to have your beginnings, but in mine to see how you would fare.

I took this journey myself and fortunately found refuge in the United States, where I hope to spend the remainder of my life. Through my personal experiences, I have learned to admire and love the American people for their infinite generosity. They are not only giving within their own borders, but most of all for their willingness to give the ultimate sacrifices of their cherished sons and daughters for the freedom of others-during World War II, the Korean War, Vietnam, Bosnia, Kuwait and now in Iraq and Afghanistan.

Communism is still spreading as in Venezuela, remaining an imminent threat to the free world. Beware!

Despite my freedom, I still fear The Knock in the Night.

-Balazs Szabo

Introduction

HUNGARY BOASTS a fascinating history. Hungarians frequently emphasize with much pride their countless countrymen who have contributed much to the world. Renowned names such as Franz Liszt, Zoltan Kodaly, Bela Bartok, Sir George Solti, Eugene Ormandy, George Szell. But they are also proud of their forebears-the nomadic Magyars who are believed to have settled the land in 896 A.D. The Magyars were pagans but the country, through the efforts of St. Stephen (997-1038), crowned as the first king of Hungary, embraced Christianity and integrated his country in the European community.

Throughout its history, the nation had been beset with a series of internal revolutions and foreign invasions. The Mongol invasion of 1241-1242 was the most horrific of all. One third of the population perished. Followed by the Turks who invaded in 1526 and brought similar devastation. After the Turkish rule that lasted 150 years the Habsburgs of Austria inherited the Hungarian crown by default to rule and tax the Hungarians.

In the Twentieth Century the 113-day Red Terror in 1919 led by Bela Kun, a disciple of Lenin, tested its power. But Hungarians will long remember the second rising of the Red Star in the wake of the Russian occupation in 1945. Some of the horrors of the Russian invasion are partly reported in Stephen Sisa 's book, *Spirit of Hungary*. Sisa quoted the Swiss Legation to Budapest to show some of the atrocious behavior of Russian soldiers.

"During the siege of Budapest and also during the following fateful weeks, Russian troops looted the *city* freely. They entered practically every habitation, the very poorest as well as the richest. They took away anything they wanted, especially food, clothing and valuables. Furniture and larger objects of art that could not be taken away were frequently simply destroyed...After several weeks, looting stopped...but Russian soldiers often arrested passers-by and dug into their pockets and stole watches, cash and even papers of identity."

Most disturbing was the report on rape, a horrendous act Hungarian women were unable to escape. Many, in fact, preferred death to being subjected to this

3

despicable act. "Rape caused the greatest suffering. Violations were so general-from the age of 10 up to 70 years. Misery was increased by the sad fact that many of the Russian soldiers were ill [with syphilis] and medicines in Hungary were completely lacking."

The fate of the peasant population was no different, especially when the Red soldiers discovered stores of wine. "Once drunk, nothing was sacred to them. They raped half-grown girls and screaming grandmothers; they robbed the peasants of their animals and stole everything they could carry.

"But the most tragic losses were the thousands of men and boys whom the Soviet army seized for deportation to Russia. `Malinka robot' (a little work) was the slogan with which the male population was taken to Siberia, which became for most a land of no return. The numbers included thousands of Hungarian Jews who had managed to survive the Nazi occupation only to be seized by their `liberators.'"

A group of Muscovite Hungarians headed by Matyas Rakosi (1892-1972) came to complete the takeover. Ironically, Rakosi was born into a wealthy Jewish family and was a hard-core member of the Bela Kun regime. With his deceptive *ways,* he reassured Hungarians of his support for a democratic and independent Hungary and with-out Soviet interference in Hungary's internal affairs. All lies, naturally. Rakosi and his cohorts lost the national elections set in November 1945. Their Communist-Socialist ticket lost to the Small Landholders, an agrarian party.

Not about to accept defeat, Rakosi began retaliating against the winning party using coercion and false accusation. His rule was characterized by police terror, with that knock in the night no one can prepare for petrifying everyone. His oppressive rule finally ended in 1953; Imre Nagy was appointed premier. Unlike Rakosi, Nagy had Hungarian affinity and wanted the abolition of the one-party system and withdrawal of Soviet troops. Demonstrators looked to him during the 1956 revolution: "Imre to the government." He was later illegally executed for his part in the revolution.

For decades, Hungary was a one-party state and a Soviet satellite dominated by the Hungarian Socialist (Communist) Workers' Party.

The Hungarian Revolution, which started as a peaceful demonstration, began October 23, 1956, with young students who wanted to be heard on their

16-points demands. (My book describes in detail these fateful days. My family and I were eyewitnesses to the massacre at the Parliament Square. My father was scheduled to recite Petofi Sandor's 1848 poem of freedom written at the time of the defeated Hungarian Revolution against the oppressive Austrian Monarchy.) After the Hungary Revolution of 1956 was abandoned by the West, the overwhelming Soviet force annihilated the resistance.

Soviet presence in Hungary ended in 1991 when all the Soviet troops left-pillaging and raping as before.

After being subjugated and repressed for decades by Mongols, Turks, Romanians, Austrians, Germans and the Soviets, and having its land dismembered by the Treaty of Trianon of 1920 then again in the Second World War at Yalta by the Allies, reducing its size to two-thirds, Hungary has recovered and is standing tall and proud. Today, it is a free, independent nation, and in 2004 became a member of the European Union (EU).

Hungarians are a spirited, resilient people who have endured the tyranny of communism without it killing their spirit. Hungary's more than 10 million people are now enjoying a multi-party political system, with free elections and rights to free speech, free press, free worship. According to recent statistics, some 67.5 percent are Catholics, 20 percent Calvinists, 5 percent Lutherans, 5 percent unaffiliated. Twenty percent live in the capital *city* of Budapest; 35 percent in other cities and towns; 45 percent in 2,892 villages.

More information on the history of Hungary can be found in *The Spirit of Hungary* by Stephen Sisa (Vista Books, Morristown, New Jersey, third edition, 1995). I credit the book for the historical facts mentioned in *Refugee # M14543.*

To comment about the book, e-mail author Balazs Szabo at **balazsart@yahoo.com;** visit the web site for more related photos and additional information about the author: **www.balazsart.com**

ONE

THE LAST RUN

HE LAY in the powdery snow, recovering from his fall, as he examined his body for glass cuts. The coal-miner had catapulted him clear through the train's closed window, and he was amazed to discover that the only injury he seemed to have received was a bump on his forehead. Balazs was only a few hundred yards from his wounded friend, the train. As the rattle of deafening machine-gun fire filled the air, he lay low, focusing on the scene. Only a few dark, shadowy figures ran from the wreckage toward him, as people bailed out and scattered in all directions.

Several of the cars were turned over or blown off the tracks. The powerful engine was somewhat dismembered and partially derailed – riddled with bullet holes releasing steam everywhere, like blood spouting from a wounded bull.

The wheels were still turning slowly – some lifted and suspended in air, others digging into the frozen ground, as the horizontal steel bar kept the motion going in some mindless reflex. The squeaking and grinding of the damaged moving parts called out to him painfully. He felt a great desire to return, not abandon it in its moment of need. He remembered with guilt the happy times they had spent together: the time the train had brought him to his grandparents' home in Fuzfo, the countless free rides about the lake, the circus trip. Balazs felt he took its faithful presence for granted. Now he watched it dying, alone and abandoned by its ungrateful and cowardly friend. But what could he do?

Russian soldiers were swarming everywhere, searching the wreckage and executing those they found alive with spurts of gunfire. They were also shooting blindly into the dark, with hopes of hitting the fleeing. He did not dare move; he lay like a hare in the brush, one with the ground, desperate not to be flushed out until it became absolutely necessary.

Suddenly, there was a bright flash of light, and a big explosion rocked the earth and the sky, followed by deadly silence and darkness. The train and all its parts blended into nothingness.

Stunned, he stared blindly into the blackness, and it was not until the tanks' searchlights began to sweep the terrain that he regained his vision.

All had evaporated in a split second before his eyes. It seemed that the last deafening explosion and flash of light took what remained of his past – the train and his childhood.

The illuminated landscape, however, brought him back to the present in an instant. Several shapes began to move near him on the white frost. He heard the muffled voices of some kids as they crawled by. Getting his courage up, he called quietly to them. "Hey, guys. Are you from the train, too?"

"Yeah," a voice came back softly. "What are you doing sitting there? Are you wounded?"

"No, I just don't know what to do."

"What do you mean, moron? Go toward the border, naturally," said a rather snotty voice with the typical jargon of the tough Csepel Island street kids.

"Okay, smart guy, if you know so well, why don't you point the way?"

"All right, kid, just fall in line. We have some idea. This here is Laci. (Latsi) I am Joska. (Yoshka) I don't know the name of the other three."

Joska was a rough-looking, well-built kid of sixteen. It was obvious to Balazs that he was working class. He had unkempt, long hair, and the smell of a wet fox.

"And this here is my brother," Joska said, brandishing a heavy, black revolver in Balazs' face, who was impressed. He had wanted a gun at the outset of the revolution, but his father would hear none of it.

Laci explained, "Joska was fighting in Budapest and Csepel, you know, and so was everybody in his family. His brother and sister were shot off the roof of the factory during the invasion. Later, he watched his father being captured with a bunch of other freedom fighters as they ran from a burning building, then executed. He was out of ammunition by that time rendering him helpless. By then, he had killed lots of those buggers! Look! Joska's pocket is full of red stars from their jackets."

Laci dipped deep into Joska's pocket and proudly produced the familiar red enamel stars that the Russian soldiers wore on their lapels and fur hats.

"All right, let's stop the social bull and move on before they catch up with us," Joska ordered. "See in front of you. The border is far beyond the flashes of light on the horizon. The flashes are the flares that the Russians and the border guards are shooting into the air to see where you are. There is no arrest here—you just get shot when they spot you. Every forty meters or so, there will be a tower at least eight meters high. The machine guns are mounted there and manned by guards. The Russians stay near them for self-defense, since lots of Hungarians come with arms. Damn it, we'd have a lot better chance with some snow fall."

As they looked up, to their surprise, they saw flakes descending a little thicker and larger. They decided to make a run for it, and sprinted across the frozen soil. A round of machine-gun fire came from close behind them, and, as Balazs turned to his side, he saw a mass of people running through the low brambles not far off. He heard another round of gunfire and saw several of the dark figures fall. He could hear screaming, shouting, commotion, but it was too dark to see clearly. He ran in mad fear now, sensing danger approaching from close behind him. He heard excited shouts in Russian, followed by the sound of rounds overlapping each other.

In front of him, Joska hit the ground, falling face first, groaning and holding his leg. "I've been hit. Oh, I've been hit!" Panic-stricken, Balazs and the others who were lagging behind the fast, strong runner dove to the ground next to him. "God Joska, where did they get you; where?" Joska looked up from the ground with a large, grin on his face, laughing at the little frightened faces around him. "You guys! I was just kidding. I was wondering when you were gonna catch up with me."

"Geez! Joska, that was stupid. This is no time to joke, " said Balazs. "What the hell were we to do if you really got wounded?"

"Well, if that happens, I want you to finish me off with this here gun, 'cuz I am not gonna fall to a Ruszki! You got that? All right, now listen. I've got something to do. As we ran, I saw only one bloody Ruszki behind us, but he hasn't spotted us yet. I think he is the one that shot at that group on our right."

As he said that, the words froze in his mouth. Three Russian soldiers towered over them, appearing out of thin air. Their machine guns were pointing into the boys' faces. They were paralyzed with fear, expecting the spray of bullets through their bodies. Balazs could not believe he had gotten this far, only to be shot now.

One of the soldiers broke the silence, speaking in Russian. "All right, you little rats, what you gonna give us if we let you go?"

They could not believe their ears. Let them go? My God, thought Balazs, do they really mean that? Lying scum, they'll probably just rob us and shoot us afterwards, he thought. But the kids next to him were already reaching into their pockets, producing cash, pocketknives and other personal treasures.

Balazs patted his jacket. He still had the two aluminum flasks filled with palinka in his inner wool pockets; the ones he had exchanged for his bike.

Knowing how much Russians valued watches and alcohol, he handed the flasks over to the soldiers. He noticed in the glow of the flares that the left arm of one of the soldiers was already covered with countless watches. He wondered what fate had befallen the previous owners.

The Russian grabbed the flasks out of his hand and laughed approvingly as he guessed its contents. He grunted over to the other two, "Now this is something worthwhile!" As the others stuffed the loot into their pockets, this one took the twist cap off the flask and took a deep swig. The Hungarian plum brandy was not like anything he had tasted in all his cheap, vodka-drinking years. The first swallow hit him so hard that he nearly choked on it. The other two laughed at him and took long hits of their own.

This drinking party on the killing field was out of place and surreal to Balazs, but the soldiers seemed very content with the loot from the kids, and were satisfied with their haul.

"Davay! Davay!" they growled, a rude way of saying, "Scram."

The kids couldn't believe their ears. Impossible, they thought. They kept on turning back to see if the Russians intended to shoot them from behind. But no! The three silhouettes slowly blended into the darkness, as they returned in the direction of the train.

"Where is Joska?" Balazs asked, suddenly noticing the older boy was missing. No one knew. They turned every which way looking for him, but he was nowhere to be found. Laci exclaimed, "Jesus Christ, while we were digging into our pockets to give all we had to these bastards, all I was thinking of was Joska's gun in his pocket, and what if they find it!"

In the midst of the longer rattle of machine-gun fire, they suddenly heard three solitary gunshots. Bam. Bam. Bam. Stunned, they waited, wondering if Joska would return. Soon, they saw a person running towards them from the direction of the train, wet, covered with slimy blood, grinning and breathless. It was he. "Joska, where the hell have you been?" "What happened?" "Why did you vanish?" they babbled at him.

"One question at a time, fellas," he pleaded, with obvious satisfaction on his face. "I couldn't let you little morons give everything to those SOB's. Especially when I saw Balazs hand them the booze. Hey, you've been holding out on us! Where did you get that stuff?"

"Never mind that," said Balazs. "Tell us what happened!"

"Well, nothing, I stole away while they were all busy with the booze tasting, worried they'd discover my gun. I was waiting for them back by the train—figuring they were the dirt from the tanks. No one was around and by the time they approached they were pretty happy from the good stuff. I hid in one of the ditches and, when they came in close enough, I just pumped them one fat bullet each. They went down like sacks. I got one for my sister, one for my brother and one for my dad. Boy, it felt good!"

He reached into his pockets and pulled out bundles of money, watches and one of the flasks with most of the palinka still in it. "We might need this if we get through the border!" The kids stuffed everything quickly back into their pockets, not bothering to divide it fairly. There was more than what they had given, since it came from other victims, too.

They each took a swig of the palinka. This potent drink burned their insides on the way down, comfortingly warming them on this freezing night.

"Now let's get going before we are caught again and get shot right here on the spot," said Joska. They turned in the direction of the flashing lights of the flares and towards the rapid machine-gun fire, which was getting louder and more constant. It was like running into the mouth of hell, running toward danger, instead of away from it. It was against all logic and, to Balazs; it began to look like a futile effort.

As they ran closer and closer, toward the ever more visible towers, the smoke from the guns began to veil everything. Yet, through the repeated flashes of the flares, they could make out thousands of people everywhere, running toward what looked like certain death. As they advanced, they fell into ditches freshly created by landmines that had been stepped on by unsuspecting feet. Dead bodies were scattered in every direction. Adults, children of all ages, fresh and old, blue frozen limbs without bodies, and bodies without limbs or heads littered the open field.

Almost somersaulting, Balazs fell deep into a hole, biting deep into his tongue in the process. As he tasted the blood, he noticed he had, bizarrely, landed on a small child's washbasin and other belongings spilled from the abandoned trunk of an earlier refugee family. It was ridiculous what people would drag with them at such times, he thought, gathering himself for the next dash.

The closer they came to the towers, the more frequently they had to dive on the ground to avoid the thick spray of machine-gun fire. The bullets incessantly pierced the air everywhere around them. The night was filled with smoke and the choking stench of spent gunpowder.

The beams of light from the towers swept the thick veil of smoke as the red and blue flares lit the entire landscape from above.

There was no wind, and the smoke was trapped low, making it harder to see, despite the constant searchlights and flares. Nevertheless, the guards, who shot blindly into this haze, in hopes of killing someone, had ample ammunition to waste, and the rattle of the guns went on uninterrupted.

There were groups of people everywhere, facing the horror of the whistling bullets. "If we can just make it through those towers," was everyone's pressing thought. They were all on their own, and no one looked to others for assistance. This was the last run!

This is what Balazs was waiting for too. Death was everywhere. There was no turning back, only the road ahead toward death or freedom. Yet that slight chance of survival, the one in a thousand, was in the heart of each and every one. Maybe I will be the one to make it to freedom! If not, I'll just die here and give up the fight. I will never return to the terror of the Russians and communism.

Joska, up front of the boys, now scattered and not together in a group any longer, fell again. Some noticed, but kept running on, no longer involved and feeling responsible for the fate of others.

Balazs, too, ran past Joska's body, thinking to himself, "Not this stupid joker again! What a jerk." But then he thought he might really be hit, because he went down so quietly. He returned quickly and saw Joska, lying in the same spot, in the same twisted position as when he had passed him.

"Joska, you're hit!" Balazs yelled as he dove to the ground next to him. It was soaked with blood all around Joska. He was lying with one arm under his body, the other thrown across his face. When he didn't respond, Balazs lifted Joska's arm, but withdrew horrified at the sight and rolled back away from the body. Joska's throat had been shot clear through, severing it from his head. It looked like the necks of the chickens his grandfather, Eugene, cut through, still attached by a loose flap of skin. In the clear light of a new barrage of flares, he could see the pipes protruding from his neck with blood spurting, bubbling out of Joska with every beat of his still pumping heart. The older boy's legs began to kick and his body jerked, shaking in that horrible death rattle with which Balazs became familiar.

He bolted from the scene with terrific speed, heading straight toward the towers. The hate and anger that filled him made him feel invincible. He felt he could run to the towers, climb the supports and tear the hearts out of every one of those murdering creeps. He would run and kill and kill, until they were all dead, until every Russian and evil person that hurt an innocent being was dead in this sick, evil world.

The lights blinded him as he ran in a numb, automatic motion between the gates of Hell with Cerberus, the three-headed hound, biting at his heels. Thousands became visible everywhere, running in front, in back and beside him, – falling in death or with screams of pain from wounds.

Nothing would stop him now, – he was determined to continue running. A memory flashed through his subconscious as he remembered the man he saw shot at the Parliament. The man's leg was separated from his body by machine-gun fire. The severed leg continued in a running motion, as if it wanted to catch up with its owner.

He neither had an idea of time or distance, nor was he aware of the numb sensation in his feet and hands from the frost. The sound of his breathing became amplified. Then there was silence as he fell exhausted to the ground. The towers were far behind him. The screams were almost inaudible, yet the flares appeared playfully dancing behind the curtain of smoke. If one were ignorant of the cruelty being played out there, one might have thought children were at a fairground, playing and screaming with delight. With extreme exhaustion and spent energy, he vomited. Balazs laid there in utter abandon and it was a while before he stirred. Finally, he sat up and washed his face in a patch of snow. He was uncertain where he was. In the confusion of the last run, he feared he may have become disoriented and ran back the wrong way. None of the other boys were anywhere to be seen.

He could, equally, be in No Man's Land, the parcel of neutral land sandwiched between the two countries' borders. If someone escaped into that area, the international rules were that no guard was allowed to shoot, but everyone knew that the communist guards and the Russians broke that rule.

Before he realized it, he was up and running again, this time, toward that strange and inviting soft ribbon of blue light in the horizon. It looked like an aurora, suspended above the white frozen land as far as the eye could see.

He slowed down and waited, then stopped altogether. All about him the landscape began to come alive with shadowy figures. The dark forms appeared from everywhere, calling out to one another in Hungarian, searching for loved ones lost in the run. Some received joyful responses; others were quiet with grief after discovering the inevitable reality of their loss. Nonetheless, it seemed that everyone was instinctively attracted to the blue lights, like so many moths drawn to a porch light.

Hesitantly, in silence, groups drew in tight formations to march together for a kilometer or so. Balazs joined a group of adults. They arrived at the edge of a quaint village aglow with fluorescent streetlights, the likes of which they had never seen in Hungary under communism.

The frightened, exhausted group stood for a while simply staring. Slowly with caution they approached a small street sign; someone read aloud for everyone to hear the name of the street in German! A confirmation to all that they had reached freedom! They were free! They had crossed the Iron Curtain! Stranger embraced stranger. Happy for each other, yet sad for those left behind or fallen.

TWO

THE TRAIN

HIS EYES SQUINTING tightly against the smoke-filled wind, Balazs strained forward to see the winding tracks come slithering toward the train. At the bends, it seemed that the steam engine ran away from the wagons, and he would catch the sparks and soot-filled steam right in his face. He wiped it off and turned his head down wind to avoid another onslaught. His destination was the northernmost point of Hungary's largest lake, Balaton. It ran a narrow stretch of 120 kilometers from east to west, with the northern tip pointing toward Budapest.

Hungary, after the Trianon agreement following World War I, and its division by the Allies after World War II, was shaped like a kidney bean on its back, a quarter of its original size, and sliced by two great rivers. It is located in the central and eastern part of Europe, flanked by Slavic nations on almost all sides, with the "Latin" Romanians on the south, and the Germanic Austrians to the west.

Since the Russian occupation of 1945 – the result of the 1943 Yalta Conference, where the map of Europe was divided by the would-be victorious Allied nations, – Hungary had formally been given to the Soviet Union, to be "administered" for a term of eight years, after which it was to govern itself freely. The Russians secured borders, – surrounding them by minefields, electric fences and miles of barbed wire. At every quarter kilometer or less, there were towers with machine guns and armed soldiers scanning the horizon to keep out the "Western Imperialists."

The River Danube (or Duna in Hungarian) splits the country down the center, east and west. The river Tisza cuts the right half in a diagonal, from north to south. The western half, where Lake Balaton is located, has fertile hills and woods. The eastern side is flat, and, at its center, lays the Hungarian prairie, the Hortobagy, famous for its exotic cattle, horses and sheep, all razed under the open skies. This has resulted in a natural selection of the fittest, given the climate extremes of hot summers and bitter cold winters.

The lake, situated in the more moderate climate of the western side, is favored for recreation by the city dwellers. The region surrounding it is a fertile land of volcanic origin, with red dirt glowing from beneath the rich, green growth. Balaton is laced with beautiful vineyards around its hilly shores and hot geyser spas. The lake itself is rich with freshwater fish, and it is not uncommon for fishermen to catch 100 kilo carp or catfish, both favorite delicacies of Hungarians. In the ancient woods of Badacsony, a volcanically created mountain plateau, roam thousands of elk, deer and wild boar.

Balazs, of course, knew none of this then, nor how much fun he would have in the discoveries that awaited him. Now, he simply stood as tall as he could on the worn, cracked-leather seat, holding the rusty metal rim on the grimy, filthy train window. The wagon smelled of smoke and urine, a combination that seemed to penetrate body and soul. As everything in the public domain then, the train had been neglected since the communist takeover. The piercing, chilled wind of the early spring burned his cheeks and temples, and gave him cramps like those caused from fast-consumed ice creams. The greenish-brown landscape of the season only added to the post-war scars of the Hungarian countryside.

The train rushed by peasants' burned-out and bombed dwellings. Scorched woods littered with the debris of war, rusting tanks and vehicles of every kind disrupted the natural landscape. The helmets of dead Russian, Hungarian and German soldiers were scattered everywhere.

Not comprehending all this with his child's mind, the passing landscape offered him pure excitement and delight.

The constant clanking and rocking had a mesmerizing effect on him and his attractive young mother, who sat beside him in distant awareness. As ever, she was well dressed, despite the poverty of the times in Soviet-occupied Hungary. Her graceful, narrowly shaped hands sported fresh, bright-red American nail polish acquired on the black market for hefty sums. Her refined figure revealed her higher birth and genteel upbringing. She was the daughter of a ministry advisor and attorney to a prewar Catholic diocese, and the wife of the most celebrated young classical actor of the times. The affluence was swept away by the war; now her years at Sacre-Coure were just a memory. The tumult of life's painful memories was also a muddle of confusion in her head, with the final blow of her divorce proceedings.

With the wind and a sound of clanking metal, the cabin door flung open. The draft of the momentary compression blew in the passenger serviceman. He had greasy hair and wore a shiny black uniform, baggy at the seat bottoms from years of wear. The dirty, half sawed-off wooden crate, strapped with leather to his bony shoulders next to his deeply grooved dirty neck, was filled with cheap postwar candies.

Almost incoherently, like a sheep, he bleated out the names of the items for sale. The young woman signaled to him, with that typically flippant gesture rich people tend to use when summoning someone of lower birth, and purchased a chocolate-covered wafer for the boy. This was offered by dirty hands and without a wrapper. Many items such as paper were in great shortage and now a luxury after the war. Toilet paper, for example, was unheard of.

Balazs received the candy with polite thanks and, within moments, had consumed it.

He was a thin boy, not yet four, with a bone structure reminiscent of his mother's, having no resemblance to his stout, monumental father. The delicate, small features of his face were a mix of both parents, but without his father's protruding jaw. His father's eyes were sky blue under an evenly wavy chestnut brown hair.

Balazs' hair was sandy blond, with streaks of reddish brown. His eyes were almost yellow-green. His mother's were a darker, angry green, framed by blonde hair. Her firstborn son, Barna, a year older, was of heavier bone structure, blond, blue-eyed, with a stronger jawbone more like his father's. His lips, however, were full like his mother's, whereas Balazs' were thinner and less pronounced.

Wife and husband had fought for the custody of the firstborn, seemingly not interested in the younger child. Eventually, the courts awarded one to each parent: Barna got his father, Balazs his mother.

Balazs turned from the window. His mother met his curiously restless eyes: she thought this was, perhaps, the look of war children, defiant of fear, not childish at all. The look disturbed her, so she averted her gaze, pretending to take an interest in the swift passing of the landscape.

For some unknown reason, he made her feel uncomfortable. She lit a cigarette inhaling deeply, relieved at the thought of leaving him with her parents. She felt him staring still, as was his habit, almost insolently, as dogs do when they sense one's fear. He would not let go, and the time seemed to stop for her. She wondered how much longer it would take to arrive at their final destination.

Her parents, in their sixties, had escaped deportation from Budapest by the simple expediency of leaving before the authorities of the new Soviet regime could ship them out with the rest of the intelligentsia. The state had confiscated their elegant Budapest home and all its belongings, but allowed them to take refuge in part of their former summer villa, overlooking Lake Balaton. (All homes with six or more rooms fell under a government confiscation quota.)

The old couple was waiting at the small train station, sitting close by each other on the hard, bright red, wooden bench facing the tracks. The parallel silver lines of the rail divided the sea of green reeds and the glistening surface of Lake Balaton from the land. The train would come from the east, the direction the old pair had arrived from some 30 years ago for the first time.

Back then, there wasn't much of a town here. Much of it was swampy land with thousands of wildly growing, giant weeping willow trees. In ancient times this land was tended by the early Avars, then the Sumerians followed by the Romans, Huns and finally the Magyars. The Hungarians, – all left it rich with thousands of years of buried artifacts.

Eugene had been assigned by the old regime to deal with the parceling of three counties and developing the land to create a resort town.

Mountains of dirt had to be moved and the swamp had to be drained, all paid for by private investors. Within a few years, much was accomplished. Valuable ancient artifacts in gold, silver and gem-laden weaponry were discovered on Eugene's lot. He built his villa on top of a hill. At the corner of it he had all the bones from the digs reverently re-buried, then covered it with red volcanic rocks with a stone cross atop. He had kept one pair of golden stirrups in his uncontrollable fascination; the rest were donated to the nearby museum in the city of Veszprem.

The villa, which Eugene had designed, had two towers. The larger contained living quarters, and the smaller one at the other end of the roof with a small lookout. This tower had a sand floor with three permanently open slits for windows, facing the lake. It was of tastefully mixed styles – Germanic and Mediterranean influences, with cream-colored stucco exterior and red slate roofing. Arched windows graced the glass-enclosed veranda. The remaining windows for the house were square with Hungarian folk-style shutters.

The house was furnished completely in the Hungarian high-peasant style. The heavy wooden chairs were fitted without nails and were hand painted with the customary Hungarian floral motifs used in traditional embroideries. In the back panels of the chairs, a tulip or a heart had been cut through. The painted wood-paneled walls and ceilings were completed at great expense by the finest artisans of the region. Slowly, the town attracted not only the vacationers, but farmers as well.

Because the willows were preserved, and more were planted along the train tracks on the lakeside, the town came to be known as Balatonfuzfo, meaning Balaton Willowhead. These were the prosperous prewar times for Hungary, and Eugene was successful in his work. He was the youngest of five children from northern Hungary in Nagyszombat (now Tvarna, in Slovakia), whose father had abandoned his young mother and the children. His mother, through her earnings as a seamstress, raised the two boys and three girls alone. The oldest boy became a priest; the oldest girl worked at the post office and later married the postmaster. The two younger girls never married and lived to ripe old ages. Eugene was a very talented artist, but knowing he would never have an easy life pursuing art, left home for Budapest's better work opportunities and higher education. He attended the Budapest University of Law and Philosophy, where he met his wife, Paula Knapp. Somehow, he ended up spending more time sitting in lectures on Hungarian studies than law.

Paula was from an upper-crust family. After her wealthy father had died in a riding accident, her mother had married the manager of a major hospital in Budapest. She had a fine upbringing. She spoke German, French, Latin, a little Greek and played the piano beautifully.

A striking beauty, she was petite, outgoing and full of pep. Her bright, pale-blue eyes shone of intelligence and integrity. She was an independent thinker and spiritual, without being dogmatic. She raised her family of two boys and a girl with the finest intellectual and spiritual guidance possible.

As the town grew, Eugene encouraged his friends to invest their wealth into building a church for the residents. Only the stone walls remained of the original ancient chapel, which had been destroyed by the invading Turks hundreds of years ago. The new church was built out of white granite, in a very clean modest design, close to the older ruins. The arched windows featured the stained-glass portraits of saints. The names of families who donated money for the project were displayed below the images. Eugene, who had given cash as well as leading the project, was given a special place of honor: the first window at the right facing the altar, where his daughter, Balazs' mother, was portrayed at age 16 with an exact likeness of her beauty as St. Hedviga, her namesake. The extraordinary artistry of the stained-glass master pleased everyone.

Those times seemed long ago now, almost a dream. Paula and Eugene sat by each other quietly, beaten and bewildered by the events of their lives. Although the old man had been against his daughter marrying the actor ("a clown," as he referred to him), he could not have guessed that things would turn out this way. He was angry and upset. He could not understand the big fuss over everyone's concern with winning the first born child in the custody fight. It seemed to him that everything had been destroyed by the war, and people had lost what little remaining common sense they held. The country fell to the Communists, people were persecuted everywhere, deportations were en masse, his oldest son had been jailed and tortured, and now his daughter was divorcing. To make things still more intolerable, the Communists denied the old couple their hard-earned pension.

****

The train turned into the sharp bend, its whistle blowing twice sharply. Paula and Eugene felt the rumble of the ground beneath them. The stationmaster, in his black uniform, walked across the red cinder gravel and, each time his weight came down, the gravel made a pleasant crackling sound beneath his shoes. As the locomotive slowed to his command, he disappeared into clouds of snow-white steam, although, comically, his red flag continued visibly flailing above it in the clear air.

The young woman called out to her parents from the window as the train came to a long, screeching halt. Suddenly she could not see them as the tears overwhelmed her. She felt overjoyed. It was always a comfort to be with them, and especially now.

Eugene helped them off the stairs with their luggage and kissed the boy's cheeks warmly while petting the top of his head. Paula held her daughter tightly with that silent understanding only a mother is able to communicate. Eugene took Balazs' hand and together they went up the stairs behind the station, and through a small park facing the elementary school. His grandfather's hand was gentle and smooth; his nails well kept and clean. His voice, mellow and warm, revealed a very pleasant and soothing nature. Although the boy could not remember ever meeting his grandfather, he felt quite comfortable with him and responded with enthusiasm to his questions regarding the train ride.

There was something very special about the train, and Balazs was certain that Eugene could answer all his questions about the workings of the steam engine.

They arrived at the top of the hill. When they turned to wait for the rest of the family they saw the train speed along the bend and disappear around the corner toward the next resort town. Suddenly, Balazs felt a special yearning to see the train again. Eugene noticed this, and reassured the boy that he would be able to see every train that passed by from the villa.

They arrived at the rusty iron-gate of the villa, a light-rust red, with straight diagonal designs and baroque curves. A narrow and steep gravel road led up to a crossing. A smaller path from there led to a mud-brick peasant hut (used as maids' quarters before the war), with a well in its small courtyard. The main gravel path led to a Swiss-style, square-shaped lattice gazebo. There was an immaculately planted flower-bedecked yard at the back. A large area, cleared and covered with white gravel, had assorted pines sporting sculptured cones, which offered wonderful refuge to a variety of birdlife.

At the far end of this plateau, occupied by the house and the front yard, stood a peculiar stone fountain (now out of service). It had a cherub-like figure, half-fish, half-boy, crawling up around a large half-shell. This was held by a similar creature, from the bottom, which, when working, spouted water upwards, so the water fell back into the shell. The courtyard was so well elevated that, when the trees were bare in the winter, one could easily see the vast lake below.

They took the four steps to enter the house through the veranda, which had wide-arched windows made of white, iron frames. The center wings were open, allowing the fresh spring air to enter. There was a lot of furniture and clutter, belongings saved from the other rooms of the house, now occupied by government-assigned tenants.

A large, baroque armoire blocked the entrance to the original main dining room, to give the old couple some privacy. It held their clothing and the large drawers were crammed with wrinkled apples preserved from last fall, walnuts, hazelnuts and almonds.

Along the wall, under the open windows, were three large peasant grapevine baskets filled with straw. Three fat Rhode Island Reds each spread their heat-filled wings gently over more than a dozen eggs in anticipation of hatching. One of the hens, however, was in for a big surprise: Eugene had put fertilized duck eggs under her. In months past, the ducks, being clumsy and heavy, broke many of their own eggs and hatched fewer than half. The hens seemed to be more careful mothers.

Now Eugene opened the two tall wings of the doors entering the bedroom – and the only living space left them, in addition to one tiny room, about 1.5-by-3 meters. Originally built as a pantry, it was now being used for their wood and butane gas stove. This was a luxury, since many households still used wood stoves for the preparation of foods. The authorities missed this during confiscation of goods.

Next to this was a three-legged stool with a white enamel lavoire or washbasin on top, and a water pail with homemade dark soap (prepared from pig's lard mixed with lye). Therefore, this was the bathroom and the kitchen. To bathe, one fetched the water from the well, then heated it before proceeding to wash body parts from top to bottom—reserving the cleanest water for the face first and doing the feet last. This helped conserve water and made for fewer trips to the well which, in bad weather, was unpleasant and something to avoid.

The French flush toilet went with the tenants' part of the house. This left the old couple to build an outhouse, which was dangerously close to the well. When the weather was bad or it was too dark to go out, they used the so-called "bili." This was quite a disgusting Roman invention of 3,000 years ago. One would relieve oneself into this porcelain or tin enamel pot with a handle, then post it under the bed, where it sat all night, filling the room with a stifling stench.

The bedroom, also known as the "everything room," held a two meter-high porcelain wood-burning stove with an iron door. Two other large armoires – one an elegant Biedermeier piece, the other a functional dark wood – faced each other. There was a double bed in the center against the facing wall, with attractive carved bedposts. On either side of the bed was a night table with drawers and two lovely antique, German bronze figurines of nude Hermes holding the post.

A card table with three chairs was pushed against the foot of the bedpost, and served as the dining area. In the remaining space a small bed was pushed against the wall with hardly a pathway between the two beds.

When Jadda (pronounced Yadda) came to visit, she slept with Balazs on the small bed.

For the few remaining days of their daughter's stay, the couple made their rounds of elderly friends who lived in similar circumstances – sharing in the events and the family sagas. The only source of news about deportations and the disappearances of relatives was through the people's grapevine. The authorities would not release any information regarding deported, jailed or tortured citizens. So the old couple and their friends discreetly discussed the many political events. News from the West came only by way of Radio Free Europe, aired by American and European Allied stations and heavily jammed by the Communists. But the short-wave radios were highly prized and in great demand on the black market. Eugene owned a fine radio from the famous Hungarian manufacturer, Orion. It was a formidable instrument, with a beautiful wood-finished casing. When turned on, one had to wait for the bulbs to heat up. In its upper center was a Cyclops-like eye, a small glass bubble. Once heated to the proper temperature, the radio's "eye" glowed a beautiful green.

The sound would come and go in waves, inaudible for much of the time, but it came from the free world, shut off by the so-called Iron Curtain. Each forbidden word caught on the airwaves was cherished and put together like a puzzle. Severe beatings, long jail sentences and deportations to unknown places without trial were the punishments that awaited anyone caught listening to the station.

****

Eugene enjoyed Balazs' company over the next couple of days, taking pleasure in his interest in flowers, animals, birds and all that fascinated a child reared in the city. Having grown up in the midst of the Second World War and moving from one dark bunker into another to escape the falling bombs, surrounded by machine-gun fire, smoke and screams of the panicked population, Balazs found magic in nature's splendor.

For Jadda, the few days spent with Eugene and Paula were filled with the warmth and comforts of parental love. She felt stronger and ready to face the chaos awaiting her in Budapest—the fight in court for her son, Barna.

THREE

THE HATCHLING

SHE HAD POSTPONED telling Balazs that she was to leave him behind until the last moment. Jadda offered some vague and shallow comforting words, in the hope that her mother would step in and help her out of the situation, something both parents duly did, without being asked.

His grandfather tried to distract him with things of interest, but the panic hit. Balazs realized that he was to be abandoned.

Although he had enjoyed the days spent with his grandparents, he was sure this was not where he wanted to stay. Frightened, he held tightly onto his mother's dress, insisting on going back with her. She tried to reason with him, explaining that it was temporary and that it was better for him to be here. He would have none of it. His grandfather had to tear him away from his mother, who took a toothbrush out of her pocketbook, left it on the table and said, "Now be a good little boy, don't forget to brush your teeth."

As she stepped outside, she felt a definite relief, putting distance between herself and the house on her way to the train station. Her steps began to quicken as her mind raced toward the coming events in the city.

Balazs was outraged at being overpowered. He cried and screamed in protest. He withdrew to the corner of the room and decided to have nothing to do with the old couple. At every loving approach, he would yell at them or cry again. Hours passed and dinnertime came. His stomach ached from hunger and crying, but he was going to win. However, as the couple was well practiced in dealing with children, now let him be and waited patiently. It was now getting dark and Paula lit the kerosene lamps, which emitted a gentle, not disagreeable scent that was familiar to him from all the blackouts of the war, and the smell of bunkers. Eugene and Paula sat down to dinner, with an extra setting waiting for him. He was desperate to eat, but didn't give in. After dinner, Eugene went to the veranda, and moments later, returned with an egg in hand. He placed a small towel in front of Balazs on the floor and placed the egg on it, gently.

He then joined Paula at the little table and they began playing cards. Balazs had no idea what that was about. If his grandfather thought that he was going to eat that egg, he was mistaken!

As he decided to look away, pretending he was not even interested, the egg moved. It actually moved by itself and rolled a bit. Balazs' heart jumped. A second later it moved again, but this time he thought he heard a tiny sound. Minutes passed and there was not another stir. He forgot his anger, not to mention his hunger.

He was fully concentrating on that egg, waiting in anticipation. He reached out and pushed the egg tenderly with his fingertips. It moved once more, and a small crack appeared at the pointed end. Suddenly, the tip of a little twig-like thing protruded. His first reaction was to run to his grandparents. He had no idea what was happening. He was frightened, but before he had a chance to act, the egg came totally alive.

A small, wet little head pushed through the opening that it had created, with the little feet folded right by its yellow beak. It lay with its head on the towel panting from the strain and the effort of birth.

With a clearly audible peep, it pushed again to kick off a large area of the shell, revealing a wet and messy-looking creature. Balazs was fascinated and unable to contain himself by the miracle which was unfolding before him.

He laughed out loud with delight and reached out for the little chick, placing it in his hand, still with some of its shell attached. He held it under his chin and blew his warm breath on it instinctively.

Maybe he felt a kinship with it, a bond of some kind. A surge of unfamiliar love engulfed him. Eugene and Paula were quietly watching. The couple knew that this moment was special in bonding them with Balazs. The thought of one-day losing him would bring great pain.

FOUR

A NEW LIFE

NATURE'S CONFETTI of fragrant, white cherry blossom flurries hovered in snow-like gusts. Plum, almond, hazelnut and pear blossoms were all bursting from their pinkish white buds, making his head swirl. Nature, however, immersed in its rebirth, took no notice of the human suffering in its womb. It went on as it had done for millions of years, undisturbed, uncaring, without the slightest compassion.

For Eugene's three hectares filled with many fruit trees and flowers, pollination was no problem. At the end of the lot, past the wine grove, was the servants' hut, with its reed roof housing thousands of wild bees. When Balazs was older, he would carefully spy out the flight of the bees returning from work, then gently pull out the reed stock that he thought was filled with the sweet honey, and suck out its aromatic contents.

Eugene was busy doing chores in the blinding spring sun. Meanwhile, in the glass-enclosed veranda, Paula was teaching Balazs how to read—partly to prepare him for kindergarten coming soon in the fall. But she also had something else in mind for her grandson's early education. She was a patient and excellent teacher, and she knew that children are impressionable at a very early stage, provided that the methods were playful and short. In the

Communist school system, children were taught concentrated Socialist dogma in many clever ways. Paula had noticed how the children parroted the government slogans without any critical or individual thought process, and soon became mental midgets, robots of the state. She was determined to prevent this from happening to Balazs. Both grandparents became very protective of him, and all their years of parenting had given them the expertise to mold his fresh little mind.

In the few months spent in Fuzfo, Balazs had almost no time to think of the city and family he had left behind. With time, they all became a blur in his memory. He was reminded daily of his mother, as her colored photos were hanging everywhere and her portrait image adorned the church window. He missed her, of course, and wanted to see her, but she never came.

Paula always spoke of her with affection and, when Eugene was not present, as now, she talked about Sandor (pronounced Shandor) his father, with admiration and love.

She recalled the first time she met him. "The first thing I saw was his beautifully expressive hands, pushing a bouquet of flowers through the crack of the door, followed by a thin, radiantly handsome face. He had wavy, chestnut brown hair, mischievous, ice blue eyes and a prominent chin. When I saw him play the roles of Romeo and Hamlet, I knew he was a genius. I was so pleased that your mother and he were in love, for they made such a handsome couple. But then this horrible woman took him away!"

Balazs heard many things about this "horrible woman" through the years. The spell she had on his father—that woman who had no refined background like his mother. That woman was famous, but an untalented, loose actress. After all, she started in circuses at an early age, carrying signs for the coming attractions, baring her breasts in public. "Pity, poor Barna, having to live under the same roof as this witch and his step-grandmother, an equally controversial actress."

****

After the reading lesson ended, Balazs ran outside to see what Eugene was doing. Almost four years old now, Balazs' curiosity knew no bounds. When

Paula knitted, he learned to knit; when she braided her hair, he wanted to do it. When she prepared the wool for knitting, he happily offered to prop his small arms up vertically, from which she unraveled the wool into a ball of yarn.

Eugene had no money and no access to toys, but with the richness of life in nature and animals, Balazs had little need for such playthings.

The weather was warm. With the weeping willow bark now tender and soft, Eugene, cut off a straight branch of 15-centimeters with his pocketknife. He beat the bark with the handle to loosen it and slid the slippery, yellow-green skin off the white slimy branch. He then fashioned a wedge-like shape at the end of the stick.

Afterwards, he clipped an angled V shape a centimeter from the edge on top, and slipped the skin back onto the stick, thus producing the nicest flute. Balazs thought it magical!

On one occasion, they were searching through the wreckage of a Russian tank, which Balazs was strictly forbidden to do alone, since many children were left without limbs or lost their lives from meddling with abandoned explosives. Among the debris next to a burned-down little farmhouse were some old, broken wine barrels.

One thin metal ring, in perfect condition, was a great treasure for them. Eugene taught him how to beat it from behind with a short stick and by running along side it, he could keep perfect control by guiding it from the sides with an occasional whack from behind to keep the momentum going.

Shortly afterwards they built him a scooter. It was cut from rough planks and two used steel bearings taken out of another wrecked vehicle.

Helping with the housework and yard chores was a lot of fun, too. He was included in every detail of life. One thing he wished he could do was to draw the water from the well, but he was too short. The water level was very low and as he stared down into the deep darkness of the well, he saw a dark circle that reflected the light like a black mirror. The water was ice cold. When Eugene was not looking, he would drop tiny pebbles down and wait for the sound of the "plop-plump." Its deep, dark mystery hypnotized him.

At the eastern end of the lot was a spring, which bubbled up from a small tunnel Eugene had built decades ago. It was two meters deep into the hillside. It was constructed of round fieldstones and featured a carved stone cross on top, representing its healing powers. The water was so clear; one could see every speck of the reddish-orange mud on the bottom.

A few, small black frogs with red-spotted bellies inhabited the icy water, which always had a thick, green alga, or "frog saliva" as the Hungarians called it, floating at the edges. It was there that the frogs hid their eggs.

In the summertime, Eugene cooled white wine given to him by some farmer friends in the icy water. One day, he noticed that someone had removed much of the wine, and carefully replaced it with water in an attempt to avoid suspicion. He and an old doctor friend were determined to catch the culprit by loading the wine with an extremely strong laxative. When the guilty neighbor came to the doctor complaining of severe diarrhea, they knew they had the culprit. He eventually confessed and the wine was safe once again.

The iodine and iron content of this underground spring had curative properties. Women with goiters from all over the countryside came to drink and take barrels back home on horse-drawn carts. Iodized salt in those days was unheard of, and Balazs saw many women afflicted with these hideous, huge, tumor-like growths under their chins.

The spring did not freeze in the winter, and was ice cold in the summer. Therefore the small

Goldfish Eugene had let loose in there some years back were happily flourishing among the occasional floating chilled wine bottles.

From the hill, the spring trickled down through a guided canal to the bottom of the property. As it traveled to the bottom, Eugene cleverly used it to irrigate all the vegetables with the fresh flow. When it reached level ground again, there was a small puddle of a pond and a little water mill generated by the speed of the flowing water from above. A gigantic weeping willow grew there, profiting from the moisture of this mini paradise. Its thick trunk and strong branches supported its grand stature. The bushes bordering the property were overgrown with layers of thick vine, also nurtured by the well and supported by a forged iron fence.

Years of this growth evolved into a natural, thick trampoline, where Balazs and his friends repeatedly hurled themselves from the branches of the weeping willow above. The effect was thrilling and yielded at least one good bounce. The leaves of the vine, though sour, were delicious. They ate handfuls of them while resting between dives. In the hot summer days, the sourness seemed to have a cooling effect.

These days were richly filled with activities and play, yet Balazs always stayed within earshot of the house. The only time he ventured farther from the boundaries of the yard was to be near his friend the train. By now, he knew every sound and every part of this fascinating contraption, and Balazs was almost convinced that it had a life of its own. He knew the times the locomotives would pull by with the passenger cars and when they would pass through the town sometimes with a hundred wagons in tow. Often it carried Russian tanks and large guns covered with canvas, or shiny mountains of black coal and hundreds of cattle or pigs.

To his delight, one day it carried an entire circus! When Eugene told him stories about the circus he could not sleep from excitement. All he thought of were those amazingly painted, colorful cars and the many animal cages housing the exotic beasts. The train, this lifeline, carried all that by him as it traveled everywhere—they said even to other countries! It was free... And oh, so beckoning.

Many children he knew jumped trains all the time. They rode to a town or two and before their parents caught them, returned on the train traveling the opposite direction. He stole across the highway several times, unnoticed by his grandparents, and hid in the tall grass of the ditch in order to be closer. From this vantage point, he could look at the people in the carriages, or watch them hanging out the windows, waving with friendly smiles at him.

Happy as he was here, he often thought that the train that had brought him could so easily take him back to Budapest. It was faithful and punctual; he could see and hear it from anywhere in or out of the house—huffing and puffing, or seeming to scream sometimes, when it whistled.

Before bedtime, he often waited for the night express to rush by, to see the little windows alight, as it slithered beside the lake on invisible tracks; then he'd go to his bed and sleep totally content.

FIVE

SETTLING IN

THE DAYS BEGAN to flow into each other smoothly and naturally, as life does in the countryside. The resident roosters started the family's morning routine, rudely waking every resting soul within earshot.

Eugene threw the shutters open to the gray early light of predawn, and attached the squeaking iron latches to the outside walls; Paula slid off the side of the bed to heat the water for the morning wash.

By the time Balazs peeked over his warm goose-feathered covers to see if he was missing anything, the aroma of coffee and burning wood filled the room. The couple sat quietly by the table, against the foot of the bed. Eugene slurped his hot, cheap coffee and dunked his "kalacs" (a light, sweet bread), while Paula delicately sipped hers like a cat. Her thick, snow-white hair would flow free and beautiful down to the middle of her back before she braided it for the day. Eugene was not so fortunate, for his thick, white hair was only sported above his upper lip. There was hardly any on his head. Yet he brushed with loving care the remaining strands about his ears.

Before the daily chores began, there was already a morning family ritual developed and enjoyed by this newly formed trio. Balazs, who crawled out of bed rubbing the sleep from his eyes, bumped into grandmother's chair and cuddled closely to her warm, little body.

She always smelled of lavender, which she grew in the yard and dried every year to keep fresh scent in the drawers. She pulled him close with a warm hug and kiss, then like an unfaithful kitten he would crawl to his grandfather's lap, which was bigger and more comfortable.

Sometimes, he would fall back asleep just for a moment or two. The old man enjoyed this special moment. Balazs would watch his mustache move as he spoke or ate. It had to be trimmed every day or so with scissors. It felt ticklish a bit, but good when the kiss came on his cheeks or eyes. His hands were also warm and comforting—always cleanly manicured and the half moons of his cuticles clearly defined. Balazs was given a bite from the coffee-soaked kalacs, which tasted particularly good if they had been able to buy sugar. (Sometimes they stood in line for hours for sugar and lard at the country store.)

After the morning coffee, Balazs would offer to brush his grandmother's hair with a beautiful silver brush. He learned to braid her long hair, and was very proud of his ability.

Shortly after, he would put on a pair of shorts and step out for some chilled morning air. The chickens would be flying out of the coop with great fanfare, waiting for Eugene to throw the seeds on the ground and put out fresh water.

Sunday was a special day for them. They would air the house, clean it, and be dressed in time for the first Mass at the church. The young priest, Lajos (pronounced Layos), had recently been allowed by the government to preach and had been "ordained" by the Marxists. It was required of him to take courses on Communist dogma before extending a license to him. The Communists wanted to show that the religious leaders, so-called "Peace Priests," were on their side. This also assured them that these priests would somehow prevent people from rebelling against their godless ideology.

Churchgoers loved congregating and listening to Lajos. However, they were all careful in their conversations, for even in church there were snitches. These "guardians" of the state were well paid and recruited from among the townsfolk in exchange for special favors from the government. They kept lists of the devout and listened for anti-government remarks. No one was certain who they were. Only in the most trusted circles would people relax. Those on the regular churchgoers' list never got promotions or help from their bosses. The government preached strict atheism.

On Sundays, Paula played the organ at the upper level of the church where the chorus sang. The children stood in front of all the pews, except for the little ones like Balazs, who sat by Eugene. They generally got the seats near the window that had his mother's image portrayed on stained glass, looking like a goddess radiating through the color and light. Whenever he missed her, he would run to the little church, crash through the doors and kneel by the window and pray. He knew three prayers his grandmother taught him by repetition every night.

The heavy scent of incense was comforting as Lajos walked down the aisle in his black frock after Mass and cast the smoke over the congregation as his last blessing of the day. The altar boys, in their long-flowing, black-and-white robes, followed behind him all the way to the door through the aisles where he stood exchanging words with the townspeople before they departed. They were a poor looking flock—the men dressed in tattered, worn-out pants and jackets, and the ladies generally wrapped in variations of black colors with scarf covered heads. The small crowd dispersed and, as was customary, Eugene welcomed the priest to his home for the Sunday lunch.

This was always exciting for Balazs. To him, Lajos was unique since he had learned in church that priests were connected to God and had a special mission in helping mankind. They were all married to Virgin Mary. Well, Balazs thought, that was fine, since Lajos was a very handsome young man, despite his wire-rimmed spectacles. He was tall and lean with delightful humor and a pleasant smile to match. Virgin Mary could not have done better! It never ceased to puzzle him, though, how Mary could remain a virgin and be married to thousands of men around the world, like some female sultan.

The adults always talked politics at lunch and news of neighbors' recent fate under the government. The meal's first course was caraway seed soup, which Balazs hated, as it tasted medicinal. It was followed by cucumber salad and on rare occasion fried chicken, the only meat they had on the table in weeks.

Occasionally, and unexpectedly, books would slide out from under Balazs' armpits and hit the floor with a thud. Lajos would pick them up and return them to Balazs, who was struggling under Paula's rigorous training on table manners. She was appalled by the deterioration of people's manners. She would have none of that for her grandchild, whom she hoped to raise in the manner befitting his class, no matter what.

Paula reminded him that elbows were kept tightly against the torso (thus the books under the arms) and never touched the table, while forks and knives should be held properly, at the end of their handles.

"Balazs, if it was meant that you hold a fork three centimeters from its base then the handle would be three centimeters, not ten centimeters, long. Besides, it looks more genteel and graceful," offered his grandmother. "Now, please sit up straight and move close to your plate.

Don't hunch and don't slurp."

With lunch over and Lajos gone to prepare for the evening Mass, the couple took out their deck of cards on the cleared table to play. Balazs curled up in Eugene's lap and sank into a deep afternoon nap while classical music filled the room from Eugene's favorite station.

SIX

THE KNOCK IN THE NIGHT

AS THE GENTLE RAYS of early summer sun turned the cherries bright shiny red, spreading comforting heat through the countryside, Balazs and Eugene would began to pick the cherries, both sweet and sour, from the lower tree limbs. Paula would be busy in the kitchen; making jams and canning hundreds of jars of fruit preserves for the winter.

The vegetables such as white parsley snips, kohlrabi, carrots, potatoes and beets were stuffed into burlap bags, then lowered into an underground hole and covered with hay. In this communal "Frigidaire," a man on horse and buggy delivered large blocks of ice, which he lowered into the hole in the spring and summer. In the winter, the ground temperature kept things from freezing as the small community retrieved their stash from time to time.

There was no refrigeration in small towns, because there often was no electricity. Most homes were lit by kerosene lamps at night, and were heated by wood stoves. In the fall they gathered the walnuts, almonds, and hazelnuts and laid them out on the attic floors surrounded by mousetraps. (It was a reverse mini iron curtain, and as effective as the one the Communists put around the Hungarians at the borders.)

There was a distinct aroma of drying nuts and preserved fruit in the attic and the veranda.

Balazs enjoyed gathering the walnuts Eugene knocked off from the branches. The walnut had thick, green meaty flesh surrounding them, and when peeled, left nicotine-colored dye from their juice on the hands, as well as an unusual pleasant scent. The dye was so permanent that it only disappeared with the erosion of layers of skin. Eugene also successfully grew figs with the helpful advice from the neighboring farmers. As they gathered through the seasons and prepared for the long winter, they also ate plenty of fresh fruit and vegetables, which supplemented their meat-deficient diet.

Despite the political horrors around them, they seemed to slip into a protective bubble. They had food and a small amount of cash, which Eugene's youngest son Gyorgy (George) sent regularly. But, like other families, they had their own woes.

The couple's older son had been taken in the night from his family, arrested by the AVO secret police, the Hungarian extension of the KGB. An engineer, like his younger brother, Eugene Jr. was accused of political crimes in collaboration with the "enemy." No one knew exactly who the enemy was, much less how to collaborate with them, as all mail was red by the government and the borders were totally secured. Eugene Jr. had not been seen for a long time and no one knew whether he had been thrown into prison, or a concentration camp in Russia or, possibly, China. His young wife, a physician, was barely able to support their two small children since doctors under Communism scarcely made more than the working class.

Then there was Balazs' uncle, Bobby, his father's older brother, who had returned from the Russian front at the end of the war with a Russian wife. He was an officer in the Hungarian army but had fought on the Soviet side against the Germans. His wife, deprived of material goods in Russia, went wild in Hungary, overindulging herself with minks, silk stockings and expensive jewelry.

One day, when Sandor and Jadda were still married, Bobby had visited his brother at Eugene's lake home. A lone drunken Russian soldier tried to steal Bobby's Jeep, parked below the villa. Just at that moment Sandor, was leaning out of the second floor balcony, flicking his cigarette butt away, and he noticed the Russian. In his drunken haste, Sandor ran down the hill, dragged the soldier from the Jeep and beat him severely. On his return he told his brother what he has done. Bobby, being an honorable young man, packed the half-dead soldier into his Jeep and gallantly delivered him to the nearest Russian headquarters for medical attention.

It wasn't long before a truckload of armed Russian soldiers showed up at Eugene's house. Sandor was terrified. Bobby told him to hide and that he would take care of everything. He was confident, since he had been on the Russian front, spoke fluent Russian, and was married to a Russian woman, that he would have some clout with them. Instead, Bobby was arrested on the spot and taken into custody, never to be heard from again. His Russian wife, too, was eventually apprehended and taken back to Russia.

Sandor's oldest sister became a victim, too, during the war. The Germans were losing and the advancing Russian army was occupying eastern and central Europe. The fast-retreating Nazi armies were followed by waves of murderous, robbing and raping Russians preying on unarmed defenseless civilians. All the population could do was to live with silent suffering; they were slaves and prisoners in their own country. While returning home from shopping, his oldest sister was forced into a passing tank by the Russian tank commander and raped repeatedly by eleven soldiers and beaten before her ordeal ended. Her mangled body was dumped on the sidewalk after they stole her groceries. When some neighbors discovered her, they carried her home. She remained in a coma for weeks. There was no authority to complain to or ask for protection since the very army that was there to liberate the Hungarians from the Nazis and "protect" them was now the law-and it was the law of barbarians.

****

Balazs and Eugene walked to the lake to fish using homemade fishing rods. The lake water, still and clear, was abundant with fish of all kinds. The afternoon overcast skies brought the promise of hungry fish. The easiest catch was the red fin Bream (keszeg, to Hungarians), but Eugene often pulled in a good-size carp, too. They went down to the docks that Eugene "used" to own, but which were now officially off limits to them, since they too had been confiscated. Eugene's old, small rowboat was still there, tied to the dock, but now with a Communist party member's name on it.

Suddenly there was a rush among the reeds. Violent splashes and jerks broke the silence making the surface boil. Calm followed. Eugene whispered and pointed out to Balazs a longer wave created by the strong tail fin of a ferocious barracuda. Quite elusive to catch, the prehistoric barracuda, with its rows of sharp teeth, was coveted by the Hungarians for its delicate, white, boneless flesh.

At the end of the day, the two had nearly 20 fat Breams strung through their pink gills, which they happily brought home to have Paula clean and cook. She fried the catch in pig's lard with onion and red Hungarian sweet paprika. After dinner, Balazs prepared for his bedtime reading, which was to be *Babar the Elephant* for the 100th time.

Paula was happy that, in a very short time, he had learned to read and was doing so at every opportunity. Eugene was quietly closing the shutters and the windows to secretly tune in to the forbidden Radio Free Europe. In the darkness, only the eye of the Orion radio glowed like a gem. The broadcasting was horribly difficult to decipher, as the Hungarian Communists spent millions on jamming interference. People behind the Iron Curtain were only allowed artificial news and fabricated documentaries of anti-American propaganda. "True" news coming from the west was secretly coveted and devoured.

Balazs dozed off listening to the announcer's voice competing with the wave of whining noise. This particular night Eugene was not successful in making out much of the report, yet he hung onto every word that penetrated through the jamming, and his heart leaped from joyous and spiteful defiance. Before retiring for the night, he shoved the radio under his bed.

****

As in a bad dream, the hard banging penetrated the peaceful, dark room. The old couple and Balazs woke to loud shouts and the vibrations of the front glass doors. Startled, they stared and groped in the darkness. Eugene fumbled to find some matches to light the kerosene lamp, but before he succeeded bright lights penetrated through the window—rendering them temporarily blind like deer on the road.

By the time he arrived at the doors, they blew open, nearly knocking him down. Two short, stocky men shoved him back. Paula finally got to light the lamp and the glow neutralized the power of the bright flashlights, making the two figures more defined. One of them emulated the typical

Lenin look with hat and beard, the other was bald and wore the black leather jacket of hoodlums. They reeked of cheap tobacco and strong Hungarian plum brandy.

"Come, you lazy capitalistic bastards," said the one with the Lenin beard. "You've rested enough for a lifetime at the expense of the people. Now it's time to work and contribute to society! Now get your rags on and hurry about it!"

The confused couple went white with fright: their first suspicion was that the tenants next door must have heard the radio and snitched on them.

Where were they being taken, were they being deported, what would be the punishment? This was the "knock in the night" that all people across the Communist-occupied countries dreaded—wondering when their time would come. "Now it is our time," Paula thought, as she nervously fretted about and wondered what would happen to Balazs.

"Do with the runt whatever you want, bring him or leave him, your choice," was the man's remark as he looked at the frightened face of a skinny child curled up in the corner of the room, holding his blanket about him. Paula and Eugene were relieved to hear this.

In their terror they dressed so hurriedly that Paula nearly forgot her dentures in the glass of water by her nightstand. They went outside into the cool night and walked down their gravel path to a dirty, old, open truck waiting for them at the bottom of the hill. The truck smelled strongly of pig droppings, most likely from the previous occupants, taken to the slaughterhouse. "Now it is the turn of the capitalistic pigs," Eugene thought darkly to himself. They were shoved up into a crowd of people. Huddled in the back among the dark figures, Eugene recognized their elderly friends from town, accompanied by their grandchildren as well. As the truck rolled down the hill, they were told that this was not a deportation, thank God, but a free labor force to the nearby collective farm. Thousands of hectares of ripe tomatoes had begun to rot, and the harvest was in danger of being lost. This was partly due in part to the farmers whose lands had been confiscated by the Stalinists and refused to work with haste. They grumbled that they fared no better now than in the times of the feudal lords, when they worked for nothing on other people's land. It made no difference now how they performed, hard work or lazy work; they all made the same wages. The Communists did not believe in the healthy incentives of the capitalists. In the "Workers' Paradise," everyone received the same pay. Except, of course, the "comrades," and the party members.

By the time the caravan of trucks had turned into the fields, the sun was up and it was turning into a hot June morning. Hundreds of people from all over the countryside were hauled in and unloaded.

They were mainly from the questionable intelligentsia or bad "Kader." This was a term used by the Communists that disqualified you from any favored population, meaning you were not of the working class or you had no relatives in the proletariat. The Communists, who preferred the helpless, impoverished, dependent working class, whom they could manipulate, distrusted farmers. The working class, the product of the industrial revolution, was forever dependent on, and slave to, any system for welfare.

The old folks were thankful and relieved to find themselves in the fields, rather than shipped off to Siberia or to some unknown Chinese concentration camp. The countless children were shoved into large circular cells corralled by rusty barbed wire. In the center of each of these open holding pens was a wooden barrel of water and a communal tin cup, hung from twine nailed to the wood. Balazs went to the barrel, dipped deeply into the still cool water and took a long drink. There were more than 50 children in his pen of similar ages up to about six-years-old. The older ones were pushed with the adults along the rows of tomatoes.

A little girl stood nearby, crying uncontrollably, her tears leaving clean tracks on the dirt of her cheeks. Another child tried to comfort her, but that just made her carry on even more. She was abandoned to her crying. Balazs tried to spot Eugene and Paula, but he could not see them, as thousands of backs were bent over toiling in the fields.

Everyone was given baskets and wooden crates, which they delivered full to the rim to the waiting trucks. Once the trucks were filled, they drove off in clouds of dust. The day wore on and the people worked hard through the miserable heat. These people, who were not used to physical labor, were from the former middle and upper classes. Eugene tried looking, but he had not seen Paula since they had separated them. He was assigned with one of his bridge partners, a retired orthopedic surgeon who was 10 years his senior and could hardly carry his full basket. Eugene was a bit stronger and was now used to everyday labor, as he tended his own garden. This was different, though. He was not humiliated by the work, simply by the treatment they received from "comrades." He had contributed a great deal to his country and everything he owned was the result of his diligent work. His intellect, ambition and hard work also accomplished his education. He was no "silver spoon" or leach, as the Communists labeled him.

They were rarely offered water, but when it came, the men in gray always distributed it with ample insults. Responding would have been suicide, so everyone tolerated the treatment from these despicable beings, which reveled in their invincibility, in dignified silence.

The children quickly made friends and began to play. Some threw pebbles at the posts that held the wires, while others played tag. Their stomachs began to burn from hunger and by the time someone came with a large pot of hot corn and tomato soup, the sun was past its zenith.

The woman who brought the food looked like a zombie. She was foul smelling as her comrades. This creature threw some more tin cups into the dust by the pot. Then, devoid of any feelings, she yelled to the children who gathered about her, "Eat!" Then abruptly left the corral, tightly hooking the wire gate behind her. Balazs began to chew the corn in his soup and realized it was the hard corn kernels, grown for farm beasts.

It was twilight when the whistles sounded to end work. The trucks lined up and were soon filled with exhausted people. Eugene, with bleeding hands and cursing under his breath, fetched Balazs first. He was a spirited man, not a sheep to be herded. He was mad, but knew better than to show it and further endanger his family. Frail little Paula's disheveled white hair was plastered with sweat to her face and forehead, and was entangled with stems of tomato branches. She looked like a mad woman who had escaped the loony house, Eugene remarked with a laugh.

At home they all washed up in fresh well water and dropped into bed, feeling lucky to be delivered to this fate. They were herded off to the fields of the collectives' six days a week. Therefore Eugene was only able to tend to his own garden on Sundays. At the end of every two weeks, they were given food tickets, which at least helped to augment their meager budget.

SEVEN

POLLUTING THE BEACH

SUMMER WAS IN full swing. City and country folks loved gathering on the shores of the lake like migrating flocks. Despite miserable conditions, Hungarians refused to relinquish the simple joys of life. Thousands of people soaked in the velvety warm lake water, with its soft, muddy bottom. They enjoyed bathing under the bright, humid-free sun. Although the lake posed dangers such as unpredictable storms, often resulting in drowning or electrocutions in the lightning storms, people kept returning every summer.

It was Sunday, a day off from the collective farms. The three decided to walk down to the lake in the still cool of the morning. Paula packed sandwiches, some spring onions, yellow Hungarian peppers and smoked sausage. After a quick dip in the water with Balazs, Paula and Eugene retired on the soft grass beneath the shade of the weeping willows. The peaceful scene of children splashing in the waters and others lounging on the shore could have been mistaken for a French Impressionist painting of eternal summer. The air was clear under the pale-blue skies, and the distant purple hills framed the green-blue water as it caressed the lush vegetation by the shore.

Suddenly, there was a big commotion. Like parent seals frantically gathering their young from the danger of an approaching polar bear, the adults were running about in search for their young, calling out names in chaotic confusion.

From the entrance to the beach, hundreds of uniformed and armed Russian soldiers appeared with their camouflaged vehicles. As the armored cars roared off the main road, the dark diesel smoke eclipsed and dirtied the gentle blue sky. They shouted orders at one another in what sounded like a mini invasion. The many consonants in each word of this hideous language to Hungarian ears, it sounded like hungry wolves barking while gorging, gnawing and ripping the flesh from their victims.

When Balazs heard the hateful language, symbolic as it was to his people of repression and occupation, he felt a deep resentment that sent cold chills into his heart. After the early years of pillaging and raping of the Hungarian people, the Russian army was now strictly confined to their bases and prohibited from fraternizing with the population for "their own safety." On extremely hot summer days, they were, however, allowed out for brief visits to the lakes. Like Mongol hoards they swooped down, almost literally attacking the water. They were permitted to use only one end of the beach, by the reeds which, unbeknownst to them, was infested with fat, black leaches. As if the waters had become contaminated, all the Hungarians withdrew, cursing while making their way back to the shore. They kept their families close and safe.

The soldiers wore ugly, large, baggy shorts as they charged into the water. Those watching wished them to be eaten alive by the leaches. As they splashed, laughed and yelled like children, others remained behind with their machine guns pointed at the frightened people. To everyone's relief, this only lasted a short while before they were herded back to their trucks. The departing vehicles reversed onto the road from where they had come in a large cloud of dark smoke. Slowly, everyone returned to resume the interrupted day of joy, although horrible tales quickly began to circulate among the bathers about those who had suffered under the hands of these villains, such as Sandor's sister's attack and rape.

The soft, large, orange sun descended slowly beyond the last hill of the horizon, but not before she had withdrawn her golden reflection from the lake's surface, like some cosmic bride gathering her train of splendor. It was time to head home. But as the air cooled and the still evening was laced with the sounds of crickets, Eugene and Balazs decided to trek up the hill for some fresh milk from the nearby farmer. By the time they arrived, the farmer had already relieved the bursting udders of his cows, and his wife served it up with her freshly baked bread out on the summer kitchen's table. The two dunked their bread into the foamy, warm milk and savored its rich, wonderful flavor. They took their two-liter fresh milk container with them, but before they descended the hill to the villa, they stopped at the summit lookout directly over the vast open lake.

The water was now silvery cool, awash in the rising moon's light. Everything in the village below them was bathed in dark French, ultramarine blue. Above, the sky,– free of any light pollution,– was thick with a blanket of shining stars. The air had the pleasant scent of drying hay, while millions of fireflies reflected the stars above with perfect mimicry blending everything into a cosmic stew of nature's inspired, everlasting beauty.

EIGHT

A POEM FOR BALAZS

FALL CAME AT last for Balazs, who was anxiously waiting to enter kindergarten, located only a kilometer from the villa. After learning his way around, he was allowed by his grandparents to walk by himself. That proved to be adventurous, for he had the opportunity to meet more of the townspeople. The women who worked at the school treated the children well, despite the early Communist indoctrination to which they had been subjected. In addition to the traditional Hungarian songs and nursery rhymes, the children had to learn Communist Russian songs and hear Russian folklore, rewritten with the system's own agenda for early brainwashing. Naturally he was unaware of these things yet. He drank acrid, cheap hot chocolate, more like muddy water. But, since he had never had the genuine article to compare it with, he was happy.

As for Eugene and Paula, their misery continued. Work at the collective farms was no longer needed, so both were shipped out to a brick distribution depot, where there were mountain loads of bricks to lift into trucks on the cold days of autumn. However, all hardships of life contain some hidden good. This hard physical labor made them stronger. Eugene lost nearly 20 kilos, which he had collected in the good times before the war.

A town crier, who announced himself with a small drum, read the news of the day, as composed by the town officials. There were several appointed stations for this event, and one happened to be under their villa across from an old tavern. The old, emaciated man beat his drum until enough people had gathered around to hear his loud orations. Sometimes he would visit all three taverns along the way. By the time he reached the villa, the information had got so jumbled up that people were annoyed and left quite disgusted. It mattered little to him, for he continued shouting the news to himself.

Like all taverns, the one near the villa had regulars even in the daytime. The runoff from the beer kegs was a primitive five-centimeter wide by five-centimeter deep trench carved into the concrete floor, and leading to the outside of the building. There, beer collected in a small puddle before slowly seeping into the ground, close to where the neighborhood goose begged for food. Mischievous patrons threw pieces of bread into the puddle, ensuring this fat, white goose would become one of the tavern's regulars, and its most popular patron. After he gobbled up a few of the beer-soaked bread pieces, the alcohol took its toll. The bird began to sway, then burped in a bird's fashion and plopped down. When very drunk, sometimes he did not make it back home, but sprawled out like a genuine drunk, his wings and his orange legs spread in every direction. If the patrons were more sober than the goose, they carried him to his home under their arms, as the bird's head swayed lifeless like a pendulum at the end of his long, white neck. (By the way, he outlived the drummer by two years, proving to the world why the goose's liver is so highly prized!)

The cold winds that whipped through the town brought with them a severe winter and snow so high that Eugene and his neighbors were forced to dig tunnels to visit each other. This was a blessing in disguise, because no one was able to go to the collectives and, instead, spent wonderful times in their warm houses with their families. They listened to classical and Hungarian folk music and read many books.

Eugene and Balazs began to draw pictures together. Eugene's oil paintings were terrific and tastefully done. He had little formal training, yet his keen eye helped him decipher the secrets of the masters, adding to his knowledge. He was what artists call a Sunday painter. Balazs particularly admired two of Eugene's large oils with one large elk in each work. They stood proudly baying in a swamp while their hot breath could be seen. Because Eugene hunted and knew the anatomy of animals, he was able to paint these elk realistically and powerfully. He also painted the little town at its inception, showing the few peasant homes beneath the hill, above the villa.

One day, Eugene decided to stretch some parchment paper on wires to replace an old lampshade. But first he drew many beautiful Hungarian folk motifs on the parchment, with colorful flowers filled in with primary and secondary colors. Since he didn't have varnish, he improvised with grease to secure the pigment. When he lit the kerosene lamp, the magic of the colors glowed like the stained glass in the church windows. One of the neighbors, who noticed the shade, asked him to make her one in exchange for some beef as payment. He happily obliged; they had not tasted beef since before the war. It was a special occasion and lucky for Lajos, because it was his Sunday with the family again. The priest encouraged Eugene to make more of the shades to improve the Sunday lunches.

By now the lake was frozen solid and the men had cleared a huge area of the lake in their vicinity for a peculiar sport the Hungarians called "wood dodging." Wooden chairs were fitted with metal tacks on the bottom of the legs for smoothness. A pole was attached to it with sheets for a sail. The person seated, more like trapped, in this contraption, flew frantically in all directions without much hope of control. Whatever the origins of the sport, the Hungarians certainly identified with and loved it. Lajos held tightly onto Balazs' chair as his black priestly frock and skirt flew every which way. Several times he let go and fell sliding on his butt with his legs irreverently pointing toward his boss in heaven. Like children, they screamed and laughed as Eugene sailed by them just to crash into a snow bank and vanish. After several well spent hours they were all blue with cold and soaked. They returned to the warm house to thaw out in front of the stove that glowed red with the burning wood. Paula heated some red wine with cloves and cinnamon as a special treat, which Balazs was allowed to indulge in, too.

Eugene took Lajos' advice and went to the local butcher the very next day to get butcher's paper, since vellum was hard to come by. He prepared many drawings for a series of shades and asked Balazs to color one like the first successful sample. Eugene was very pleased at the neat rendering his grandson had done, and so they established their little cottage industry. They were easily able to exchange the shades for cash, food and tobacco. They felt proud and prosperous when they returned home, sometimes with items such as sugar or butter they could otherwise not afford to buy.

There were occasional letters from Jadda, but never from his father. Her letters were quite impersonal when she inquired about him and his brushing habits. His bonding with her, long since eroded, had been replaced by the deep love he felt toward his grandparents. One cozy winter evening, while they busied themselves making lampshades and listening to the radio, the music ceased. The voice announced Maestro Sandor Szabo, who was to recite poetry by Attila Jozsef, a great Hungarian poet. The poem's title was *Go To Sleep Little Balazs*. Balazs saw Eugene stiffen in his chair, but Paula sat up with interest. Balazs was overwhelmed at having heard his father's name, and that he would be reading a poem addressed to him. Was he sending a message, he wondered?

"It's Papa on the radio, did you hear, it's Papa!" he shouted, and before he had settled down, the famous, deep, beautiful baritone voice of his father filled the little room. He was a master not only on stage and film, but was also one of the best in the recitation of poetry.

Balazs was swept away, not only by the beauty of the Hungarian poetry, but by the closeness he felt hearing his father's voice for the first time that he could remember. His voice was energetic, sometimes dramatic, then gentle, filling the room, speaking just to him.

Suddenly, he felt deep sadness, wanting to run and run until he reached his father and jump into his arms, kiss him and tell him how much he missed him! Then a thought crossed his mind—why has he not come for him? By the time the voice disappeared, he felt empty, betrayed and hurt.

He looked over at Eugene, who was like a wounded animal, sitting small, reduced by a power which he could not compete. He was frightened and tried to hide his emotions, sensing Balazs' thoughts. He had grown so attached to this child that he could not face sharing or losing him even for a moment. Competing with the father, even a phantom voice on the radio, was a reminder of a day surely approaching. Yet he tried to deny it. Eugene had a fleeting image of the little ducklings that hatched under the hen's care, bolting for the lake as soon as they were able. While they were splashing and frolicking in their natural habitat, the surrogate mother hen ran frantically on the shore, bewildered and miserable at the loss of her chicks. Balazs seemed to instinctively feel what was going through Eugene's heart and within a split second landed in his lap, crying pitifully. Paula approached to embrace them both, and joined in a good cry.

NINE

LITTLE CSILLA

SHE CAME DOWN the hill from the government apartment compound that had been converted from a private resort. Csilla (Tchilla) wore her usual shabby clothes. She was only a year or so older than Balazs, whom she found fun to play with, despite his wild and over-energetic personality. She was also drawn to the villa and its two towers, especially the small one. They spent hours spying on the world about them while raiding the adjoining attic, crammed as it was with dried fruits and walnuts. The tower afforded a clear view not only of the lake, but also of the road below the villa. Since it was the only major road around the lake and its neighboring villages, it was busy with trucks and the ever present armed military vehicles.

They played in the healing spring of the garden, and caught the frogs with red-spotted bellies. Balazs liked to build for her small water mills. They both enjoyed watching as the water cascaded down the hill. He climbed the highest branches to fetch for her the last few sweet fruits of the season that the birds had missed. Clearly, he enjoyed clowning around to entertain her. He loved being in her company, too.

She was very pretty, and always clean, despite the poverty in which she was raised. Her parents worked at the chemical factory four kilometers from the town. The plant, which manufactured components for bombs and other military weapons for the Soviets, drained waste water into the lake. This eventually killed much of the fish life and vegetation, slowly turning the water into a putrid, opaque-green. There were no provisions, under the Communists, for the prevention of pollutants.

The hillside above the little town and the villa had no houses on it. It was covered with grass that grew tall by the end of spring. Among the grass were beautiful, bittersweet smelling, purple wild tulips with fuzzy petals. A small, yellow, waxy flower called the "herald of the storks" – so called because it appeared just before the storks returned from Africa every spring to build their nests – popped its pretty head up from the tall grass too. The grass reached a meter high, and had fuzzy stems toward the tips. When a breeze blew over the hill, the tall grass moved in waves, much like long, blond hair on a girl's head, and, indeed, the country folks called this Orphan Girl's Hair. Csilla's hair reminded Balazs of this vision. He often stroked her long, blond locks, which she allowed him to brush and braid hours at a time while they chatted.

With his friends he played soccer and did many rough things, which he enjoyed. But she was special—with her he could talk of personal things, things he was afraid to talk to his grandparents about, for fear that it would hurt their feelings. Mostly he wondered about his father, and what it would be like to have young parents like she had. Every summer his mother came for a brief visit, but spent little time with him. She played bridge with her parents' friends and others who came to vacation. Strange men, who were irritated by Balazs' presence, surrounded her, and she obliged them by getting rid of him most of the time. She often reminded him that she was looking for a new dad for him. He resented hearing that, for he already had a dad and didn't want a new one. Her shallow, meaningless kisses and strokes annoyed him. Somehow, he sensed insincerity in her.

Little Csilla seemed much like a grown-up; she would always know what was on his mind, or what to say to soothe him. Csilla told Balazs that her parents saw his dad in the movies, and he was tall and very handsome. Balazs had not been to the movies yet, but neither had most of the townspeople. The only movie theatre was outside at the end of the town, where millions of ferocious bloodsucking mosquitoes from the swaps waited to feed on the people. Because money was scarce, and the Communists made books cheaper and more readily available in libraries, not many worried about missing the luxury of movies.

Families who owned radios gathered around it for music, plays and poetry readings. Hungarians love poetry and the arts. Every time Sandor's name was announced on the radio, Eugene made certain it was not on. He hated to see his grandson hurt in the anticipation of the visits that never came. Almost every time a train sped by toward Budapest, Balazs thought of stowing away on it to visit his father. Maybe, Csilla thought, Balazs should write to his father and secretly mail the letter.

With that in mind, Csilla brought letter paper and an envelope to instigate the project. She was determined to do this because she knew how much Balazs hurt. He was also curious to meet his new mom, who was known for her beauty. The more negatives he heard from his grandmother and his mother regarding her, the more he seemed to like her. They sat in the little tower and composed the letter:

Dear Dad:

I am your son Balazs and I miss you very much. Please come to Fuzfo.

Million kisses,

Balazs

She stuffed the folded paper into the envelope, licked the glue and sealed it. She addressed it to the Maestro, the famous actor Sandor Szabo, in Budapest. Csilla promised to mail the letter the next day at the post office, and assured him that even without the correct address, it would get to him because he was famous and everyone knew him. They both got excited about their project, but Balazs felt guilty about doing this without his grandfather's knowledge. Csilla calmed him by telling him that everyone had a right to meet his or her dad at least once in a lifetime. Also, Eugene was a nice man and she did not think he would even mind. Balazs loved her for saying that as he walked her up the street to her building. On the way, they caught low-flying brown beetles for their collection jars. There was a rumor among the kids that someone would pay lots of money for them, because they made medicine out of them, though Balazs didn't know anyone who had ever sold even a single beetle. The next day he always released them anyway.

The night seemed long and restless for Balazs as he thought about the letter. He went through the whole scene over and over in his mind. What would his father do upon opening the letter? He decided that, by mid-morning, Csilla should have returned from the post office, so he ran down the gravel path to meet her. As he approached the gate, he noticed an unusual commotion in the neighbor's yard. In the shade of the big cherry tree, by a large summer table, a group of peasant women were gathered, screaming at the top of their lungs. He could see them as they rang their hands in prayer toward the heavens, "Oh, dear God, Oh, dear God!"

The odd gathering looked like a mad group of crows flapping their black wings, as village women often wore black after they reached the age of 40. There were other neighbors too, men who crowded around and tried to get a glimpse over the women's heads of something on the table. Balazs had enough of the mysterious theatrics. He energetically pushed his way through the circle of adults to see for himself what it was all about.

Before anyone was able to tear him away, he became rooted like stone as he beheld the bloated, naked, blue body of a little, skinny girl, prostrate on the roughly hewn wooden boards. Her hands were stiff as they clenched in a frozen, pleading gesture to the skies. Her eyes protruded from their sockets, as did her tongue from her distorted swollen lips. The once blond, beautiful hair was soiled and green, covered with human feces. The hideous expression of a silent scream stifled by her swollen black lips terrified Balazs. He went into denial upon hearing Csilla's name called out by the bewildered, grieving crowd, and then his mind went blank as he vomited uncontrollably, until he felt his eyes would burst. The men dragged him away, cussing at each other for allowing the child to penetrate the crowd.

Later that night, he awoke totally disoriented and feverish, without any recall of the ordeal. He drifted back to sleep. He slept for days, almost as if he were entering a coma. Eugene had his physician friend pay a visit to examine him. The doctor diagnosed severe trauma, which he said would pass after Balazs' subconscious had dealt with it in his sleep. He encouraged close attention and nothing more, knowing that they themselves felt traumatized by the incident. They knew how close Balazs was to Csilla.

The evening Csilla and Balazs had separated; she took the letter and the jar of beetles. On the way home, she stopped at the only toilet for the compound of more than fifty people, an outhouse. As she sat on the bench with the hole in it, the evening breeze must have slammed the heavy door shut. She had tried to open it, but it was stuck beyond her strength to move it. She kept shouting for help, for someone to come, but nobody responded. Nobody heard her. She grew frustrated and panicked. She decided to get up and stand on the bench. She leaned forward to yell through the small heart-shaped hole to be better heard. The door gave a little and she lost her balance. As she leaned so far out, her foot slipped backward and she plunged down and was enveloped in fecal matter. She suffered as she struggled for survival, until eventually this most vile form of death overcame her. She wasn't found until the next morning, when one of the tenants noticed the top of her head.

Balazs was told of the events a few days after he readjusted to life. He seemed to shut the world out and did not respond to the news. He did not cry, but called his pet pig, and the two went for a walk in the woods. He had lost his best friend forever, and with her, and the letter, and his hopes of ever meeting his father. The world had become a very empty place.

TEN

CATS' FATE

IT WAS A CRISP, clear, invigorating morning. The countless fruit trees were well past their prime and the young, pastel-green leaves matured into darker viridian hues, softly veiling the thick netting of branches. The scent of flowers was carried intermittently by the stirring breeze through the open doors of the veranda.

In the little bedroom, there was much excitement and bustle. Eugene had finally convinced Balazs that the newborn kittens must be done away with. There was no extra food to feed any more animals, and the hungry cats would resort to eating the birds or even the small chickens. The cat shared what leftovers there were with the dog. In Hungary, there was no such phenomenon as pet food. The Hungarian Puli, an ancient Shepherd breed whose ancestors probably originated from Tibet in the ninth century, was a gift to Balazs from Paula in memory of the one they had for him at their Buda house, when he was just a toddler at the end of the war. As the advancing, occupying Soviet forces drove their tanks through the street in front of their house; the Puli went into a mad barking frenzy. One tank commander spotted him behind the iron gate and slowly turned his vehicle with sadistic pleasure into the gate to crush the barking animal. The beautiful wrought iron, baroque design gate fell flat on the unsuspecting animal like a horrifying cookie cutter. The terrified grandparents had whisked the bewildered child from the scene of cruelty to prevent further trauma.

Eugene was always gentle and patient with his approaches, respectful of the child's feelings and concerns. He made all the preparations as if it were a ritual for an ancient act. As Balazs approached the wooden box containing the tiny bodies in tight formation suckling from their mother, he accidentally bumped the box. The kittens stirred into a chorus of thread-thin meows. The mother responded by purring with half-mast eyes at the familiar intruder. Balazs already knew that the kittens would be put into a burlap bag with a rock tied to it as the sinker. They would be eased into the deep water below the fishing dock. Eugene assured him that the kittens wouldn't suffer, just get dizzy for a moment and fall asleep.

However, Balazs found this a bit hard to believe. Every time he swallowed water or it ran up his nose while swimming, the sensation was traumatic and frightening. He decided not to give his grandfather any grief about this, remembering the first time he threw a tantrum about the chicken's throat being cut for the Sunday dinner.

He understood that every animal he raised from birth eventually would come to the same fate—into the family's hungry bellies. As the preparations were made, the quiet morning was suddenly broken by the neighbor's loud intrusion as she burst through the veranda door. "Master [it was still customary even in those days for the older country folk to address people of higher class thus], I am terribly sorry to intrude like this," she said with an exasperated expression on her face, "but last night they came and took Janos (Yanosh). It was terrible! This shiny Pobjeda [a Russian knock-off of the American Chevrolet] pulled up to the vegetable garden with its headlights off, three men jumped out leaving the doors open. I was still up, since Janos snored so loud, you know when he drinks he snores something awful. Anyway I ran to the front door to see what this was all about, but before I got to open it they just broke the glass on the front door and ripped my crocheted curtains off! They said they were taking Janos! I said, he done nothing, what did they want with him? They said they just want to ask him some questions. So, I suggested they do it in the morning after he had sobered up, besides he didn't have the morning shift at the factory. They just shoved me to the wall, lit the kerosene lamp and went to the bedroom where he lay asleep. One dragged him out of bed while another kept me in the hallway. I could hear Janos protesting, but I think he thought it was a dream until that bastard started twisting his arm and slugging him. He threw his clothes at him and shouted, 'You've got a big mouth, Janos, and we are gonna find out if you are an enemy of the movement. We heard you were shooting your mouth off at the tavern about the movement and how the five-year Plan didn't work.' They said they were going to take him to see how much he knew about running the government better."

Evidently, Janos had sobered up pretty quickly and was terrified. He realized that one of his friends must be an informer and told on him. The last time one of his friends had been taken for questioning by the authorities disappeared all together. No one knew what happened to him. The local Communist Party office would only respond that he went where all the enemies of the people go, to re-education. Frightened, he begged them, losing his pride as he cried like a child and pleaded not to be taken away. He would not get off the ground, but held onto the man's legs.

"I have never seen Janos like that, so scared like a child, totally out of control and without shame. I said he has done nothing; he is a hardworking man. So what if he gets drunk once in a while and shoots off his stupid drunken mouth? It's only words, it isn't gonna change the system or nothing. It's just a bunch of harmless drunks feeling important. It's innocent and harmless."

They had stuffed Janos's limp, unwilling body into the car and took him off. At first light, she had mounted her bike and ridden to the local Communist office, located at the center of town. It used to be home to an unfortunate family that had been deported to make way for the headquarters, and a large, red Communist star had been welded to the apex of the roof.

The door of the orange-yellow, neglected farmhouse was closed, so she waited, sitting on the steps crying. When someone finally opened the door, she entered the already smoke-filled room. It had filthy wood floors with a chipped, old bench pushed against a wall. There were two old chairs facing a scratched-up desk. Behind it sat the silhouette of a short, fat man, engulfed in smoke so he more resembled a large steaming lump of smoked ham, she thought. She squinted, but could not make out his face, only the large, black and white photo of Stalin on a sidewall, with his thick, Georgian mustache. Next to it was the fat, baldheaded Rakosi, the Hungarian puppet Premier. Every school and public building had these two photos as a reminder that Big Brother was watching you. There was the red star above them and the red Soviet flag leaned against a corner. The revised red, white and green Hungarian flag, with the Russian sickle, hammer and wheat pods in the center was in the opposite corner. In response to her inquiry, she was told that Janos was taken for further questioning at the AVO office in Veszprem, a larger city nearby. She understood the meaning of that. She was exhausted and looked terrified. She had run all over the neighborhood looking for some comfort.

The peasant woman sank to her knees, hopelessly lost and cried uncontrollably in the arms of his grandparents, who realized that this could have been their fate as well.

Balazs sat and listened to the woman's story in frightened silence, as he recalled his teachers encouraging the children to report the conversations of their families at home, to see if there were any reactionary remarks against our brothers and protectors, the Russian people. They would be well rewarded! He knew better than to fall for this, as his grandparents had prepared him early on for the traps of the Communists and their methods. After all, he was the offspring of the intelligentsia, the enemy of the people from birth. He knew where he belonged. He was made quite aware of this as his grandparents were regularly herded out to do forced labor in the fields and to brick factories.

Later, as Eugene eased the kittens into the burlap bag, they began to stir with repeated meows of panic. Then Balazs thought of Janos. Like these kittens, he had scratched and whined but to no avail. His fate was sealed like these cats, which couldn't be altered now! What price for the loose tongue of a drunk under Communism? The boy felt nauseous at the thought of these irreversible fates that were so absolute and final. He lay on the docks and watched below as the full burlap-bag sank slowly into the deep dark abyss. He imagined a tiny Janos among the kittens, screaming, clawing, gasping for air and trying to escape from the sinking bag.

Eugene and Balazs stood silently at the edge of the docks in the bright sunlight. The lake had swallowed the event without leaving a trace, not even a ripple. The birds chirped, as the silver guppies flashed undisturbed in the shallows. He thought he heard the kitten's meow from the depth rise to the surface with the ascending bubbles.

Or was it just an echo of his guilty thoughts, for having had a hand in their fate?

ELEVEN

PIG TALK

THE SEASONS passed with much learning and personal growth for Balazs. The forced labor for his grandparents lasted a few years, until it was finally determined that Eugene and Paula were too old. The country had fallen into greater economic decay with the lack of incentives that came with collectivization and with further mismanagement of the infrastructure by the inexperienced Communist government. The shelves were empty of food, and to acquire anything such as clothing and shoes became a real problem. Eugene had shoes that dated back more than 20 years. They had been resoled countless times.

The Gypsy tinkers, at least, were getting prosperous from the demands of mending holes in everyone's old pots. They pushed their knife-sharpening millstones about the countryside and on the city streets, propelled by homemade, sawn-off bicycle contraptions.

Balazs outgrew the last pair of ankle boots the family was able to scrounge up for him. Cheaply made, the shoes were so hard and coarse that all his toes bled. He developed permanent corns. Eventually, they had to slice the tip of the toes off to make room for his growing feet. Buying new ones had to be postponed for lack of money.

By now the whole country was suffering greater shortages even than during the war. The population seemed to form one endless, hopeless line in front of stores that ran out of provisions long before they could satisfy everyone's needs. People resorted to bartering to acquire some necessities. Balazs was old enough to walk to town daily and stand in line for sugar and other items when available. Often, he found to his disappointment, the doors were closed right in front of him for lack of merchandise. Curiously, when the local party members arrived, merchandise suddenly appeared. They came to the back door of the stores to get all the sugar they needed. They later sold it on the black market, to the very same unfortunate people who had been standing in line all day before, without success. The black markets flourished, filling the needs of people, despite the severe punishments dealt out to those who were caught. Eugene and Balazs were part of that system and became experts in the lampshade business, as they traded for goods with the local farmers. The farmers began to farm small plots, though it was against the rules. They were only allowed to work on the collectives for their meager wages. Ironically, the collectives were on the very same land they used to own before the confiscation started to collectivize "for the greater good of the people."

Third grade was approaching for Balazs. Another beautiful summer was coming to an end. The small, red, late-summer pears were juicy and sweet. The swallows were busy teaching their young the "aerobatics" of fly chasing, and soon their artfully built mud nests would be beaten and cast to the ground by the fall's wind and rain.

The little pink pig that his grandfather had given him the year before grew into a giant, round, walking lard lump of 200 kilos. Despite its heavy weight, it trotted faithfully with Balazs over the hills and into the woods on lonely walks in search of solitude or some acorns. They spent much time together, and Balazs felt that he was able to decipher most of the pig's vocabulary of various grunts and groans. Sometimes, they would spend all day in each other's company even skipping the midday meal and only returning at dusk. They were content just mulling about the bushes and the hills; Balazs observing the pig's little habits or watching his long blond eyelashes cast lazily half-mast as he expelled deep sighs when napping.

One warm August afternoon, high on the hill, the pig and Balazs were lounging together on the summit of the plateau where a deep crater had been dug during the war for the anti-aircraft guns. Over time, it had filled in with thick brush and soft grass. The edges were lined with a variety of wild rosebushes. Plenty of small, spent, old blossom petals carpeted its basin like an artist's palette.

The young boy found it pleasant to hide out in the shades of these holes and take afternoon naps. He propped himself against the pig's soft stomach, and listened for his even, but strained, breathing. The pig's flat circular nose was wet and his scent, which would surely have repulsed any city person, was warm and comforting to Balazs.

The pair fell into a gentle sleep. Subconsciously, they listened to each other's breathing, but began to sense a third or maybe even a fourth layer of breathing too. It was out of sync and not in harmony with theirs! It was more heaving, quicker and sometimes broken into short, sharp segments. Balazs and the pig were being rudely derailed from their sleep, back into reality, by the persistence of the sounds. Balazs gently rolled off his pig, not to wake him, and slithered to the edge of the crater to examine the disturbance. The pig grunted in acknowledgment and drifted back to sleep.

Apparently, the adjacent crater also had some occupants in it. He crawled closer to spy. He heard some soft giggling and some rather deep groans. Some sounds seemed familiar to him even though he could not make out what was going on, or who was making them. He decided to brave it and crawl closer on his stomach to the edge, under the thick undergrowth, where he could not be detected.

He could hardly believe his eyes! There was a young peasant woman, the oldest daughter of the farmer from whom his family got their milk. She had a pretty, round face, nice light-brown hair, and was a bit on the plump side. Her layered peasant skirt was pushed up under her armpits, making her look like the over-bloomed rose blossoms on the bushes. From this mess of colorful petals, two snow-white legs, terminating in worn, red peasant boots, were alternatively flying and kicking in the air, or digging deep into the grass and the soft dirt bottom of the crater for leverage.

She was heaving and clawing at the back of the man who was between her legs, rising and falling toward her. Two pale, pink bottom cheeks flashed from tangled and hastily removed trousers. For a moment Balazs could not tell whether she was pushing the man away, pulling him in towards her, or both!

Her expression was of pain and ecstasy mixed with giggles, laughter and short screams. He tried to move closer to get a better view of the scene, which by now was pretty clear to him. He was no longer a city boy, and he had seen animals do that, but never before people!

He began to look for more details, but to no avail. If he moved in any closer, he might be discovered. As the heaving and the grunting reached its crescendo, another, competitive grunting, became evident. The lovers had also become aware of it. Irritated and distracted, they tried to turn and find its source. Too late! The grunting pig stood above them, looking for Balazs. Following the boy's scent, he scurried too close to the edge and lost his balance. Down came tumbling the enormous mass of raw fat and meat wrapped in bristles of steel, right on top of the lovers, snorting, squealing and crushing everything in its path.

But Balazs now beheld a sight he was not prepared for; the man who rolled off her was none other than Eugene—struggling to push the pig off him and the girl. Balazs laughed so hard at the absurdity of the situation that tears ran down his cheeks. Eugene was surprised, confused and embarrassed. But, as always, humor got the best of him too and he too roared with laughter. He struggled hastily to pull his trousers up, fighting with his suspenders, which kept snapping back. The young woman had still not found her composure by the time Balazs and his pig reached the bottom of the hill. As they descended, the pig continued to grunt in a peculiar fashion. Balazs was convinced that the pig was laughing, if there ever was such a thing.

He recalled how Paula had once humorously told him of her aversion to sex and how the very act for her was something done only out of "duty" to please the husband she loved. She was relieved when he nagged someone else with it. She had been sheltered as a young woman; so much that, on her honeymoon, Paula had been so frightened by what Eugene presented her with, that she had run home to her parents in panic.

TWELVE

THE FORTUNE TELLER

THE COLD WINDS blew in from the angry, gray, murky autumn lake. The waves crashed against the shore, where the rocks were piled up to prevent erosion. The thick sea of golden reeds lining the lake swayed and rode wildly on roller coaster of waves as the gusts of cold rain whipped it relentlessly.

The skies became dark with thick, black clouds turning the early morning into twilight. He leaned out of the window contemplating the empty landscape. The vacationers were all gone and the little town had settled back quickly into its routine.

Drops of cold rain began to hit the windowpane. Balazs smelled the warm aroma from his grandma's kitchen, making the room inviting, so he closed the window and tuned the radio to the classical station. Vivaldi's *Four Seasons* was playing; it matched his mood perfectly.

He entered the kitchen and hugged his grandma from behind. She reached back with her free arm while stirring the pot and pinched his side teasingly. Eugene was still outside cleaning the pigsty and the chicken coop. When he returned from the well with a large bucket of cold water, his clothes had the aroma of fresh rain.

Paula had gone to the library and taken out several of James Fennimore Cooper's novels, including *The Last of the Mohicans*. Balazs read often and very well for a child of his age. This was primarily due to Paula, who taught him early to read. When chores were done, and other children were not available or the weather was not practical for play, he read sitting in the corner of his bed, leaning against the wall. His imagination carried him into the wilderness of the early Americas filled with Indians. He had read many books by Cooper and Mark Twain.

Most impressive to him, however, were novels that dealt with the Turkish invasion of Hungary. Tangible evidence of the presence of the Turks was presented by the ruins behind the church the city of Veszprem, a few kilometers away with its castle, was the victim of years of occupation. Silent minarets still stood there, empty now of the mullah's eerie calls to prayer. No matter where he turned, he bumped into fascinating bits of history.

Last Spring, Eugene and Balazs were digging around the foundation of the house to make a new bed of flowers, when they hit upon many skeletal parts, including some well-preserved skulls, embedded in the red clay. Eugene told him of the villa's excavation and the discovery of an ancient graveyard from early battles of Buda. Many brave warriors were found buried facing east, toward the rising sun, as was customary, and surrounded by their bejeweled weaponry and earthly riches.

Reluctantly, Eugene in the end, decided to donate all that was found to the Veszprem museum's archaeological department. His find was not only historically valuable, but monetarily as well. He kept one set of gold stirrups and spurs that he could not resist. Eugene, well read in Hungarian history, knew that it was the "barbarian" Huns, with their Chinese origins, who introduced stirrups to the West. They also brought with them writings from the Sumerian culture, as Europe still lingered in the dark ages. They were credited for introducing from China such spices as paprika and ginger, as well as live silkworms.

After the Communists took over, all the gold treasures disappeared from the museum, and, to his chagrin, Eugene could only show Balazs his pair of finely fashioned golden stirrups and spurs. Upon seeing this treasure, Balazs was left with a fever to discover additional items to add to his growing collection of rocks, butterflies and bugs. For months, the yard appeared under siege by dozens of moles, because of the numerous holes the boy dug. He never discovered any treasure.

Winter hit with a severity unlike any Balazs had experienced in his short life. The snowstorms were frequent and without pause. Since it was bitterly cold, there was little opportunity to go and play. Instead, Balazs continued to spend a lot of time with Eugene making lampshades.

They drew pictures of Hungarian forts and castles under siege by the Turks. When the weather improved somewhat, he dragged through the high snow, sometimes disappearing all together, burrowing into tunnels that led from earlier ones, dug by others.

The snow could be more than two and a half meters deep in places, and higher in the drifts: the windows of the house would be totally covered. On such occasions, Eugene and Balazs would have to make burrows to the coop and the pigsty. Once, they noticed the shadow of a large crow above them—almost frozen onto the surface. Eugene and Balazs devised a plan to catch it.

Eugene would slowly and carefully dig under the crow, while Balazs would distract it with a twig pierced through the surface to keep the bird busy watching it. When sufficiently close, Eugene thrust both hands upwards and scooped the surprised bird from below. It screeched and fought, but Eugene held him tightly and stuffed it into the snow to grab its neck. With just a twist and a crack, the big black bird became limp, ready to be plucked.

Paula was so disgusted; she would have nothing to do with it. The two excited hunters had to clean the bird and make their own crow soup. It was a skinny, starved bird, but the two rascals enjoyed the whole thing and ate it all.

The winter wore on. The magical Christmas season arrived, and the townspeople celebrated the birth of Jesus with beautiful Christmas songs and prayers for deliverance from the Soviet occupation. The manger was set up in a corner of the church porch, and candlelight danced in the dark of the evening mass. Paula played the organ while the chorus of peasant ladies sang like so many angels. Mass being over, the three walked home under the clear evening sky with billions of stars twinkling above. They looked up toward its mystical beauty, recalling the story of the birth of Christ, wondering whether it was on such a peaceful night that the three kings saw the star that led them to Bethlehem.

As they looked up, a large V formation of wild geese flew overhead, honking their peculiar horn calls. Eugene stopped dead in his tracks and, as in his old hunting days, took his stance, holding his cherry-wood walking stick and pointed toward the sky at the passing birds. He sounded off two rounds of imaginary shots. Bang! Bang!

With a sigh of satisfaction, he lowered his cane. As he did, a dark object fell not far in the distance from above, thud—it landed in the frozen snow, near the bewildered family.

They hurried to the spot and saw a freshly shot fat gander, lying with prostrate wings in the snow. The following day they solved the mystery, as a local hunter complained of a missing goose. Eugene's loud imitation of the two shots, almost unbelievably, must have rung out simultaneously with the real ones of the hunter so they never heard them. Balazs became the owner of the newfound treasure of multi-colored feathers—shiny blue, green and purple.

That winter, on one of their bright moonlight walks as fresh snow sparkled and cracked below their boots, a solitary Gypsy woman appeared in front of them, as if by magic. All three were startled, especially Balazs, who was frightened by the old, witch-like woman, bundled in rags.

Staring at Balazs, her eyes seemed to burn like amber beneath the shade of her scarf. She spoke first, "Kiss yer hands and feet and have pity on a starvin' old Gypsy. I beg yer Excellencies' pardon. I can tell you are of higher breedin'. Let me tell the fortune of this young gentleman?" The Gypsy woman carried on with her honey-sweet compliments to earn her few coins.

Paula and Eugene felt spellbound, almost in a trance. Paula reached into her winter coat and put a few aluminum forints into the skeletal hands of the Gypsy woman. "May yer bless your generosity, always," said the shaky old voice as she reached for Balazs' reluctant hand. The moon was so bright that his little upturned white hand glowed against the darker one of the Gypsy. He could make out the lines of dirt in the old wrinkles. Her touch was hot, despite the cold. As she spoke in strange words he saw no trace of her breath in the frozen air. She frightened him and he tried to pull his hand back, but she held it fast and tight.

With meaningless mutterings, she ran her sharp fingernails along the lines in his palm and pronounced him a very fortunate child who would live in America, rich and happy. He pulled his hand back as soon as she loosened her tight hold with the relief of an animal that has escaped from a hunter's trap. Before Paula could even cynically remark at the pitiful and obvious fortune just told, the Gypsy woman had vanished without a trace. Eugene remarked jokingly, "Well, of course, if someone gives you money you are going to say something pleasant, even if it is impossible! I am certain none of us will ever see the free West as long as we live."

America! Balazs thought to himself, the West, the Indians and the cowboys, where everyone was free, happy and rich. The Gypsy woman had said he would be there one day! He did not want to argue with his grandparents, but somehow he believed the old woman. She seemed special and possessing mysterious knowledge. For many days he could not get her out of his mind, and secretly thought about her prediction. He told some of his friends at school, but they only laughed at his gullibility. So he stopped talking about it. But he never forgot.

THIRTEEN

THE MEETING

ON AN OVERCAST day, he took his grandmother's rusty bicycle out on the garden path that led steeply down to the iron-gate. It was a good place to jump on the pedal and ride the rest of the way down. When he gathered enough speed, he could stand with his left foot firmly on the pedal, then cross his right foot easily over to the right pedal to balance himself. After he shifted his entire weight onto his right foot, he could break before hitting the gate. Some of his friends already knew how to ride, and he could hardly wait to have the freedom and go with them around town.

Balazs was growing fast. His thin, little body was quick and beautiful, as children's often are at seven or so. The baby fat had been absorbed, more or less, from his face to match his skinny body. He was happy and adjusted, immersed fully into the life where fate brought him, despite the abuse he frequently received in school from his Communist teachers. As the teachers lectured the children on the evils of the old regime and the values of "The Communist Democracy" (a contradictory term if ever there was one, and typical of the double talk employed by the Party), Balazs was repeatedly asked to stand in front of the class as an example of the corrupt fascist, imperialistic and capitalistic system. He supposedly embodied all the evil caused to the people by his grandfather's generation, the traitors of the people and the enemy of the government. All lies, of course.

Before he reached his seat, he was often spit upon by some riled up children of the working class, but never by the children of the peasants. Balazs was so often called out that it no longer mattered to him. His grandparents explained to him about the politics of the day and of the world that had existed before to avoid confusion. He had no doubts about the lies the teachers taught. Early on he learned to understand to live between two worlds.

The neighborhood was quiet and uneventful on the third overcast day running as he practiced rolling down the hill. Only the crushing sound of gravel and his own puffing was audible as he pushed the bike back up the hill. He turned at the top with renewed confidence after his last success and sailed down the path again. Perfectly balancing and controlling the bike made him euphoric.

Upon reaching the bottom, he noticed he was not alone. A tall, strange figure of a man was leaning against the gate, intently staring at him. The unexpected presence threw him totally off balance and out of control. The bike and child came crashing into the iron-gate with full force.

Confused and embarrassed, he gathered himself from the wreckage and withdrew quickly from the helping hand offered by the stranger. He knew everyone in the small town and, as country children often were, he was shy and distrustful of strangers. Yet, he felt a very strange sensation—fear and attraction mixed with his curiosity. There was also an urgent desire to run for his life, indescribable and confusing. He glanced at the superficial wound on his bleeding knee, when the tall, strange man spoke in a deep voice.

"Are you hurt?" "No, I'm all right, it's just a scrape," replied Balazs, readying himself to bolt. "Stay," said the man, calmly, looking down at him and still leaning against the gate with his hands holding the vertical bars. Balazs turned and noticed just how very handsome and different this man was from any man he had ever seen. He was broad-shouldered and wore a stylish dress shirt casually opened at the collar; his sleeves were fitted with large, gold cufflinks. His grandfather had one of those, he remembered, but Balazs only saw him wear it once when Eugene went to the city, with written permission from the local government.

He had on a pair of light-gray pants and shiny, expensive shoes. Balazs noticed the man's extraordinarily beautiful hands and his aquamarine blue eyes. Eugene had an engraving called *The Kiss*, by the famous French sculptor August Rodin; these hands looked like the exact replica of the ones owned by the male statue, sinking into the nude woman's tender flesh.

However, being shy, he tried to avert eye contact with the man. After the first glance at them, he withdrew his eyes and returned his gaze to his hands. His skin was soft; the man smelled clean and sweet. He spoke again to the boy in what seemed like a hypnotic, baritone voice, "Do you see that big bus down the road?"

Balazs looked where the man pointed and saw what he had not noticed until now—a large, new, shiny bus. "Yes, I see it," he replied. "Well, how would you like to take a ride with me in that for a while?" "God, could I?" Balazs surprised himself, with his unguarded willingness. After he realized what he just said to a stranger in his excitement, he immediately withdrew the reply, knowing full well that it was not safe even talking to him. Nonetheless, he found himself curiously attracted to this stranger.

He was not afraid of him, and, although he could not explain why. It felt like he knew him. His eyes were warm despite their cold blue color. His voice mesmerized him. Yet, Balazs remained anxious.

"Wait here a minute," said the man, as he turned and walked across the street to the neighbor's house. Zsuzsa (as in Zsazsa) opened the door of the kitchen, as he was about to knock on the glass. Rooted to his spot, Balazs could not make out the conversation, but he noticed an excited Zsuzsa seemed visibly shaken. He overheard her saying something like,

"Yes, Maestro, I will be honored. Oh what a blessing from God!" She totally changed, finding new composure as she backed off, bowing in her retreat. She ran into her house, hurriedly tied a scarf about her hair and hastily rushed to Balazs, who was now quite curious.

What was the big fuss and excitement about? He wanted to get on that bus. He had once seen one like it pass through the town with lots of city people in it. It sped through, but did not stop. As the children stood to wave from the ditch, he recalled that only one person had returned the wave, but all the kids were happy for that little acknowledgement.

If he were to get on such a bus in view of his friends, he would be the envy of them all. He could not wait! Zsuzsa grabbed his hand and they ran up the hill to the house, while the man turned and walked down toward the bus. She whispered something to Paula and they went to the bedroom, leaving Balazs waiting outside. There was a big commotion inside the house and he heard his grandfather protesting and disagreeing about something. As the minutes passed, Balazs could no longer wait. He ran around to the other side of the villa and crawled into the little tower room. He peered down the road and watched the movements around the bus. The man was outside with a group of men and women, chatting and smoking cigarettes. The women, who wore red lipstick and lots of makeup, were dressed in bright, beautiful colors. The men, attired in handsome casuals, stood around blowing puffs of smoke into the air.

Balazs was called and he ran down. His grandfather seemed agitated, but Balazs knew that he must have lost the debate, because when the women folk decided on something, there was no way a man could win. Zsuzsa was smiling radiantly and as Paula addressed Balazs, she seemed very nervous. "Grandpa and I have decided that you can go with the man on the bus, but it won't be just a ride. They want you to go with them to Fured for a couple of days."

"You mean I can miss school?" asked the excited Balazs, without even suspecting or asking what this was all about. "Yes, and I have packed some changes of clothes for you. You will be gone for a few days. Now remember to be a good boy, polite, and make your grandparents proud. We are going to miss you." He hugged both of them, dismissing Eugene's discomfort, and ran down to the bus. Balazs looked around and was disappointed that none of the other kids were out to see him board the bus.

The man lifted him up the steps with ease. Balazs felt horrified that he was suddenly in the company of these strangers. The smell of perfume and smoke was overwhelming from all the made-up women, who were chatting and laughing. They seemed unable to keep their hands off him. They said nice things and asked him all sorts of questions, which he was very timid in answering. The beautiful man sat next to him and let him sit by the window. It all happened so fast that Balazs was frightened now and wondered if he had done the right thing.

The bus roared by the familiar sights of the lake that Balazs knew well. On days when the long freight trains came slowly through the town, he and his friends ran along the tracks, grabbing the handles, pulling themselves up the steps to get rides. He had taken many trips to other towns on the train, his cherished friend. If caught, they would have been in big trouble with the town officials and, of course, his grandparents. Especially since, not long ago, a boy fell under a train and had his leg cut off by the wheels. By the time help arrived, he had bled to death.

The bus ride was fun. The interior of this Icarus coach was new and clean. These buses were well designed and built, despite their Communist label. They were one of the few items exported, winning awards in Western Europe.

The soft sway of the well-built system made him sleepy. One of the attractive women moved up across from her seat and asked Balazs to sit on her lap. She had a son his age and she said she missed him. Balazs gladly obliged. He became more relaxed and comfortable. The conversations were about theater, acting and reminiscing about past anecdotes on stage. He just listened and answered only when spoken to. He didn't say anything about his father being a famous actor too and decided not to ask if they knew him. For the most part, Balazs had pretty much given up thinking about his father, since the drowning of little Csilla.

The late afternoon sun was large and golden as it broke through the softly painted, overcast gray skies. It settled into a brilliant orange, crimson glow before sinking into the lake. Grandpa always said some things only nature can get away with because, if an artist attempted to copy them, they end up just creating distasteful and mediocre kitsch. He drifted gently into sleep as the bus swayed and the twilight melted in with the muted chatter of the tired occupants.

The man didn't say much to him on the ride, but was satisfied just observing him for long periods of time when he felt the boy was not looking. As Balazs was about to drift off, the woman stroked his head and leaned near the man, "Sandor, there is no doubt in my mind that this child is yours. Just look at him. He is the spitting image of you!" "Yes, I think you are right," he responded with a somewhat broken tone.

Balazs overheard the woman's comment. He opened his eyes and stared directly at the man, whom this woman had addressed as Sandor! He was overwhelmed with the sudden and shocking realization. Tricked, cheated and betrayed! He turned to the woman who appeared caught and frightened. It came to him that everyone had lied to him and played a terrible, cruel trick! He was unprepared and was shocked at the discovery.

Sandor, overcome at his son's visible distress, reached toward him. Balazs instinctively withdrew in panic, then in the next split second, as if propelled by an unknown force, found himself in his father's arms crying uncontrollably. "Dad, oh, you are my dad!" He was shaking as he buried his face into his dad's comforting embrace. Father and son held each other tightly as they cried from pain and happiness combined.

Balazs now found an explanation for the man's mysterious magnetism over him, the many secret and loving glances. "I knew you would come, I knew you would, one day!" Balazs exclaimed, laughing and simultaneously sobbing. Sandor stroked his son gently and lovingly. His mixed emotions of guilt and love for his son were indescribable.

For an instant the moment was filled with confusion for father and son. The strain of this long-awaited moment was so overwhelming for Balazs, that he fell fast asleep in his father's arms.

Sandor looked down at his son with renewed love, knowing that he wanted his child with him. He feared and anticipated the answers he must give Balazs the following day. He knew how cheated his son would feel the day the bus would return him to his grandparents' home. He wished he could take his son with him, but that was not possible. He realized how unprepared he was in his heart for this visit.

The two days were filled with deep bonding, joy and play. The father devoted every moment to his newly found son. Balazs asked Sandor about his brother, Barna. Sandor told him about the wonderful woman that he had married, whom loved and cared for them. She was also a famous actress and her name was Kati. Of course Balazs knew of her, but from different descriptions.

Sandor rented an air gun at the hotel where they stayed with the cast for the few days of the Summer Stock. The two of them practiced target shooting at an old, white, chipped iron bedpost on a grassy hill. The air was aglow with the wet green day and in the still of an overcast sky everything seemed fresh. They strode by the lakeside, and beneath the boat docks discovered a huge lobster skeleton bleached white by time. They attempted to pull it out of the water, but it fell apart, so they abandoned the project.

Night came and the play began at the local theater. When the curtains were drawn, an unbelievably rich and stunning stage set appeared. The whole atmosphere was tantalizing with hundreds of hands applauding the entrance of Sandor, his father on the stage. Balazs was intoxicated with admiration and pride in his father, the father who had returned, who had come back for him, who loved him, who was the most wonderful man on earth.

He had never seen a photo of his father, and had no visual recall of him. He found pleasure in looking at him. He thought he was the most handsome and heroic man he had laid eyes on. Now he felt he would never be afraid of anything. His father would always protect him, unlike his grandfather, Eugene, who was small and weak, more a victim than a hero. Sandor, on the other-hand, was on top of the world and admired by all.

Balazs felt guilty for feeling this way and realized why Eugene was protesting this visit on the bus. They knew who this man was! Eugene was devastated and feared losing the love of his grandson—now truly a son to him, whom he loved deeply.

Balazs' thoughts of Eugene vanished quickly in the speed of events. Before he knew it the bus was on its way to Fuzfo to redeposit him back into the past. "But I thought you came back for me, so we can all be together," exclaimed the disappointed child with tears running down his cheeks. Frustrated and uncomfortably guilty, Sandor did not know how to handle the situation.

He tried to explain to Balazs logically that things are not as simple as they seem. There were laws; he couldn't just walk away with him.

None of that made any difference to Balazs. He felt cheated and lied to again. His father did not really love him. He couldn't just leave him behind again! Sandor tried everything to console the broken-hearted child, but to no avail. The boy retreated to the far end of the bus and would not respond. Now he realized fully that nothing had changed. He had been happy in the world he accepted and lived in, until his father showed up and ruined it all. Now he feared he would never fit in it again, that it would never be the same.

The bus pulled up the road of the twin-towered villa. The town children were out at play, but it did not matter anymore. Balazs pushed past his father, who stood by, sad and depressed. He watched him walk from the bus toward the villa, never looking back. In pain and in utter confusion, he sank quietly into the seat as the vehicle rolled down the path toward an obscure future.

FOURTEEN

SOVIET MAY PARADE

"ACTUALLY THAT WAS really funny, don't you think?" Eugene asked Balazs as they laughed about the calamity that had interrupted the May Day parade. The May 1st was the biggest annual Communist rally, and commemorated the "grand" Socialist system.

As the Soviets marched their armies and flexed their military muscle in Moscow's Red Square, so did the Hungarians, and all the other occupied countries. All had to attend: roll call was taken, with serious consequences for those not showing up. The school children were marched out too, and they were made to carry large, heavy posters.

This particular parade was organized up on the factory settlement, where the authorities had built an enormous paved area, large enough to accommodate thousands of people. The settlement, where they had the paper factory and the chemical factory, also included the apartments that housed several thousand workers and their families. Combined with that of lower Balatonfuzfo, the population here was more than three thousand.

The old folks were no longer required to march or listen to the boring speeches, but Eugene decided to come along anyway with the bike. The gentle spring breeze kept the crowds somewhat cool in the morning, but these events took long hours. Everyone was made to hold red flags or signs. Balazs, along with his classmates, were given a gigantic portrait of Stalin. The Party leaders were boasting of their wonderful accomplishments and conducted sing-a-longs of many Russian and Hungarian marching and party songs, played from scratchy old recordings, amplified by tin-can sounding speakers.

It was a joke, since everyone knew that this was a forced celebration. All that was cheered were phony events, followed by phony promises from phony people. Balazs wore the required red scarf of the Communist youth "pioneers," almost identical to the Nazi Hitler-Jugend organization, who had green scarves. He stood for hours on the burning concrete in the sweltering heat, while his grandfather waited in the cool shade of the blossoming chestnut trees, rolling his homemade cigarettes.

Like all his friends, Balazs was bored by it all, but he stood patiently. Sometimes he was stirred from his day dreaming by the sound of some new marching music that enlivened a meaningless speech. At times, flies would land on the kid's shirt in front of him, distracting his attention for a while, helping the time to pass.

He was not allowed to wear a cap out of respect. So the sun began to burn his scalp severely, while the concrete felt like it was boiling his toes, through the soles of his shoes. The sweat began to pour down his face and trickled down his sides from his armpits. He planted the pole of the large sign firmly on the ground for support, only raising it in the air when the signal was given for them to all cheer. He was thinking of a nice, cool swim in the lake after this ordeal. Almost, as if in a dream, he felt light and relaxed, with his feet gliding above ground. Suddenly, he woke to a hard knock on his face and forehead. His face was pressing against the hot concrete, totally disorienting him. He sat upright and found himself in the midst of a great commotion. When he was finally able to focus, the scene around him resembled a battlefield. Everywhere, children were on the ground in contorted positions, lying over each, and with broken signs and poles in every direction. Balazs was sun struck and, as he fell, hundreds of others came down with him in a domino effect, disrupting the entire affair.

Balazs and Eugene mused over the humor of the event as they worked side by side, hoeing the weeds from the young carrot patch.

He was now able to plant the vegetables and tend to them by himself, and even loved doing it. He knew that the young carrots would be about his hand's length, which he would pick and eat, freshly washed in the spring's cool water. The vegetable garden became an open-air set table for him, and he would return to it throughout the summer.

The betrayal he felt by his father's departure, and the remaining guilt of his abandoning Eugene, slowly subsided. Indeed, lately, he found being with Eugene more interesting than playing with his friends, not that he did not play wildly and vigorously whenever possible. When Eugene was not around, Paula asked about every detail of Sandor's visit and, to Balazs' surprise, he realized just how much she adored his father.

Unfortunately, as in the past, he had not received any communication from his father: no letters or cards at Christmas, on birthdays or for any occasion at all. Deep inside, he forgave his father. Unbidden, Balazs seemed to have developed the same love relationship with his father that his grandmother had.

****

The little kitchen became a sauna from the iron stove as the flames leaped from beneath the iron disk supporting the pan. Paula was frying breaded apple slices, while Balazs helped peel the potatoes for dinner. Eugene went to release the pig and fetch some water from the well.

Suddenly, Paula wavered, lost her balance and accidentally leaned onto the pan's handle. The pan flipped and the boiling hot grease spilled on her delicate, white skin, severely burning her. She fell, faint.

Balazs jumped to her aid and struggled to pull her through the little door. Eugene, arriving on the scene, immediately doused her burned arm with the cool bucket of well water as Paula made feeble attempts to regain her composure. She had severe third degree burns. They put her on the bed. Eugene ran around the room, frantically searching for the phone.

"Grandfather, we don't have a phone, it was taken from you after the war."

"Oh, God!" the old man broke down in desperation. "I keep forgetting, every damn thing was taken away. Balazs, honey, go see if Erzsi is home next door, while I put some wet cloth on your grandmother's burns and forehead."

When Erzsi arrived to help, Paula was still in pain on the bed. Eugene decided that he must get some medical help. He got on the bike with Balazs behind him on the metal rack and pedaled off to the local Communist Party headquarters. This was where Erzsi's husband had been dragged off, severely beaten, and later put in jail. Eugene wanted to ask permission to use the phone and call for help at the Veszprem Hospital.

Frightened and out of his wits, Eugene kept repeating how much he loved Paula and begged God not to take her from him. What would he do without her? He would make any promise to God, just to save her. Balazs began to panic, too, realizing how serious this must be, with Eugene talking about death, about losing her. Sitting on the back rack, he held on tightly and urged Eugene to pedal faster.

They arrived at the shabby farmhouse with the red metal star on the roof. It was the office of the fat little Communist the boy had learned to hate so much. His son attended the same classes and encouraged Balazs' harassment. The man stood with his back to them at the side of the yard—pissing across the neighbor's fence onto the fruit laden raspberry bushes.

Irritated, he turned to see who had opened the squeaky gate as Eugene, in his haste, dropped the bike against it. The man's penis slid back slowly through his unzipped fly, leaving yellow beads of urine running inside and outside his pant legs.

Layers of pigeon droppings from the suspended coop under the roof were piled on the threshold of the door. Chickens were scratching mindlessly in the dirt of the neglected, grassless yard, making small clouds of dust. The dog, with his empty water dish, parched and mad from thirst, barked viciously at the strangers, hopelessly trying to tear himself from his chain. "

What you want?" he grunted at the obviously panicked old man.

"We need, with your permission, sir, ah, excuse me, comrade, we need to use the phone for a family emergency," Eugene stuttered.

Once they stepped into the office, the man having noticed his visitor's urgency and frustration, deliberately and slowly walked around his desk. This kind of torture, which he employed to exercise and emphasize his power over helpless people, was one of his sickest specialties. His pleasure in life was actually the pain he could cause these formerly well-to-do people.

What right did they have to live so well, he thought? It serves them right to have nothing and to answer to the likes of him.

Eugene had never had any dealings with him before. It was obvious this man had been waiting a long time for the opportunity to cross Eugene's path.

"So, the capitalistic pig wants to use the people's phone?"

"Yes, sir, err comrade, I implore you. We are desperate. My wife has had an accident. We urgently need a doctor," begged Eugene, ignoring the sarcastic remark.

"I am comrade to you always, pig! There are no sirs in this era, if you have not noticed," the red faced official screamed.

"Perhaps you need a little rehabilitation, like your son got, to bring you up to date!"

"No, sir, I mean comrade." The form of address sounded so foreign to Balazs, coming from his grandfather's lips.

"You know it's a communist phone, it might just contaminate your bourgeoisie ears," he teased the old man further.

"Please comrade, please," Eugene pleaded in fear that time was wasting and might prove fatal to his wife. He would do anything to prevent that from happening. The man read Eugene's mind and said, "I suppose you would even get down on your knees and beg to use this here phone?"

"Yes, comrade, I would," replied the humbled old man, broken and powerless.

"Don't, grandfather, don't," implored the outraged child. "Why don't we just get back on the bike and hurry to Veszprem?"

"Hush, Balazs, we don't have that time," said his grandfather, who leaned on the edge of the desk, then knelt like a disciplined school boy to the visible satisfaction of the pompous, worthless Communist official.

A moment of suspenseful silence held the room. Then the man said, "I could also make you sing like a canary if I wanted, but to show how lenient I am with scum like you, I'll let it pass."

He lit a cigarette, took a deep breath and exhaled, filling the room with a cloud of smoke. With that he cleared his throat, hawked up a mouthful of yellow phlegm, which he spat right into Eugene's shocked face. Balazs watched the old man's kind blue eyes fill with tears that riveted down his face.

Balazs was so filled with hate and anger that he did not see the man depart, or hear his departing words to the old man, delivered with a triumphant smile, "The phone is yours, pig."

"My father would never ever let this happen to him," Balazs shouted in Eugene's face in utter frustration. But as soon as he said those words, he felt his grandfather's pain and the humiliation he had just endured, and he felt ashamed.

Eugene did not respond to the pain caused by Balazs's remark, but reached for his handkerchief and slowly wiped the spit from his face. Painstakingly, he stood up, reached over the desk, removed the heavy black receiver and, with shaking fingers, dialed the operator.

FIFTEEN

FIRST MOVIE

HE WAS AT the crossroads of his life. Everything was becoming more complicated, when it should have been easier. Ever since his father had paid him that unexpected visit, Balazs felt like he was unintentionally hurting his grandfather at every turn.

Now there was an excitement in the air. The town was looking forward to some kind of film attraction. There were posters announcing the film showing Sandor, his father, in the main role. Everybody was talking about the movie. Children, even those related to the Communist Party members, became more lenient with Balazs and gave him more respect after they found out that the featured actor was his famous father. Now everyone wanted to know whether he was going to the movies or not.

Certainly, he wanted to go. But how was he to ask Eugene for money to see his father's film, knowing the pain that request might cause? He could ask Paula, but it would still get back to Eugene. He did not want to play one against the other.

He decided that the only way to get the money was to swipe it from the drawer, where Eugene always dropped change or leftover coins after shopping. He had never stolen, or even thought of stealing anything, before. He followed his Ten Commandments very strictly, now that he was an altar boy, helping Lajos at Sunday Mass, baptisms and other celebrations. He did admit in the dark confessional booth of the church to cussing a lot. After he confessed his sins, Lajos made him say hundreds of prayers over the stages of the Cross.

But stealing was something different. They were still dirt poor, and the lampshade trade was absolutely necessary to them. Their little garden brought in the badly needed produce. It was still insufficient with the rising prices. To make ends meet, they made most of their basic necessities themselves. Paula joined the peasant women of the village in boiling pigs' fat and mixing it with lye to make soap. Balazs hated the disgusting tasting soap. He was also told to use it to brush his teeth, because there was no real toothpaste available. A disease that swept the region infected the chickens they had raised, and they lost more than 60 out of 70 birds.

The painful day had even arrived last fall when his grandparents gently informed him that his pig had to be slaughtered for food. He knew that the time would come one day, but somehow duped himself into thinking that it only happened to his friends' pigs, not his. His first reaction was to hide the pig in the nearby woods, but the pig chewed its rope and returned home. Then he hid him in several sties of trusting buddies, but to no avail. In the end, he gave up the fight and released his loyal friend to the ultimate fate of all pigs.

The village butcher came one early November morning to do the butchering. He was known to do the best job, causing the beasts the least amount of suffering. The neighbor's roughly hewn table (the same place where little Csilla's body had been stretched out) was used for the prepping. The hand-held coal torch was ready to burn the bristles from the surface of the skin as the peasant women readied large cauldrons of hot water to clean the intestines. They were to be filled with the finest of spices and ground meat to create the famous Hungarian sausage. The hoofs and head made up the base for aspic in the aromatic garlic broth. The brain was prepared in various ways as a gift of delicacy for the major contributors to the work. The sausages and the thighs were later smoked as an ancient preservative for prolonging the shelf life of the food.

All of this was going to be done to his friend. Like Judas, he sold him out. He was miserable and guilty, yet helpless. His self-consoling promise was his determination that, even if starved to death, he was not going to eat any part of his friend. He stayed inside the house to avoid being seen by his pig, yet he could not tear himself away from spying through the wooden shutters, which Eugene closed in order to protect him from this painful sight. The pig was brought out and the men tied his front and hind legs together.

As he lay, unsuspecting and trusting, on his side, a sharp knife penetrated through the more than 12cm layer of fat on his chest, just slightly above his front legs. As the knife slashed through the first real flesh and nerves on its way to the deeply hidden heart, a piercing scream came from the beast. It ripped the air and ricocheted off the walls of the house, the trunks of trees and echoed back from across the hill. The butcher struck deeper, cutting the vitals and passing into the lungs as well.

It was awful. Thankfully, the bloody ordeal did not last long, though it felt like an eternity. It left him feeling empty. He opened the veranda door and entered the scene to everyone's surprise. He saw the body lying on the table with a clean, open cut on his chest. He was dead. Just like the table below him, he had become an object. The pig saw nothing through his glassy eyes of death, but Balazs felt somehow that his friend's spirit was lingering about him watching. He had leaned over, kissed the peaceful head and walked away toward the lake in dazed numbness.

Now Balazs stood, looking into the drawer with fear and indecision—aching to take the money from his grandfather. This would be his first film, and he wanted to be near his father, if only through the fleeting projection on the screen. Again the same nagging feeling of guilt came over him with the knowledge that he was causing Eugene pain. Nevertheless, he snuck into the last row of folding chairs, under a great big tree, by the old creaking projector. The film started over several times and broke down often with the strips of film flapping furiously about like a chicken with its head cut off. None of this seemed to distract him from the trance that possessed him.

The enlarged image of his handsome father on the screen, coupled with his strong and graceful stature, captivated him completely. He yearned and ached and loved all at the same time. As much as he loved his grandparents, he knew with all his heart where he belonged – by his father's side.

The thrill of having seen his first movie starring his father filled him with much pride as he walked through the veranda door. Flushed like a young lover, caught sneaking home from a night's passion, so Balazs was caught totally off guard when he found Eugene sitting up with a reproachful look on his face.

"You could have asked me for the money, Balazs. You know my love better than to resort to stealing." That was all he said, as he turned and went out into the darkness to hide his pain. The blow of that simple pronouncement stunned the boy. A good spanking would have been a much easier punishment to bear. Now he was left with the permanent burden of guilt. He could not bring himself to run after his grandfather and comfort him. He had cheated and deceived him. His guilt turned to anger and resentment toward him—this was not fair!

He threw himself onto his bed, looked over to his grandmother who was pretending to be asleep. Balazs felt for the first time in his life that he wanted to run away, to run and it didn't matter where. The room seemed very small and stifling. He slid off the side of his bed with his pillow in hand—turned the corner of the house, mounted the stairs for the tower and opened the hinged door to settle in on the sun-warmed sand. Lying there, he peered out through the slits and cast longing gazes across the silvery surface of the tranquil lake.

SIXTEEN

THE CIRCUS TRAIN

IT WAS EARLY the following morning, the 5am express was not even halfway around the lake, and nothing was stirring. On a peaceful summer morning like this, he liked to wait in complete stillness to catch the very first faint vibrations of the train. Balazs regularly jumped undetected on the trains to get a free ride and visit towns bordering the lake. Now and then, he was able to deceive the conductors into thinking that he belonged to the families with which he shared window seats. He enjoyed the magic of the continuously flowing landscapes. The rhythmic clanking of the metal wheels, repeatedly hitting against the steel track joints, sometimes rocked him into a hypnotic slumber. Some of these deep sleeps were interrupted by the sharp whistle calls from his friend jolting him back to reality. With haste, he would jump off the moving train to catch the returning ride back. He was home before anyone missed him.

The train sometimes had to wait long periods for the oncoming trains to avoid collision. This gave ample time for his inquisitive hands to touch every part of the engine within his reach, that wasn't too hot. As he felt the huge iron wheels with their bright red spokes, he imagined that the great patient beast had some sort of awareness of him.

Sometimes, the soft huffing and puffing sounded to Balazs like expressions of approval by the trusting Avatar, tolerating and yielding to his inquiring presence. Balazs had no doubt that there was a secret, special bond between them. Perhaps the thing was not merely so much metal and steam. It had a free spirit and a thundering personality—not to mention its speed and strength. Even the smell of soot created by the glowing and smoking coal being digested in the hot belly had a special resonance for him. It sent sparks flying into the dark night sky as it rushed past the villa, slithering like a smoldering dragon, screeching as it made its way around the sharp turns.

Balazs tried gazing through the slow rising fog. He sensed the first gentle vibrations beneath the villa from the distant rumbling of the train. He did not return to the house, but as soon as he reached ground level, he mounted the old, rusty bike and rolled down the hill to intercept his friend. Some sparrows began early to chirp in the trees, but did not leave the safety of their perches. The greenish-white fog still lingered.

He did not go as far as the station, but turned and crossed the tracks, dumped the bike into the ditch and sat on the soft, uncut, tall wet grass. Through the fog he faced the hardly visible villa, which looked like an enchanted castle suspended in the sky.

He heard his friend as the wheels screeched while entering the tight bend, followed by the triple-whistle warning. The nozzle of the whistle atop the engine looked like the spout of some giant whale depicted in the old engravings Eugene had in Jules Verne novels. In his mind, he could clearly see every detail, the wheels, the wagons and the black locomotive with the chimney appearing first, erect and proud through the fog. The wagons followed, like a serpent's tail, whipped in any direction at the will of the behemoth.

As the anticipated image of the engine with the red star penetrated the fog and flew towards him, the most surprising scene unfolded to test his imagination. Colorful, large, painted wagons hitched behind the locomotive unraveled from the mist. As if in some happy celebration, the whistle blew again countless times. These wagons were the type that carried closed freight, but had bright murals painted on them, depicting exotic animals such as tigers and elephants jumping through circles of fire, or clowns and half-naked women balancing on large balls. None of this resembled the drab, rust-colored wagons he was expecting. These colorful cars brightened the otherwise monotonous landscape around him, which seemed as bland as he felt his life to be, compared to this jubilant barrage of fantasy rushing upon his tranquil, sleepy town.

He saw equally colorful people shouting and yelling through the windows—laughing, blowing kisses toward him and throwing bright flyers into the air. Some blew trumpets, some beat on brass plates and some even danced atop the moving vehicle's rooftops, with clowns jumping from wagon to wagon with ease and great precision. Balazs was spellbound—his heart raced with imagination far ahead of this train, which, he now saw, had accelerated rather than slowed at the station.

As the noisy, chaotic scene ran past his bedazzled eyes, he realized he was holding the circus prospectus announcing the following week as the date of the performance in Fuzfo. He ran in mad, frenzied delight to gather the flyers, which decorated the green ditch like hundreds of red poppies in bloom. Forgetting the bike, he ran up the hill, burst into the sleepy villa, breathlessly trying to explain everything he had just experienced, totally incoherent from the muddle in his mind. He attempted it over several times, waving the leaflets like a windmill in the face of his grandparents.

****

Around this time, there was renewed anti-Semitism instigated by the ruling leaders, called "The Red Gang of Four," ironically with Matyas Rakosi, a Jew, at the helm. The Gang of Four, Jews who were survivors of the Nazi era and later trained in the Soviet Union as Communists, did not retaliate on the few who were guilty Nazi sympathizers, but on the entire nation. They used Fascists' methods too, combined with those of Stalin, to purge the intelligentsia. They executed hundreds of thousands and banished as many to Soviet Gulags in Siberia or China to forced labor camps.

They reigned with terror—labeling all that questioned their rule, even if they were of the same Communist stock, as "subversive." They viewed every idea with suspicion and as potentially representing ideological betrayal. Therefore, no one felt safe.

Rakosi's terror on this small nation made Eugene feel betrayed and furious. He could not comprehend how a Jew, who had suffered under Nazi terror and survived, had not learned anything from it, but continued simply repeated their evil works against humanity under another excuse.

Before the war, Hungary was not affected to the same degree by the wave of anti-Semitic hysteria of Europe and other neighboring countries (although it is true the first openly anti-Semitic laws were passed here in the 1920s). It generally had a history of tolerance—allowing Jews to own land unlike the other European countries. Through hundreds of years, a large Jewish population evolved—drawing more and more Jews to the land for better and higher opportunities in government and business. It was only here that the Jewish aristocracy evolved (as landowners with titles) These Jews lived freely in wealth and unchallenged pomp.

As a result of the occupation of Hungary by Austria (against whom the Hungarians revolted in 1848), there were thousands of resident German sympathizers to the Nazi cause still loyal to their fatherland. While living in Hungary, their voices of sick fascism were often mistaken for those of the Hungarian's.

Jews were not interned into camps in Hungary, at least until the Germans marched in and took over the country, because the government didn't allow the camps or the persecutions to exist. Many attempts to destroy the Jewish population of Hungary by Hitler's regime were derailed. (The 1941 census counted some 825,000 Hungarian Jews, 6% of the total population. This number included 100,000 converts to Christianity who, under Hungarian race laws which were passed between 1938 and 1941, they were still considered Jews. In 1942, the German government kept pressuring Hungary to hand over Hungarian Jews into their custody. But Prime Minister Miklos Kallay refused.)

Eugene was in a high-ranking advisory position to the ministry of the Catholic Diocese in the previous regime. He was open minded and respected different views in life; he reared his children in the same manner. His younger son, Gyorgy, happened to fall in love with, and marry, a Sephardic Jewess at a time when the long German arm was beginning to reach out for the destruction of the Jewish people. Eugene, seeing the situation for what it was, quickly used his influence, and had papers forged for his daughter-in-law and her family, proving them to be Catholics. Eugene thus managed to save the lives of hundreds of Jews from being deported and taken by the Germans. Had some Nazi sympathizer discovered his actions, Eugene knew he could have ended up in some concentration camp and gassed like the other three million non-Jewish victims of Hitler. Despite the dangers, Eugene continued to practice what he felt was morally correct.

Ironically, the local Soviet-trained Communists in Fuzfo, despite the country's Jewish Communist leadership, hated the Jews as much as the Nazis. They began to bully Eugene for being a Jew-lover. So Balazs also had the pleasure of not only being condemned as the descendant of capitalist pigs, but also a Jew-lover to boot. The madness of human prejudice and ignorance was as confusing to Balazs as it was to his grandparents. And it seemed to permeate the educational system too.

****

The days dragged on and he could not concentrate on anything, especially at school, as his mind was totally preoccupied with the circus. There were only a few days left, which made it all the harder for the children. Spring fever accompanied by the rare, forthcoming circus in such a small village, sent children and adults alike into a frenzy of anticipation.

The run up to the arrival of the circus was also Soviet week, which meant that all the children were forced to speak only Russian. Balazs so hated Soviet week, or, indeed, anything Russian, that he found it psychologically debilitating and burdensome to memorize his homework. He developed an angry aversion—a mental block to it. It was far from a unique affliction—the symptom had affected millions of children across the Iron Curtain countries, especially those families who had suffered personally from the occupation.

His excitement was so extreme that he slipped and broke the rules, just as he was standing by the Russian language teacher. This freshly brainwashed

Communist woman, who had recently returned from Moscow's Marxist school, hated Balazs for one reason or another. Her persecution was so vividly concentrated that even his classmates, who often made his life miserable, turned with sympathy and consoling glances toward him. This short, skinny, unhealthy looking woman with charcoal-black hair would hit Balazs with a wooden ruler anytime she had an opportunity. She would whip him across his bare neck as she passed in the aisles. Worse yet, when he gave an unsatisfactory answer to her question, she would have him hold his small hands vertically with fingers tightly closed together, With full force, and lightning speed, she would bring the ruler down hard on its mark on the tip of his nails.

The blood would squirt from under the bed of his nails as he suffered an agony that seemed to reverberate through his entire body. He flinched as he held the other hand, waiting for her to deliver the second assault. He could see from the evil glow in her passionate, coal-black eyes the pleasure she derived from the torment. He wished her dead and imagined her demise in many ways. For days following these beatings, he was unable to do his homework or help Eugene in the yard.

Strict rules of conduct and obedience were enforced throughout the Communist school system. All students had to sit straight up in their chairs with hands folded behind them. The only time it was allowed to bring one forth was when raised for questions or writing. The classrooms were always silent and undisturbed places for "education." No time was wasted on discipline, but when it happened it was carried out with severe corporal methods at the teacher's discretion. When his grandparents went to plead with the principal, their complaint fell on deaf ears. Balazs witnessed the abuse of others as well.

When Balazs accidentally spoke in Hungarian about the circus to the child next to him, the Russian teacher overheard. She didn't waste a second in letting him know he had broken an important rule. Before he was able to duck, she hit him with full force, almost puncturing his eyeball. As a small vein spurted with blood, Balazs dropped instinctively to the floor covering his face in fear that he might lose the eye.

After the initial shock and the realization of what happened, he was consumed with hate. Spying the open door, he jumped up and bolted through it, not stopping until he reached the villa.

Paula carefully examined the damage and determined that his sight was in no permanent danger. There was a temporary scratch on the cornea and a deep wound to the flesh. There could be no consolation, though, for the inner damage was more lasting and cut deeper than the flesh wound. Only Eugene's reminder of the forthcoming circus restored his sanity.

SEVENTEEN

THE RUNAWAY

THEY WALKED through town under a gigantic, dull orange sun, and were joined by groups of excited villagers. The circus train had pulled in at dawn to give their workers time to set up the huge tents in the green meadows at the far end of town.

The town's folk showed up willingly, unlike for the compulsory parades in May. All were excited to have this momentary escape from their otherwise miserable existence. The soft, gentle breeze carried the pleasant scent of the muscular stallions that snorted and dug their hoofs into the dirt. Lions roared somewhere in the distance, while large Indian elephants calmly reached out their trunks for the carrots offered by the more precocious children. Jugglers teased the delighted crowds, and numerous competitive clowns ran mischievously among the children, handing out cotton candy or multi-colored popcorn.

A man on what seemed like incredibly high stilts took giant steps around the campground, announcing the coming events, as colorfully garbed Gypsies read the palms of the gullible. The crowd pushed the three of them through the entrance. Balazs was dazzled. The band played festive music, while the circus attendants tidied up the equipment for the show. Sawdust was thrown into the rink inside the red-velvet border that circled the stage. Trapeze artists' ropes and ladders hung over head like the web of a giant spider. They cut the bright lights into angles, crisscrossing the flying dust like a cubist painting. Children shouted and screamed as horses neighed, tigers roared and dogs barked in a happy mix of sounds.

With all the seats occupied, the repeated blinking of lights heralded the beginning of the show. A heavy, mustachioed circus master appeared in the arena and, as all the floodlights focused on his stumpy figure; he graciously swung his top hat into the air to acknowledge the audience and to introduce the performers.

Balazs sat spellbound with his mouth agape at the masterful performances, and felt envious of such an exotic, exciting life. These people seemed so free, not like those of his village, he thought. The men and women were masters of their skills—riding while standing on the backs of fast horses, juggling and twirling plates with flawless precision, throwing knives around a woman spinning on a wheel. There were dangerous stunts by fearless tamers of tigers and bears. All the color, pageantry and music brought nonstop applause from the happy, delighted crowd.

The boy had heard that the circus performers, like the Hungarian athletes, were allowed to travel not only throughout the Eastern Bloc countries, but also to the West. As he was dreaming about circus life and comparing it to the drab existence in his village, an attractive family of trapeze artists in glittering outfits entered the arena. With swift agility, they climbed the ropes to the utmost heights of the great tent, accomplishing stunts that defied gravity and fear.

The couple's little daughter, a beautiful girl around Balazs' age with sparkling blond hair, held a long, slightly bent rod in her hands as she walked along a tightrope. She was crossing at least 14 meters or so above the spectators, without a safety net. The audience was silent for fear that she would lose her concentration and fall to her death. She stood on one foot in the center of the rope as the drums began to beat faster to accent the zenith of her performance. Her young parents stood on the sides with unwavering confidence, admiring their child's stunning skill.

The little girl, fragile-looking but with well-formed muscular legs, wore makeup and lipstick that made her look quite mature. After she had completed numerous heart-stopping stunts, she took to the vertical ropes and slid onto the *terra firma* below to execute her graceful bow and receive the well-deserved applause from the relieved audience.

As the show continued, Balazs kept thinking about this superhuman little girl, and how wonderful it would be to travel with the show; to earn money while performing something, or tend to the animals, anything to be gone from this life. He felt the scab on his temple throbbing at his touch. The difficulty of seeing the show through one swollen eye reminded him of his condition.

It made him all the more determined for a change of venue. Perhaps he could work with the circus train and be by his faithful old friend forever. He loved his grandparents and did not want to hurt them, but he would not have to attend school. He could earn money to send them. He would no longer be a burden to them, since it would be easier to feed two mouths than it would three. Eugene and Paula could not, anyway, protect him from the people who hurt him.

Perhaps, one day, he'd become a famous performer like his father and show up in Budapest with the circus, inviting him to a show. What great fun that would be. He was now determined to join the circus, but how? His grandparents would naturally never consent to his leaving, so he had no other choice but to run away. He had to act fast and think of a way to accomplish this, knowing that the circus was there for one night only, and would be packing up after the show. He knew no one at the circus, so what if they did not want him and rejected him? Looking very innocent, he turned to his grandparents and excused himself to go outside. He exited into the fresh cool air of the night. He ran to some wagons holding the cages of the performing animals. He glanced back at the great tent. In the night, it looked like a giant Japanese lantern, rocked by music and laughter.

He almost returned, reluctant to miss anything, but, then again, what would it matter anyway if he were to go away with the circus? Just as he was about to seek someone out for advice, a door opened from the adjacent wagon, casting light on him. He was about to bolt but there in the doorway, was none other than the little tightrope dancer.

"You came to see the animals?" she asked as she found him standing dumbfounded and lost for words.

"Yeah," he replied. Before he knew it, they were skipping from cage to cage while she entertained him with an informative dialogue about the animals. She was very open and personable, not as cautious and shy as he was with strangers. She made him feel so much at ease that it seemed as if they had known each other for a long time. He could not help casting secret looks at her beauty. She still wore her costume, which made her look like a miniature copy of her beautiful mother.

Abruptly, Balazs asked, "How can I get a job with the circus?"

"I don't know, I guess one has to be born into it. Everyone here is like me— either they are the kids of someone or they came from another circus," she replied innocently, not realizing his full drift.

"No, I mean how could I, if I wanted to come and work for this circus?" asked Balazs, now a little irritated in not getting a direct answer.

"I told you already, I never heard of anyone joining the circus unless they were born into it," snapped back the little girl, now a bit annoyed with him. Then, with light laughter as she finally realized the *real* meaning of his inquiry, she added, "Well, if you really want to run away with us, I will help you. There are not many kids at the circus for me to play with. The other children are much older or much younger than I am, so I can't even talk to them. Oh! I have an idea!"

"What?" Balazs asked so loudly that he frightened himself, lest someone overheard and would unmask their conspiracy.

"Well, perhaps you could come back after everyone has gone to sleep at your house. I will let you in the wagon while everyone here is busy dismantling the camp; my parents will be helping, too. You can hide in the back, where I sleep, and, by the time they find you, we will be far enough away for anyone to be able to do anything about it! It will also be easier then to talking them into keeping you."

Balazs thought that sounded great, but asked, "Are you sure your parents won't mind?"

The girl thought for a moment and a shadow of doubt passed across the so-far enthusiastic expression. "My parents could be persuaded by me, but I forgot about the two AVO among us! We don't exactly know who they are, but we think one of them is a clown. If they catch you, you will be in big trouble."

"What do you mean?" asked a downhearted Balazs.

"Well, the AVO were planted among us and they are everywhere, so none of us are sure who our friends are. Mom and Dad told me never to talk about what we say at home, because they will be taken away to camps or tortured, as others were in the circus last year. We just don't know who they are and it's really scary. Now my parents don't talk to anyone, because the AVO could even be their best friends. Everybody is afraid now."

"But maybe because I am a kid they won't notice," Balazs said, not wanting to give up his plans. They agreed to meet later in the night. He returned to the bright lights. The noisy performance was still in full swing. Hurriedly, he snuggled up to Paula, who reproached him for worrying Eugene, who had gone looking for him. Eugene returned from his search with a smile, telling Paula that he ran into the circus manager, who had turned out to be an old attorney colleague of his. Denied law practice, too, for being an enemy of the people, he had, however, been allowed this new position. It lifted Eugene's spirits to have found someone from his past and class with relative good fortune.

They were all tired from the late circus night. Balazs again faked the brushing of his teeth with the dreadful-smelling pig's lard soap. He kissed and wished them goodnight. He thought for a moment of his flight and returned again to their bedside, kissing them with more passion, uncertain when he would see them again. He felt guilty, but his excitement for a new life soon overcame it as he stared at the ceiling wide-eyed, awaiting the first signs of their deep sleep. Before quietly dressing, he made coughed a few times to test the depths of their sleep. Slowly, like a shadow, he stole across the floor and exited the villa.

He crossed the village—passing the church on the street parallel to the main road to avoid being detected. A few solitary dogs barked in the night, but he safely reached the sidings where most of the circus wagons were parked. The camp was already bustling with circus people—feeding animals, dismantling equipment, generally doing anything that could be accomplished in the light of the tent.

The girl had been right—the commotion was so big that no one noticed him walking across the camp. As he worked his way to her wagon, he realized he had forgotten even to ask her name. Nervously, he looked about once more and, with his heart pounding fast, reached for the handle of the door. Just as he touched it, it swung open almost hitting him in the face. With her strong, athletic arm, she hoisted him up by his reaching hand, into the semi-dark wagon.

"Hurry! What took you so long? My parents are almost back from their chores." Before he could reply she added, "My name is Ildiko, come let's hurry and go to the back of the wagon. You can hide among the clothing and go to sleep near me."

She laid down in what seemed like an open trunk, with lots of linen beneath her. He burrowed under more cast-aside clothes in a bigger pile in the adjoining corner.

"What's your name, runaway?" she whispered coyly.

"I am sorry, it's Balazs."

"Don't be sorry, it's a nice name, and unusual. I never met anyone called Balazs. Goodnight." "Goodnight, and thanks," he replied as he covered his body and head in the scent of dried lavender, just like the type used by his grandmother, and, exhausted, fell asleep.

EIGHTEEN

THE END OF THE RIDE

THE HARD JOLT and the abrupt push of the locomotive as it banked shook the sleeping occupants of the last wagon. Balazs opened his eyes in the dark, but fell instantly back into deep sleep. The colorful wagons slowly and quietly pulled out of town, leaving behind only traces of trampled grass and many pleasant memories. This one night seemed for many villagers like a day of sunshine in the midst of a bleak and dreary winter.

The cabin's temperature began to rise rapidly from the bright noon sun that beat down on the metal roofs. The sweat was pouring from his temples as he slowly woke to the movement of the train, and what he found to be a loud family quarrel.

"Ildiko, you know better than to do such a thing to your parents. How many times do we have to explain that there are AVO men among us and anything that brings attention to us can endanger all of our lives?" Balazs presumed it was her father's voice.

"But Karcsi [pronounced Karchi], it isn't a political thing. The little boy is just filled with fantasy for the circus like so many children are. Let him stay a while. We can make up some story that he is a visiting nephew and return him in a few days," suggested the mother.

"Yes, please, Papa," implored the little girl, now that she felt she had her mother's support. Ildiko was desperate for company of her own age. After all, her days were spent as an adult, filled with the rigors of daily practice with her parents and a few hours of studies, but hardly anyone to play with in her free time.

The three of them were still debating furiously as Balazs appeared in the small door of the "main everything room" of the wagon. A variety of shiny theatrical costumes hung decorating the walls. Trunks crammed with personal things under lock and key and several kerosene lamps filled the cabin. On the walls posters featured the young couple as star acrobats. A small table and a few chairs took up most of the floor space. The three were having a typical Hungarian breakfast of smoked sausage, rye bread, green and yellow bell peppers, with hard-boiled eggs. A small kerosene burner heated the teapot in the middle of the table, which was shooting out streams of steam like a miniature locomotive.

"So, young man, you are the runaway causing us all the fuss?"

Balazs, embarrassed and feeling very guilty for not having thought this all out clearly, stood there blushing beat red. "Yes, sir, I am sorry." He hurriedly added, "I can take the next train back to Fuzfo if you want. I am sorry. I don't want to cause you any harm by this."

"Well, come on in and let's have breakfast first before we make another foolish decision," said the father, comforting the boy with a warm and winning smile. Balazs sat by the table but did not dare to look the couple in the eye and hid in his shyness. He began filling his hungry belly with sausage and bread.

The conversation went on regarding the dangers and the chances they were taking in harboring a runaway child. The AVO was, of course, quite aware of the number of people in the circus, and would know every detail about their private lives. The pretense that he was a visiting nephew could only be maintained for a limited amount of time before it was found to be untrue: then what? Any bending of the rules was punished, in the interests of the people and the protection of the workers' paradise from the capitalistic elements trying to undermine the success of Socialism, of course.

However simple and poor their lives were, the family considered themselves lucky to be serving in a state-run circus. They received salaries from the government and, by most standards, they were free. They traveled throughout the land and often performed in neighboring Soviet-occupied countries. There was talk of perhaps giving performances in Austria in the near future.

They sat for many hours deliberating and getting to know each other. Balazs told them his life story and about his grandparents. They, in turn, told him about theirs. He liked them and the feeling seemed mutual. So, soon the young couple began to entertain an approach to help him stay with the circus, since he really showed such enthusiasm and desire.

Karcsi suggested that the best way was not to hide Balazs, just to be found out later and punished. Better, he thought, to ask the circus manager, whom he liked and trusted. He knew the manager could not be one of the AVO men since he had been an attorney in the former regime; he could decide what to do. If he decided against the child staying with them, Karcsi would personally take Balazs back to his grandparents and smooth things over for him.

The train pulled to a stop near a village station, where it was granted permission to park on tributary tracks. A circus cook prepared the two main meals of the day for everyone. This was done to avoid fires caused by cooking in the wagons. Despite the simplicity of the government-supplied provisions, Hungarian ingenuity worked its magic. Everyone ate well and the aroma of his cuisine was appreciated as it permeated the little camp. Some came to fetch the meals in stacked aluminum canteens, and others brought their folding chairs to eat communally. Hungarians are a very social people who love company. Good local wines accompanied all the meals.

Karcsi invited the manager to have lunch in their wagon, hoping to enhance things with a good bottle of Eger Bulls Blood, an especially cherished Hungarian red wine and a rare commodity under Communism, until it was decided to produce it in great quantity, and poor quality. A government worker and admirer had given the bottle to Karcsi after a Budapest performance. He thought this to be an excellent time to pop the cork. The spectacled old man arduously and slowly pulled his portly body up the steep narrow stairs of the wagon.

Jolanka [pronounced Yolanka], Karcsi's wife set a lovely table with a bouquet of wild poppies that Ildiko had picked by the train tracks. Balazs was hiding in the back and agreed not to come out until he was called to do so.

As the old gentleman entered the room, he wore the pleasant smile of which they were familiar. Graciously, as was the custom of the old days, he kissed Jolanka's hand and slightly bowed. "Well, it has been a while since we dined together. It is so nice to be here again, but why the sudden invitation?" he asked, slightly suspicious, and with a faint smile at the corner of his mouth.

"Karcsi, you go ahead," said Jolanka. Before her husband was able to proceed, the old gentleman, noticing the five-place table setting, asked, "Are we expecting another guest?"

"Well, sir, that is exactly what we would like to talk to you about." So, the cat was out of the bag and, within a few minutes, they had told him what was happening and called the frightened Balazs to come out.

The boy was totally terrified and expected the worst, but his fears were unfounded. The old man was actually very kind and receptive. He offered Balazs a job helping with cleaning and feeding the animals. After a few glasses of the good wine and delicious food, he said there was a chance to consider Balazs, if he showed any talent, to do one of the stunts. Everyone was pleased. The fear of doom was lifted. Ildiko was so delighted to secure herself a permanent playmate that she rushed into the old man's arms and kissed his round face all over.

Thus began the happiest days of Balazs' childhood. The dream of every child had fallen into his lap. Everyday was filled with adventure and learning. There were so many things to see, so many things to help out with, including preparations for the show and dismantling the equipment. There was also the anticipation coupled with the excitement of travel. Each town received them with much love and people often came bearing gifts to show their appreciation.

Hungarians loved theater, arts and sports, admiring anyone whom excelled in these endeavors.

Balazs was not only happy to help, but was tireless and could not be grateful enough. He offered to help wherever they would have him. One day he was allowed to help the engineer in the locomotive to shovel coal with the fireman.

They fed the hungry steam engine and, as a reward, he was allowed to pull the train's whistle.

His heart nearly burst as he stood on a ledge pulling the lever as children and grownups alike observed him while lining up near the tracks to greet the circus.

He spent the evenings with his new young family when there were no duties to perform. They made campfires at night and hung bacon on sticks, letting the juicy fat drip on the fresh bread below. He sang songs with them and listened to the circus people tell great stories with much humor, making everyone laugh.

As the week passed and he missed church on Sunday morning, he felt guilty thinking about how much joy he had in his life, and how his grandparents must be worried over his disappearance. He decided to write a letter to comfort them and tell them not to worry. He sat at a table, chewing the end of his pencil and wondering how to begin. Suddenly, he noticed the most unexpected scene from the large window of the wagon.

His grandfather was standing outside in the middle of the camp, immersed in a jovial conversation with the manager of the circus. He held two little fryers, which were tied together at the legs, hanging upside-down, wings apart, and combs bright red with the rush of blood.

The two old men, arm in arm, walked together toward his wagon as Eugene handed the other the two chickens. Balazs could not believe his eyes: he didn't know what to do, run or hide, but what difference would it make now? How was he found out, how could his grandfather know where he was, and what was all that backslapping between the two men? He felt helpless and confused.

NINETEEN

FAMILY REUNION

BALAZS MATURED faster than most children his age because he was raised by the elderly couple who gave him wisdom and knowledge of the world around him. He was a political child, aware and informed about conditions in Hungary and was taught by his grandparents about the democracies in the West. He understood the differences of the totalitarian Communist regime in the East through first-hand experience. The ideas of democracy he understood only in theory, and as a dream, as it was for millions behind the Iron Curtain.

While poverty deepened and Hungary sank into economic despair, likened to the times after the Turkish Wars, the Communist Party members and the privileged AVO continued to enjoy luxurious lives at the expense of the people. None of the promises of Communism had been kept. By now, it was not only the intelligentsia, but also the "beloved" working class who began to see the hopelessness, and became disillusioned with the system. Yet, the Workers' Paradise was persistently promised to them, if they would only be more patient.

Slowly but surely, it became evident to all that the system fed off the people, as had the feudal systems of the middle Ages. With one major difference: the terror.

Under no other system was the political and ideological persecution so acute. The Soviets not only rivaled the Nazis, but also managed to surpass them. The torture, executions, forced labor to Siberia and China was all the result of a nation unwilling to submit to Soviet imperialism. Out of fear, more and more people reported each other to the authorities. They were afraid that they were being tested by a secret member of the party, and in failing to report anti-government "subversive behavior", they would be the ones to suffer and languish in the torture chambers.

Balazs' uncle, Eugene Jr., after his release from an "ideological correction center," was so destroyed, mentally and emotionally, that he refused to offer any information about what had happened to him. He feared that his family might suffer the same fate if the authorities found out that he talked.

Children under harsh conditions will always find ways to play and find freedom; Balazs was no different. He enjoyed his short stint at the circus and the reunion with his grandfather ended in good spirits. They spent two more days at the circus together before departing for home.

Eugene, knowing the boy and the capacity of his imagination, coupled with his recent disappointments, had anticipated his next step. At the circus reunion, where had encountered his former colleague the circus manager, Eugene revealed his suspicions of Balazs' possible flight.

They had decided to allow it to happen; it would be a good break for Balazs after the recent events. Eugene was to pick him up, with the local government's permission, at an appointed town after a week's time. The two chickens, which the boy had seen his grandfather carrying, were payment for the favor. Balazs was not upset at Eugene. In fact, he saw it as a demonstration of his deep love and understanding, and of the humor that he kept through the worst of times.

****

In the middle of a sizzling hot July, Balazs was informed that he was to visit the Szabo family, two towns away. The information sent an incredible jolt through his system. He knew of his father's parents' small summerhouse. In the summers, his brother, whom he could no longer remember well, and all the boy cousins gathered. There was a single girl cousin, but she was much older.

It all happened so fast that, before he realized it, he was on the train with a small bundle of clothes his grandmother packed for him. He waved to the two old people as the train pulled slowly out of the station, all the time wondering what had brought on this change between the families. He knew quite well how much they disliked each other. Nonetheless, he was not really concerned, for his desire was to meet his brother and father again.

The train entered a grove of weeping willows, forming an almost perfect tunnel of foliage and blocking the ever-shrinking image of his grandparents. He continued to hang out of the window, examining his much-traveled landscapes. Finally, it pulled into the small, white stucco train station. The red wooden benches ran along the front of a long row of thick honeysuckle and acacia trees.

Five cheerful boys were jumping up and down on the benches waving and calling out his name. Since he was the only child getting off the train, there was no mistaking him to be the right one. They were all bigger than he was. There was one skinny little blond kid, kind of introverted, who stood back from the others. Two older boys were brothers—Csaba (Chaba) and Atilla—the children of Sandor's closest sister in age, the other two each from older sisters, one called Domi and the other Lorant.

With the backslapping and general welcoming over, the brothers Barna and Balazs drifted timidly toward each other to hug and get acquainted. Balazs felt a painful yet wonderful sensation of belonging.

****

The reunion, and so much that came before it, might never have happened. Shortly after the war, as the advancing Soviet Red army was in pursuit of the defeated, fleeing German soldiers, rumors of Russian's cruelty and ruthlessness preceded them. Thousands of Hungarians, including Sandor and Jadda, fled them by every possible means available. With their two infants, they managed to be swept onto an open cattle-car, headed for Austria. They were exposed to painful cold, with no stops to relieve themselves or any space to change baby diapers as bodies were tightly pressed to one another.

After many hours, their train finally approached its destination in the Austrian mountains. A German fighter pilot spotted the refugee train from the skies and descended to spray the hundreds of terrified passengers with a barrage of machine-gun fire. Warm blood sprayed into the couple's faces as the bullets hit struck flesh around them. The plane was like a hawk on its prey, repeatedly diving out of the clouds with its rattling machine guns. On each pass, more people were killed. Packed against each other, the tight formation prevented the dead and wounded from falling to the ground. They hung headless and lifeless between their companions like butchered red meat. Amidst the screaming wounded came a chorus of shouts rang out urging the engineers to stop the train and allow people to get off and run for cover. Naturally, the engineers could not hear the pleas, but were keenly aware of what was happening. They went into a robotic mode, shoveling coal as fast as they could into the already bursting furnace of the steam engine. Faster and faster they shoveled with one purpose in mind. Behind them in the wagons, people began jumping off the speeding train into the ditches taking the chance with a fall rather than what seemed a sure death on the train amid the next passing shower of deadly bullets.

Sandor glanced at Jadda and without a word he knew their next move. Each held an infant as tightly as they could and pushed through the dead or panicked people to reach a side opening and make their fateful plunge. Just as they were ready to jump everything turned dark. Smoke and steam filled their throats as the train rushed into a narrow valley, carved out of the mountain long ago for the passage of the train.

Two cliffs rose high and tight creating a crevasse, making it too dangerous for the plane to attempt further attacks as it lost visibility. All along, the conductors were aiming for this to deliver their passengers—knowing that if they stopped before reaching the valley, they would all be facing death.

Nearby, in a small alpine village, an elderly widow took them in. They passed more than six months in this quiet Austrian settlement, slowly recovering from the shock of the bombardment of Budapest and from their near-death experience on the train. They listened intently to the radio for news about Hungary. Jadda was fluent in four languages and was able to communicate with their hostess. When the false news came that the Soviets were not planning on staying in Hungary permanently, Sandor immediately decided to return with his family. After all, his career was something to go back to, and the Hungarian language was the tool of his art. Having little knowledge of other languages, save a little Italian and German, he would not attempt to live in another country. With the Germans finally defeated, he was one of millions of Hungarians hoping for an independent country.

Upon their return, Sandor's father in-law, Eugene, thought it would be better for them to keep a low profile at his country villa while things settled in the destroyed and ruined city, but the family eventually resettled in Budapest. One memory did flash through Balazs' mind from that time, but it did not have his brother's face attached to it.

After the war, when the family returned from their short escape into Austria, the bomb-damaged apartment in Budapest was not repaired for several years. A bomb had taken more than half off one of the corner bedrooms of the building. The ceilings in this elegant building were four meters high. Two glossy, white heavy doors were generally locked to keep everyone out of the half-existing room.

The children were strictly forbidden to go in there so, naturally, they were curious. Even adults dared not enter for fear of crashing down into the apartment below, or falling to the street.

Consequently, a wooden rocking horse was still in that room, because no one dared to fetch it. One day, when the children were unattended for a few seconds, they managed to make their way to the door with a large, black iron key. They were unable to reach the lock, but, with the aid of a low footstool, they succeeded in unlocking the door. They pulled the many old rags that were stuffed under the door to keep winter's howling cold drafts out away from the front, and entered the bombed-out ruin of the bedroom. Balazs, then three, and Barna, almost five, were thrilled and excited. The snow was falling outside and in the room, covering everything in it with drifts.

They could see the entire avenue with the yellow streetcars and the people below. The little rocking horse was there, too, so they wasted no time brushing the snow off and mounted it immediately. They were so engrossed in the joys of play and adventure with the novelty of the open room in snow that while wildly rocking the horse they didn't notice the edge, almost falling to their deaths three flights below. Someone from the street noticed the children and rang apartment's doorbell. They were saved by their mother and the stranger, and got severe spankings that neither child ever forgot.

There was one other vivid memory of his brother that Balazs recalled. The young couple was planning an evening out and, as they were getting ready, the children became difficult and cranky—unwilling to part with their parents. It was past their bedtime, but they found excuses not to stay in bed. Balazs whined that he was hungry; Barna insisted on going to the bathroom for the tenth time. Their mother, Jadda, was unusually impatient and easily exasperated. Barna was standing on the edge of the bed that abutted the wall next to the bathroom door, with his little fingers in the crack of the door. Jadda shouted at him and slammed the door, crushing his small, delicate fingers. The blood sprayed on both children. Barna wailed from pain and hung by his small fingers from the shut door, unable to free his hand.

Horrified, Sandor entered the children's room to free Barna's crushed fingers. He was in such excruciating pain and shock that he temporarily went mute. He was only able to utter silent screams and this was the face that Balazs remembered as it was etched in his memory. Barna lost all the fingernails on that hand, though not permanently.

They ran up the hill almost a kilometer to the small summerhouse. Since this little house had only one bedroom, it wasn't subject to state confiscation—neither were the small summer homes of their cousins' parents. Balazs knew the way since he had spied the town the year before in hopes of getting a glance of his brother or cousins, but his timing was always off—the kids were either at the lake or at other relatives' houses.

On one of his afternoon adventures, Balazs was able to spy on his paternal grandparents. He saw his grandfather, a handsome man but shorter than Eugene, with a full mustache, working along the raspberry patch that lined his fence. An obese, slow-moving woman approached the path from the direction of the local patisserie with her aluminum take-out lunch set. Balazs stood by the fence watching the old man inside the garden working. Upon seeing him there, the fat woman gave the intruder an unkind glance and gruffly asked what he wanted. Balazs looked at her, terrified, and ran all the way back to the train station to board the next train home.

Coming near the house with the noisy gang, he saw to his dismay, that the same mean woman, who had questioned his presence, was the one now welcoming him. By some good fortune, his paternal grandmother did not recognize him. He gave respectful hugs and kisses to both, but felt no sincere emotions. They were strangers to him.

Grandpa Szabo seemed pleasant, with a nice voice, and the yard he tended was beautiful. There were roses, cosmos and other flowering plants. Weeping berry, cherry, apple and walnut trees completed the garden. It wasn't even an eighth of the size his grandpa Eugene had, but it was immaculate and earned the boy's respect.

Old Grandma Kati, on the other hand, was overweight and had a screechy, sharp voice—not to mention an unpleasant body odor.

The children ran from house to house, introducing the boy to the many aunts and uncles in the Szabo clan. Though shy, he made it through all the obligatory introductions.

They raided the fruit trees like locusts, and ran to the lake for swims that lasted the whole day.

On their return, they ate the restaurant food, which they were sent to fetch by their grandmother, who did not particularly like to cook. Three days went by fast, but on the morning of the fourth day an automobile pulled up to the front gate.

His heart leaped. It was his father! He got out and towered over the small Czechoslovakian Tatra car. His radiant smile and light summer outfit made him look like a star from the West rather than an actor from poor Communist Hungary. Barna jumped through the door from behind him screaming, "Dad! Mom!"

As Barna ran toward the car, his father came around and opened the other door facing the yard. Balazs was sure this must be Kati, the "witch," the "whore," the "evil woman" who was accused of breaking up his parents' marriage.

Sandor reached out for a slender white alabaster arm that ended in a graceful hand. She was beautiful, with sparkling, silky, thick, blond hair. Her cheekbones were high; her lips full yet not exaggerated, with fine contours that needed no art from a lip liner. Her chin line was gentle with a defined cut, ending with a sensuous neck. Most of all, she had a perfectly straight nose—with just an ever so slight, aquiline bend to it. Her green eyes, which played in the changing light, shone with intelligence and a capacity for deep thought.

By any measure, she was a lady—with such grace, charm and poise, the kind not taught nor borrowed. It was a special, inborn quality, an inner refinement of birth that comes from the luckiest mingling of rare and exceptional genes. She rose from the car with Sandor's help and kissed Barna, who gave her a tight, loving hug. Then she approached Balazs directly with total and unexpected openness. Not sentimental, not trying to win him, but simply with sincere warmth and genuine feeling. She reached toward him and gently stroked his head, just once, and said, "I have been looking forward to meeting you in person for a long time. This indeed is a special day."

Her presence and her unfathomable beauty stunned Balazs. She seemed to him like a goddess. If it were not for her one-piece, light, flowery summer dress and sandals strapped high around her young ankles, he would have thought she floated from the sky. But no, she was real and positively the most beautiful woman he could imagine. Her voice was unexpectedly deep, somehow musical.

His father shook him back to reality, picked him off the ground to his height and warmly kissed him. Balazs returned the affection and felt complete—so much part of something; something he should have had from the start; his family. It was all there, all around him, yet just a taste, not really his. It belonged to his brother, but why not him? A deep, sickening feeling seized him; the happiness that he felt momentarily was swept away by his jealousy.

Fortunately, it had no time to linger for everyone gathered in the little house for a happy reunion of sharing tales from the city life and stage life. All the uncles and aunts arrived, as well, full of admiration for the young couple. This was not simply because they were famous and well off, which brought hope in their hearts under such a regime, but because they were such a magnetic couple. They were well matched and full of robust, youthful life.

Kati had everyone laughing as she spoke of Sandor's recent performance. In one of Shakespeare's plays, he had to stab his opponent to death. The actor's hard backward fall to the ground resulted in his releasing a loud fart. All heard it, actors on stage as well as the audience. For a millisecond, there was shocked silence. Then Sandor composed himself and loudly responded, "Are you still groaning, you swine?" With a grand theatrical gesture he stabbed the man on the ground again. He brought the house down with such uncontrollable laughter and applause that they had to start the next scene six times over before the audience got hold of itself.

Balazs was caught up in the audience of admirers, but Kati reached out for him to sit by her side. As the hours passed into the night, he fell asleep against her lap. After the other children retired to their homes, Sandor laid the two sleeping boys side by side, looking at his wife with wishful thinking.

TWENTY

KATI

TWO SLEEPY BOYS squinted into the bright summer morning. Waking next to each other was a new and strange feeling. However, within minutes this newly formed family had gathered at the breakfast table to make plans for the day. After Sandor and Kati's second cup of black espresso, they decided to drive to Tihany, a famous summer resort of old. This postcard-picture town was high above Lake Balaton. Tihany was built on rich, red volcanic soil, striped by blankets of green vineyards that looked like a Persian tapestry from a distance. On the summit over looking the lake stood a 17 Th. Century Baroque church. Its earthy, cadmium-yellow walls could be seen for miles across the glittering lake. A kilometer from the church was a popular lookout. From this strategic point, people yelled or whistled to receive one of the clearest echoes from the church walls.

Balazs was thrilled to be riding in a private car. Not just any, but his father's. He could not help wondering how rich his father must be, and, with a child's typical innocence, he posed the question to Sandor directly. Instead of getting a satisfactory reply, they all laughed at his inquiry. As they continued toward their destination, Sandor decided to take the scenic route, which passed Fuzfo.

Balazs sat in the back seat next to Kati in the cramped little car as it puttered along the lake's one-lane deteriorating highway. Poorly maintained since the occupation, it looked like snails of tar had left their black oily tracks behind.

The boy was proudly pointing out all the familiar landmarks of the region, spicing his commentary with anecdotes to impress Kati with his knowledge. This was his world and with the help of jumping trains and of cycling long distances on his grandmother's rickety bike, he boasted keen familiarity of the area.

By the late morning's heat, they took the turn around the bend to his town. Balazs pointed toward their villa, which stood on the hilltop protruding above the rich vegetation of healthy fruit trees and thick foliage of weeping willows. In the distance, rolling hills glowed in soft cobalt and azure blue. Nature's paintbrush tinted this mixture and slightly mixed it in crimson and varieties of green, to challenge any French Impressionist.

The two towers were in direct sight as Sandor slowed for Balazs to point out the medicinal spring with its stone cross that overlooked the vegetable garden. Below it, in the garden, bent over the soft dirt with hoe in hand, toiled a lonely figure. The boy felt strange—looking at his grandfather as he pointed him out. It was as if he were looking at him from another world, another time. He seemed very small, lonely and far, far away. There was silence in the car for a moment that seemed eternal. The car pulled to the side of the ditch, but when Barna suggested they stop and say hello to grandfather, the atmosphere turned tense. Sandor felt uneasy, and Balazs was gripped with a sense of guilt at watching Eugene working as hard as usual, but alone. He turned to Sandor, who suddenly looked terrified.

****

The noon train came rumbling around the corner like a black devil pounding the rails, shaking the earth and spewing a black stream of soot. In the little church, the boy appointed to assist the priest was bouncing up and down on the rope to toll the heavy bronze bell. The altar boy had to pull with his entire weight in order to wrestle the rope to the ground. With the return of the pendulum, the bell would swing him high into the air.

Eugene heard the sound of the train and the church bell converging. Slowly, he straightened his stiff back. Sweat poured from his forehead to his eyebrow and into his eyes, stinging them a little. He reached for his white lavender scented handkerchief in his back pocket, and wiped the perspiration from his eyes and face. He removed his pocket watch from his vest and, with a satisfied look that everything was in order, glanced toward the train. He observed a small, gray Czechoslovakian sedan challenge a race with the steam engine.

A strange sensation passed through him. Something inside him stirred; he looked around, but saw nothing out of order. The strange feeling subsided as fast as it came. He used his hoe like a staff to support his weight as he made his slow progress up the hill to Paula's kitchen of inviting aromas.

****

To avoid the tense moment, Sandor suggested a race against the train. Both boys screamed with delight: distracted and engaged in the challenge, they cheered on their little car. The tracks that ran parallel to the road for many kilometers offered them a long race; sometimes the train, and sometimes the car would take the lead. They blew the horn to get the attention of the smiling conductor and engineer who waved back playfully at the excited occupants in the little gray car.

At breakfast the next morning, Kati sat by Balazs. Her perfume brushed his face whenever the morning breeze changed direction. She was very curious about Eugene and Paula and asked many questions. It pleased Balazs to talk about his grandparents. Kati was genuinely interested about the feelings and depth of people, as was Balazs, who was an introverted and reflective child. What pleased him most was the fact that Kati spoke to him on his level and valued his opinions on things as if he were an adult. After a short while, they discovered their similar childhoods and were lost in a deep conversation.

Kati's mother Eta, a petite brunette with a fiery personality, was also an actress. Many years ago she fell in love and married a young Jewish aristocrat. This affluent gentleman traveled Europe frequently with Eta, which led to

Kati's birth in Abazia, a small Italian resort town. The marriage did not work out and, as a child of three, just like Balazs, she was taken to her grandmother in the small town of Oroshaza, situated in the Hungarian prairie. She grew up in poverty, but, again, like Balazs, she was loved and surrounded by farm animals and nature.

Her actress mother, who was the sole support for her daughter, worked in far away theaters and could seldom visit her daughter. Kati's grandfather had committed suicide long ago and her step-grandfather abandoned his wife and Kati for America. In her teens, Kati went to the city of Gyor to live with her mother, who had remarried. This time, it was the director of the theater in which she performed. This gentleman, Lazslo Rado, also Jewish, loved Kati and treated her as if she were his own.

Naturally the theater became her life and blood. By age 16, she had begun starring in films and soon became successful. Her arranged marriage to a young chemist and the owner of his own drugstore was looked upon as a suitable match by the standards of the times. Society did not take artists of any kind seriously, no matter how successful and renowned. She was forced to live under the same roof as her mother-in-law, who was disdainful and jealous of her.

When Kati was pregnant, the woman forced her to sleep in the hallway on a cot, because she said her pregnancy disgusted her. Both pregnancies ended in stillborn birth. Years after their divorce, there was strong evidence that her husband was administering questionable medications which caused her to lose the babies. The two boys she lost were born, coincidentally, in the same year and months as Sandor's two children.

After her marriage failed, disillusioned, Kati returned to the theater, totally consumed by her work. She finally met and fell in love with a young man, the Count Cziraky, a dandy and sweetheart of Hungarian and Austrian society who was a few years younger than Kati. Thereafter, her life changed considerably.

Although she continued her theatrical appearances, she now lived in elegant grand residences in Budapest and in a mansion at Lake Velence, a short car ride from the capitol. Hundreds of servants maintained the properties, stables and residences. They hitched up her own set of white stallions, presented to her as a gift (one of many lavished on her) to the family carriage. Kati entered the life of the cultured and the elegant. With her fame as an actress, she had it all.

Then the Second World War broke out, to be followed by Communism which, like a tornado, swept the land barren of everything. The Count lost everything in the confiscations and was jailed for life, proclaimed an enemy of the people. Cziraky later escaped from jail and settled in Canada. Kati told Balazs incredible stories about how the servants helped to bury valuables from the Communists before they took everything from the mansions. Unfortunately, the "loyal" servants stole all of it later.

TWENTY ONE

THIEF

THE FEW DAYS went by faster than any of them would have liked. Kati and Sandor returned to Budapest. Barna stayed on in Akarattya to spend the rest of the summer as usual. Balazs was to stay a few more days, but, even though he enjoyed the visit with his brother, the guilt of leaving his grandparents was too strong. He told Sandor's parents that he wished to return home and, to his surprise, old Kati offered to accompany him home. Balazs, aware of the ongoing conflict between the two families, strongly protested, telling her that he was familiar with the trains and would not mind going alone, but she was insistent.

The next morning, after hugging his brother goodbye, the two of them caught the train. It proved quite a performance to get Kati on board; two station managers, struggling with her huge weight, pushed from behind as she mounted the stairs. She got this special attention strictly from the accomplishments and fame of her son, and they respectfully called her the mother of the "Maestro."

Balazs was looking forward to coming home to Fuzfo. But with old Kati with him, he worried about the intrusion on his grandparents' privacy. When the awkward moment arrived with old Kati's entrance at the villa, Balazs felt bad and was apologetic. He tried to convey to Paula that this was not his idea. Eugene was visibly sick to his stomach, but Paula, true to her tactful and amiable character, made every effort to welcome this visitor. With civility mingled undoubtedly with feminine curiosity, a dimension and talent most men necessarily lack, she began her diplomacy…

Balazs and Eugene freed themselves from the strained atmosphere by pretending to do chores outside. Paula, a wonderful hostess, put out some cookies and pastries on the table (despite the shortages). Old Kati, a sweetaholic, wasted no time sampling the sweets. The two then entered into a strategic conversation of trivia cloaked and loaded with interpretable meanings only women's complex minds are capable of comprehending.

After a little while, Eugene asked Balazs to go and check on the two ladies in the house. He used the excuse of bringing in their hen's freshly laid eggs, which he placed in the usual basket on the sunny veranda table. The ladies seemed fine as they chatted about the prices of things and the many hardships of the present-day life, wishing back the good old days.

Paula left to fetch some more tea from the kitchen and Balazs headed back to report to Eugene. On his way out, he glanced over his shoulder. He was shocked to see the heavy, slow-footed old woman swiftly getting to her feet. She reached toward the eggs in the basket like a fox in a chicken coop, filled her blue apron quickly with the freshly laid eggs, and returned to her chair as if nothing happened; unaware that Balazs had seen it all.

This shameless woman, who received a handsome monthly stipend from her successful son, and who lived, in every way, more affluently and securely than his grandparents, had actually stolen their freshly laid eggs. He returned to the garden where Eugene was sitting under an apple tree, smoking one of his self-rolled cigarettes. The boy decided to say nothing.

The time arrived when old Kati had to make her slow trek to the train station. Balazs decided to say goodbye and thank her for her hospitality in taking him into her home. With Eugene and Paula standing by, he ran into his paternal grandmother's arms, surprising her with a hug as fierce as he could muster. Pressing against her tremendous bulging stomach, where he knew the eggs were hidden in her apron. They popped, squirting and oozing in every direction. The apron went limp and wet. Balazs looked with great satisfaction into the face of the greedy old woman as he dealt out the final strokes of his loving goodbyes!

Unveiled, embarrassed and angry, Grandma Kati, was lost for words. She spun about and with what seemed like wings of youth she flew down toward the station. In the distance, they saw her liberating herself from the puckish apron, which she angrily discarded in a nearby ditch.

TWENTY TWO

STALIN IS DEAD

NO ONE FELT safe. Everyone was isolated, even from his or her closest friends. Rumors of disappearances continued to sweep the country. The people lived in fear. Each night, the old couple turned the lights out and huddled in silent fear of the darkness that had engulfed their lives and the country. Few families were left in Fuzfo of their generation and their class—and all were now expecting deportation at some unspecified point. Across the street lived a family who, like them, were middle class and had been successful in the previous regime. They had two boys. These friends often came to join Eugene and Paula for some nights of bridge and hushed political discussions. It was a small support system for both families.

One morning, Balazs went to the house to play with the boys. As he burst through the already open door, he found himself in an absolutely empty space—void of furniture and all. Balazs stood bewildered and saw what looked like a hurriedly abandoned house. A strange chill went through his body. Spooked, he ran in panic to his grandparents, who froze upon hearing Balazs' discovery. They hugged each other tightly, surrounding Balazs as if the invisible and inevitable danger were to befall them right then. After some time, Paula spoke in a whisper. "My God, Eugene, are we next?" The boy was asked to stay in sight and not to go anywhere. Every sound, every gust of wind, triggered shivers. They felt vulnerable and helpless, waiting for something for which no one could prepare. "They" would simply come and take the family away. And that would be it–gone without a trace. No one would ever hear from them again.

Eugene and Paula tried to strategize. What should Balazs know and "never forget" in case they were separated. It all became a muddle in his frightened mind as the panic sank in with images of being taken from his grandparents. Balazs remembered from reading Hungarian history how the Turks had captured and enslaved Hungarian children. Took them back to Turkey and trained them into *Janicsar* warriors. They converted them to Islam and raised them in camps to be the fiercest fighters—marching them back to fight against their own people.

The next morning, Balazs cautiously peered into the yard through the shutters of the bedroom. The garden, clear of danger, was empty save for the chickens scratching and pecking invisible things out of the dirt. After the morning sip of tea and usual hugs, and despite the warnings from his grandparents, the boy's curiosity got the better of him. He headed toward the empty house, imagining all the tortures and beatings his friends might be enduring somewhere, perhaps in Russia.

As he took a second look across the street, he could not believe his eyes. The neighbors' yard was not empty. There were two little girls playing, screaming and chasing each other with laughter and shrills. The house was alive once again, as if nothing had changed. But something had. There was this strange family living there now, as if they belonged there.

A tall, robust young woman appeared in the doorway calling for the girls to come in for hot chocolate. When she saw Balazs' face plastered to the iron-gate of the yard, she called out to him with a familiar grin. "Hey Balazs! You can come for hot chocolate too, if you want."

Confused by this stranger using his name, he forgot his fear. He found himself in what had been his friends' house, then an empty space yesterday, and now today was filled with the smells of good cooking in the warm kitchen and with furnishings in every room. He stood there dumbfounded, drinking "real hot chocolate" for the first time. The girls sat at the kitchen table beaming with smiles and waiting for him to join them there; a baby boy was in the next room. He did not dare ask any questions and no one offered an explanation.

The woman's husband, a tall, good-looking man, came in, smiled at Balazs then went about his chores. The mother happily chatted with the girls and talked to Balazs, as if she had known him and his family for years. He could hardly wait to tear himself away, run home and tell his grandparents all this incredible news. It made him quite dizzy.

****

After he had laid out all the details to the worried couple, Balazs was told the terrible news. The new family, they told him, were most likely planted by the Communists and were probably Party members themselves. That was why they knew everything about Balazs and the old couple.

They were also the ones who probably destroyed the lives of the family that lived there before them. Balazs understood now why there was such an abundance of food: sugar, hot chocolate and who knows what else that he had not seen before in anybody's house in town. They were informants: they were there to spy on people.

The boy was completely trained about what to say and what not to say. Eugene hid his short-wave radio again in another secret place lest he was reported for it. In anticipation of a future surprise visit from the new government informants, Eugene combed their entire living space for any incriminating clues.

Eugene and Paula had not invited the priest to the usual Sunday luncheons; they were afraid of the consequences. They felt grateful just to be allowed to stay in the one room of their villa. They protected Balazs with every ounce of their strength and cunning. He was the very center of their lives. For the past six years, one purpose alone kept them sane—the welfare of their grandson. Seeing their grandchild renewed their strength to face another day in an existence of terror.

****

One gray dreary day, the local drummer shocked the small group of people waiting for the daily Communist propaganda. He actually did have big news to announce—Stalin was dead! As if an enormous burden had lifted from the group, they straightened up to hear it over, again and again. Either they could not believe their ears or they could not get enough of this good, most welcome news. The same emotions were felt unanimously across the land, over the borders and in all points of the globe. The world had been liberated from a ruthless dictator. It reminded people of the emotions they had felt when the news of Hitler's death was announced.

What would follow next was not a concern, because life could only be better than what they already endured. A sense of hope sprouted like a tiny seed, felt by all those who suffered under this regime. Paula and Eugene immediately contacted their friends in town to verify the news and rejoice with them. The country was in an invisible wave of positive emotion that no one dared to express in public, only in the most trusted circles of devoted friends.

The Communists of the Soviet Union and in the rest of the Eastern Bloc prepared for international mourning in homage of "the loss of our great comrade." Black flags draped every building and every photo of Stalin on classroom walls. All places of work were decorated with black ribbons. There was news that his body would be preserved and placed in the mausoleum on Red Square in Moscow, next to their great leader Lenin, the very one he had murdered. Thousands of brainwashed Russians, who benefited and became the privileged class through the Party, came to view his body. Hysteria swept the ruling class of the Soviet Union. Meanwhile a new leader had already been chosen by the Politburo, a man of "peasant birth" whom many hoped would be moderate and less sadistic than his predecessor had been.

TWENTY THREE

JADDA RECLAIMS HER SON

EUGENE AND PAULA continued to struggle through the six years they had Balazs. Even with the changes after Stalin's death, and the release of some political prisoners from the Gulags of Siberia, all real hopes for the future of Hungary were nonexistent. The eight-year promise made at Yalta was a lie. The Soviets were well entrenched and continued to rob the country of its resources.

One of their ingenious ways was to remove the raw materials from Hungary, and take it to the Soviet Union "free of charge." Agricultural equipment and trucks "exchanged' for raw materials were then manufactured and sold back to the Hungarian government at premium prices. Most of these machines were poorly built; however, Hungary was only allowed to purchase Soviet-made products. Throughout the years, these things piled up in rusty abandoned industrial dumps and were a total loss to the Hungarian economy.

Before Stalin's death, the Cold War had reached its height between the US and the Soviet Union. Stalin felt powerful with his possession of the secrets of the Atomic bomb. He played a direct role in the Korean War hoping to weaken the United States and spread Communism.

Unbeknownst to the American Air Force until later, it was the Soviet Air Force that they encountered in the skies over Korea. The great blunders of the questionable leadership of FDR sealed the lives of millions behind the Iron Curtain after the war. Stalin was totally successful in infiltrating FDR's presidency with spies both American-born and Soviet, either through their mercenary greed or their incredible stupidity and gullibility regarding the benefits of Communism. For that reason FDR became the laughing stock of the non-Communist population behind the Iron Curtain. Now the Soviets were openly hailing their KGB-reared babies—Julius and Ethel Rosenberg, and hundreds of their associates, as heroes of their cause. They named boulevards in their honor and arranged forced, much publicized "protest marches" on their behalf against America, through all Russian-occupied countries and in Russia itself. These "protests" were aired worldwide and believed as legitimate!

Meanwhile, the media and American pseudo-intellectuals were busy sympathizing and protecting those in the USA who sided with the Communists. The very people that enjoyed and prospered in the free US system worked toward its demise. They attacked to destroy Senator Joseph McCarthy, an American patriot who sacrificed his career, life, and family to defend the country by warning the American people of the great dangers of Communism.

Eugene and his small group of friends, despite the lack of free world news media, were able to piece together a very clear picture of what was going on in the US and the West. They worried for the survival of democracy. They were glad when FDR was gone, too. From the beginning, the American leaders would not listen to Churchill's warnings regarding the dangers of trusting Stalin and the consequences resulted in the Cold War that followed. So, things became bleaker and bleaker for the future of Hungary.

The family income from making artistic lampshades was indeed small. They had their chickens and every three years they slaughtered a pig with the neighbors' help. Balazs' shoes still had to be cut out to give space for his growing feet. He suffered with them through the cold months. Eugene labored in his small vegetable garden with help from Balazs, and tended to the fruit trees. They added beast corn for animal feed. After an incident with a fox that had taken some chickens and killed many more, they erected a small knoll out of mud and hay with a solid door to it.

Eugene's older son survived the prison and was released. A broken man, he went back to his family in Budapest. He and his pediatrician wife now worked for the Government like everyone else in the country. Despite their small incomes and their additional third child, they managed to send some money every month to Eugene and Paula; so did their younger son, whose wife suffered from tuberculosis and was unable to work.

Balazs' mother, Jadda, had a job in an architectural firm, but claimed to have no money left. She lied to Eugene and Paula that she was not receiving alimony or child support. She was off the hook as everyone felt sorry for her.

But the law had changed regarding the payments which Balazs' mother was allegedly not receiving. Parents who did not have children living with them became ineligible to collect. In fear of losing that money, which she had been receiving all along, she was forced to bring her son back into her carefree, single lifestyle. She made arrangements and miraculously got married overnight to an engineer some years younger. Jadda then appeared at her parents' doorstep and, without warning, tore her son from their lives, just as abruptly as she dumped him there years ago.

Before Balazs knew it, he was being hurriedly ushered onto the train for Budapest—with hardly a moment to bid his beloved grandparents goodbye. He hugged Paula and Eugene who, stood next to him lovingly running his fingers through Balazs' hair. Eugene was unable to contain his emotions and allowed his tears to run freely down his cheeks into his white, bristly mustache.

Hanging out the train window, Balazs etched into his heart and mind those two loving figures, the people who had nurtured him through the most painful period of his childhood. He could never have imagined his life without them. Never for a moment had the likelihood of this sad and unexpected separation occurred to him. The whistle blew three times as the train huffed and puffed. The wheels began to roll on the iron tracks. Clouds of white steam blew from the sides of the locomotive, engulfing and then obscuring his grandparents from the scene. They stood there lost and broken, torn from the most precious reason to carry on their struggle.

As the train sped into the distance, Balazs felt a heavy pain in his heart and a sense of emptiness. This woman, his mother, was practically a stranger to him. Her visits were rare, but always included the company of some strange, male friend, never allowing mother and son space or time to bond. Balazs did not feel comfortable in getting consolation from Jadda, so he continued to look out at the familiar landscape, rapidly vanishing with every passing moment.

When he finally wiped his tears, he sat back onto the old, green leather seat and starred at the familiar, filthy, oily floor of the cabin. Next to him stretched his mother's long, exquisitely shaped legs, as usual sporting expensive honey-colored silk stockings from the black-markets of Budapest. His grandparents wore clothes more than 40 years old, mended over and over. Eugene's sweet image in his old Austrian hunting britches and 100-times resoled boots flashed through his mind. Balazs tried to hold his breath to prevent inhaling her expensive, stifling, perfume. Slowly he found consolation with thoughts of Budapest, where he could be near his father and Kati, his stepmother.

The brothers Barna and Balazs with Father Sandor,
(taken in 1946 before their separation).

Paula and Eugene.

Eugene and Paula's villa and nearby healing spring in 1930.
The villa in 1948 with full vegetation.

The church at Balatonfuzfo, established by Eugene and Paula
In the background stand the ruins of the original church,
destroyed in 1520 by the Turks.

Balazs at his First Communion with Father Lajos at center at the church in Balatonfuzfo.

Balazs on the right with brother Barna and Kati, whom
he met for the first time on this occasion in 1950.

Balazs, age ten at the shores of Lake Balaton in 1953.

Sandor in Budapest in 1938.

Kati was as popular and in
demand onstage as Sandor. Taken in 1950.

Sandor and Kati onstage together in 1953.

Kati, 1951

A room filled with antiques at Sandor and Kati's Budapest apartment.

The brothers Balazs and Barna 1955.

Eugena with Balazs, Jadda, Barna, and Sandor, at Eugene's home in
Budapest before the communist confiscation.
Unidentified child in the foreground.

Eta, Kati's mom also a celebrated actress. (Taken in 1930)

Sandor as the prince in Shakespeare's *Hamlet*.

Sandor, a classical actor and recipient of the famous Kossuth
Award, in Rostand's *Cyrano de Bergerac* in 1955.

Balazs on a Russian tank, captured by the freedom fighters (1956) Photo courtesy of Mr. Laszlo Papp.

The avenues of Budapest littered with the ruins of Soviet tanks and armored vehicles, destroyed by the freedom fighters in 1956. Photo courtesy of Mr. Laszlo Papp.

Balazs, reunited with his family in Vienna 1956.
Photo by Sandor Schwartz

TWENTY FOUR

CITY LIFE

LATE AT NIGHT THEY ARRIVED at the Southern Railway Station, then took a cab. He held onto his small luggage, containing a few personal things. Balazs would have rather brought his cat, Cindra, along. But, knowing full well that city life would have been death for a country cat (as it might well be for him, he thought grimly), he abandoned the idea.

Budapest had become a dark, gloomy city since the Communists had become custodians of this once bright capital. It had been likened to the French capital, and nicknamed "the Paris of the East" before the war for its gaiety and nightlife. The silhouette of the Royal Palace on the western, Buda bank loomed darkly against the clear, night sky. Beneath it, Balazs saw the well-lit monument of Socialist realism. A tumult of workers, with rolled-up shirtsleeves, rushed forward into some imaginary wind, hammers and flags in their powerful grasp, representing the false aspirations and idealization of Socialist collectivization.

Their cab continued its route along the west bank of the Danube, passing two bridges and an ancient Turkish bath built by the Sultan Suleiman the

Magnificent (one of many the Sultan built in Budapest). After more than 400 years, the baths were still in use. At the foot of the waterfall and the statue of St. Gellert was a third Bridge, named after a Hungarian queen called Elizabeth. Bombed during the war, it was still partially submerged in the currents of the Danube. Its wreck, with its ornate, twisted metal, looked like a modern sculpture. On this side of the rocky Gellert Hill, above the ruins of the submerged bridge, stood a dark, unlit bronze figure holding a small cross in his right hand toward the city.

The cross, of course, was and is an important symbol of Christianity, which the country embraced through the efforts of its first King, St. Stephen. After his death, there was chaos and confusion, including the question of succession. The German Holy Roman Emperor, who long wanted to subdue Hungary, helped Peter, the king's half-Italian nephew and the heir to the throne, but who was unable to rule without German support. He humbly knelt before the Emperor and pledged his whole-hearted allegiance.

Hungarians were infuriated by Peter's declaration of loyalty and openly rebelled—provoking a pagan uprising as well. Pagan rebels, believing that the country's problems were caused by foreign influences, began turning against foreigners and Christians. One casualty was the saintly and loved bishop, Gerard (Gellert). The rebels captured him and put him in a barrel pierced with stakes, nailed it shut and rolled him down the steep hill that now bears the Saint's name. Many considered it a miracle that the Soviets did not demolish this statue with the cross in his hand.

The dome-shaped roof of the great Art Nouveau architecture of the Hotel Gellert is nestled nearby. At a distance, the somber sound of a solo Gypsy violin could be heard from its now run-down and shabbily furnished riverfront restaurant. This 100-year-old, world-famous architectural work of art boasted the world's first artificial wave pool; also the world's first almost Olympic-size "champagne" pool, a precursor to whirlpools. Designed in the 19th century, it had hot Turkish baths, separate for women and men, offering massages and medicinal baths, which were fed by natural geysers beneath the city. The pools inside and outside were exquisitely decorated in the styles of the time.

Throughout Hungary, and especially concentrated in Budapest, there were many such ancient baths built by the Romans before the Hun occupation of what was then Pannonia, a Roman province. (The Magyar tribes arrived sometime later, around 896 AD, lead by Árpád, St Stephen's father.) Later in the 16th century, during the 150 years of the occupying Ottoman Empire, baths and minarets were built while fighting and converting the resisting Hungarians to Islam in order to gain access to Western Europe.

Two blocks down from the great edifice of the Gellert Hotel, the cab pulled over to an ornate, large, hand wrought-iron gate. Jadda paid the cab driver and together they hauled up five flights of stairs (the elevator had not worked for years). She rang the doorbell that was deafening even from outside. An old, skinny, hook-nosed lady's face appeared in the window's frame. After a few clicks, the door quietly opened to a dim, long hallway. There was a strong, trapped smell of long-ago fried onions, reminding Balazs that he had not eaten and was famished. The hallway led to an old-style, elegant living room, typical of the gentry. An exquisite crystal chandelier (somehow saved from Government confiscations) hung in the midst of Biedermeier furniture untouched by age and wars. The dining table was set with ornamental silverware. The heavy and decoratively carved, crystal glasses and water decanters were surrounded by the finest hand painted Herend china. Balazs had only ever heard of such beautiful things from his grandmother, Jadda's mother Paula, whose entire possessions were confiscated and distributed among the legal Communist Party looters after the war.

The old woman reminded Balazs of the lady who took in the little elephant Babar, in the story "Babar The Elephant." She greeted them with reserved warmth. The door to one of many bedrooms opened and a handsome young man in his early 30s came out. With a smile, he announced himself as Balazs' new dad and hugged Jadda flirtatiously, which struck Balazs as wrong, but he let it slide because of the young man's sincere warmth and candor.

The boy noticed a peculiar relationship between the elderly mother and her son. Even though all three shared the one room—Jadda, her husband and Balazs—the mother insisted every night on hot ironing the sheets in the bed for her only son before he retired. His grandmother had spoiled Balazs, but he had never seen anything so ridiculous in his life as this, and felt sorry for the man.

Several other tenants lived in the apartment. There was a government ruling on a determined number of bedrooms—if the original owners of the intelligentsia had not been deported, they had to allow government-assigned families to move in. These families were hostile working-class people already prejudiced against the upper class. They were brainwashed by the propaganda machine. Convinced that they were the rightful owners of the people's democracy and everything that was in it, even if they had not earned it as the previous owners had.

The next morning he was glad to find out that Jadda's brother, his wife and their two daughters (the family Eugene had saved from the Nazis) lived across the hall. One of the girls was older than he and the other younger. The older girl resembled the father's family in complexion, but the younger was a little dark Sephardic beauty, looking like her olive-skinned, stunning Jewish mother. He had played with them on many of their visits in the summers at his grandparents' home.

Soon, after Jadda's marriage fell apart, she was offered a share of her aunt Eugena's apartment. Paula's sister lived near the Eastern Railway Station on the Pest side of town, facing the largest animal hospital built before the war.

TWENTY FIVE

EUGENA

EUGENA'S BUILDING consisted of three flights of stairs, with her apartment on the second floor. She shared it with her half-sister Brigita, whose drunkard husband, a former history teacher, was now assigned to the coalmines. He would come home from the pubs nightly and beat Brigita senseless. Balazs hated hearing the screaming and the sounds of the thuds and blows on Brigita's frail body.

This building shared a courtyard with another, identical building, but was divided from it by a high wall. A large chestnut tree grew next to the wall, and reached all the way to the rooftops. In the hot summer it provided a green, thick canopy against the hot sun. The branches were a haven for many species of birds, which kept the courtyard echoing with lively songs.

Eugena was a petite, lovely woman, with a round face of goodness. She radiated the same sweetness and sharp intelligence as her older sister Paula. College-educated and liberated, she had taught art at the Fine Arts Academy of Budapest, while Paula taught at the school of philosophy, before the war. Now the government had forced her into retirement and re-evaluated what would have been her legitimate retirement income to a level of starvation. This was all part of the Communists' plan to starve out the intelligentsia. Having Jadda there with her son now helped her a little.

There were three bedrooms. Jadda and the boy stayed in one room, using Eugena's furniture, and sharing one bed. Next to them was the room that used to be the living room, which they now had to cross through to get to the hallway. Eugena slept here among giant, beautiful tropical plants she tended for more than 25 years and through the war. Her beautiful watercolors decorated the walls. Some were painted in Hungary, and some during her travels and schooling abroad in Italy before the war. The forth room, was, naturally, occupied by a government-appointed person, another in-plant. Next to it was Brigita's bedroom.

All seven people shared the facilities, one toilet, one kitchen and one bathroom. The hot water for the bath came from a wood burning stove with a water tank in it. (Balazs loved this luxury, because they had no bathtub on their side of the house at Lake Balaton.) When the water was heated in this boiler the bathroom also became hot as a sauna.

When she was still a young lady, Eugena had been formally introduced to a young Japanese student living in Budapest. He finished his studies at the university and became as fluent in her language as any native Hungarian. He remained in Hungary beyond his language studies to soak up the culture as well. He fell in love with Eugena, because she reminded him of the petite Japanese women back home. She was shy and had the tiniest and most beautifully shaped hands and feet. Her unusual talent in painting impressed him as well. His visits or "calls" at the parental home were always restricted. Tea was served and the chaperones were never beyond earshot of the young couple's whispers. On every occasion, Imaoka Iushiro would show up with a white lily, no matter what the season. Their passion grew as the years passed.

Unfortunately, Imaoka was called back to Tokyo at the beginning of World War I. He dared to ask Eugena's parents for her hand in marriage and their departure to Japan. The heartbreaking decision of her parents, to allow their marriage only with the condition that Imaoka remained in Hungary, hit both of them hard. They were loyal children to their own culture, respecting parental decisions, but did not abandon their love. Imaoka left, but vowed to return and live with her in Budapest.

Imaoka, who became stranded in Japan by the events of history, was forced to remain in Tokyo. He eventually gained the position of director of the international studies division at Tokyo University. He married and had two daughters, and yet remained faithfully in love with Eugena. She did the same thing—married a young man of breeding her family arranged for her: as it was in the Japanese tradition, so it was in old Europe.

After an uneventful but respectable 20-year marriage, Eugena's husband died. Childless and a widow, she tried to carry on and survive the difficult war years. Meanwhile, in Japan, Imaoka was busy translating the Hungarian classics into his own language, and completed the first concise Japanese-Hungarian dictionary. His wife also passed away, leaving him with two daughters. Through the years of his marriage Imaoka continued his intense correspondence with Eugena. The collection of 30 some years of love letters was tenderly stored in a drawer. Now, with both spouses dead, they could communicate guilt free—although Eugena still had some concerns. Receiving letters from a foreign country, she worried the Communists would accuse her of collaboration with the enemy and feared the "knock in the night."

Balazs and Eugena became very close and spent much time painting together. They read the letters from Imaoka and the beautiful love poems he composed for her. When Balazs needed help with school, Eugena was there to assist him. Balazs found school in the big city more challenging. His classmates were very self-assured and felt superior; the teachers were more intimidating. In the larger classrooms learning was more difficult. Eugena proved to be a big help with his schoolwork.

Jadda, however, wasn't dependable. She was preoccupied with dating and wasn't around much. When she did come home, Eugena and Balazs had to leave the apartment to sit out the "visits" at very cheap news theaters.

(The government knew that many people had no heat in the winter and were forced to sit in the 24-hour movie theaters all day just to stay warm. They were a captive audience for the Soviet propaganda machine. These theatres projected ongoing "documentaries" of the Soviet Army defeating the Nazis and liberating Europe without ever mentioning the Allies. They also fabricated films of American capitalists torturing blacks and using them as guinea pigs for scientific experiments.)

Because Jadda was always on the go, she and her son never bonded. She was impeccably made up and had "good" clothes, relatively speaking for the times. She always had expensive French perfumes, silk stockings, and French lipstick, none of which were available or affordable for the general public. These items were still only in special stores reserved for Communist Party members and their families who were the only ones allowed travel outside of the Iron Curtain. Ironically, they were the ones supplying the black markets at home. The country was filled with "off limit" stores where only Party members were allowed to shop, but they could only shop with U.S. dollars. If non-Party members were caught with currency other than Hungarian Forints, they were arrested and never seen again.

Jadda's temper was incendiary and her hands even quicker. She slapped Balazs frequently, back-handed across his face, at the slightest provocation. Many times Eugena had to jump between them to prevent these physical outbursts, which were totally alien to him. His grandparents were kind, loving people who never laid a hand on him. To him, Jadda's presence always meant the possibility of unpredictable, violent attacks.

TWENTY SIX

SANDOR IS DEPORTED

BALAZS WAS LEARNING to adjust to city life filled with diverse new experiences. But his heart was still in the country. He missed the natural rhythm of life, the closeness and communion with nature. He knew the names of all the plants and flowers around him and understood animals, wild or domestic. He missed seeing the vast lake at the crack of dawn and at sunset.

Now a city resident, he had to remember street and boulevard names and which streetcar went where. He had to acquaint himself with all the tall structures and many historic places. On his return from school, the scent of "poverty soup" (as Eugene called it) would hang in the air of the gangway. Times were harder for the city folks who depended on supplies from the inefficient collective farms of the "Workers' Paradise." So it was, too, for this little family, as they settled down to their meal of caraway seed soup. The soup was simply hot water, onions, and boiled seeds of caraway seasoned with salt. They ate this for three days in a row at three meals accompanied by some Hungarian bread. Balazs remembered that, back in the country, Eugene had always tried to humor him, while having trouble himself in forcing it down.

He used to say that it would cleanse everyone's colons and medical researchers would one day discover that it prevents cancers and prolongs life.

The boy's father had finally prevailed over his mother's stubbornness about letting Balazs visit. The law had a provision that he was to see his father regularly, but Jadda always invented some excuse for him not being able to make it there. Finally, the threat of not getting child support from Sandor worked. This was the first time since his move to Budapest that Balazs had been allowed to visit his father and stepmother, Kati.

Up to 1950 from the end of the war, Sandor was a very successful young star, even in the new regime. He filled the theaters of Budapest whenever he played. His brilliance, energy and charm drew the depressed city dwellers to his performances. In 1950, the Communist Party saw an opportunity and put tremendous pressure on him to join the Party, to set an example to the people in supporting Communism. He declined, using his art as an excuse not to meddle in politics.

"Look," he said finally to the Party delegation, "I don't meddle in politics and you don't meddle in the arts because I know more about my art. You know more about your politics."

"You are totally right," replied the Party member.

The next day, Sandor and his family were deported to a small, artistically insignificant city at the other end of Hungary. All their belongings were confiscated. Sandor and Kati took Barna, then nine, to an uncertain future.

Meanwhile, the theaters in Budapest lingered in financial uncertainty in Sandor's absence. The Communists were forced within a year to recall him. Rather than admit total defeat, however, they put him at the lowest level of a beginner's theatre, where he stagnated for a year. Sandor and Kati slowly worked their way back to the top theaters by the sheer demand of their public. Kati, played at the first-rate Budapest Kis Madacs Theater just across from their apartment building, and was enjoying the conveniences, the fame, and the pleasure of working alongside her mother, a celebrated old-time actress.

He was forgiven, for the moment, because, instantly, he turned the theater profitable with his return. They felt fortunate, knowing full well that many of their colleagues had been sent to prison, or even Russia, for lesser offenses, and were still missing. The pressure to join the Party was eased for a while and his income was raised several times above the average citizen's of the times because the Communists continued to use the arts as part of their propaganda machine.

Sandor and Kati were passionate decorators and lovers of fine antiques. The black-market in antiques (because you could not sell anything on your own and make a profit like a "capitalist") was filled with beautiful bargains. They purchased some of these bargains to furnish their new apartment in the middle of Pest. The room was filled with 500-year-old furniture carved by masters in the field both from the Austria and the Hungarian Rakoczi era. Ceiling-to-floor, handmade velvet drapes separated rooms that were four meters high. Silver chalices, crystals, and the finest Herend porcelain filled the three meter long table where they entertained. The dark, massive tabletop was covered with an antique gold, hand-embroidered cloak of a Catholic priest dating back several hundred years. A "maid" took care of the parquet floors covered with expensive Persian rugs.

The pomp and elegance reflected the privileged class of the former regime. Kati recreated a small image of the years she spent married to Count Cziraky, showing her excellent taste in decorating.

Only the Communist members, the country's privileged elite, the sport stars and the theater people in the Party's favor lived in such opulent surroundings. The only difference was that the others, the Party ruling class, were allowed to travel beyond the Iron Curtain. These privileges were put out of reach for Sandor and his family for not joining.

The sparkle of wealth that greeted Balazs as he entered the apartment seemed to him out of place in this broken-down country. He could not believe his eyes, especially since he came from the countryside where the Soviets had robbed each village they "liberated".

Balazs was deeply affected by the general feeling of depression of the city folks. He saw fear, hopelessness and poverty everywhere. The infrastructure of the city was in dismal shape after the war and the Communists' bad management was evident everywhere. Without private ownership, no one cared and no one had incentives because it all belonged to everyone, and to no one. The government boasted to the Western nations that they did not tax the people in the Workers' Paradise and there was no crime. Naturally, since everyone was paid by the same government that decided on salaries, no one actually knew how much was withheld. So, the amount of tax was a secret known only to the officials.

Crimes were never reported, since all the newspapers and radio stations were now in the ownership of the state. There was only rosy propaganda, 24/7, about how well things going. They claimed that the oppressed, poverty-stricken people exploited by the capitalists of the west tried to cross the borders into Hungary in order to escape. All the borders had barbed-wired, minefields and machine-gun towers to prevent entry and for 'the protection of the people." The funny thing was that everyone knew that the minefields and towers were on the Hungarian side of the border, to prevent escape out. On the Soviet side it was done correctly, and the minefields and watchtowers were all on their side of the border. No one would be mad enough to escape to the Soviet Union from the Hungary. To the poor Russians, who fared even worse under the Bolsheviks than they had under the Czars, Hungary was sheer heaven.

TWENTY SEVEN

WRIGLEY'S SPEARMINT GUM

BALAZS WAS LOOKING forward to Christmas, his first with his father. The brothers were excited as Sandor, a Christmas enthusiast, began preparing the living room for the main event on the evening of December 24. Wall-to-wall and floor-to-ceiling, the antique glass doors divided the living room from the rest of the apartment. Barna and Balazs could not see through them clearly, but could make out the blurred shapes of things. A beautifully trimmed Christmas tree stood in the room. Sandor was quietly whispering in the company of angels, as they brought the gifts and placed them beneath the tree. (Children held on to their beliefs in angels as the Europeans don't combine the Christmas holiday with St Nicholas day on December 6, although the more modern tradition in Hungary is that the presents are delivered by the baby Jesus). The brothers could hear the sounds of their wings and could smell the fresh winter air as the draft streamed through the open windows. The small candles were lit on the very ornately decorated tree—laden with lots of angel hair and thin strips of silver foil. It was a dazzling spectacle under Sandor's creative hands. The sparklers were lit as the little crystal bell was rung for the third time. The family would enter the room together and recite prayers in honor of Christ, followed by the sad lyrics of the outlawed Hungarian anthem.

All this delay was a torture for the already highly excited kids. Balazs entered the living room of Heaven and, without observing any of the traditions, rushed past the entire setup to the open window, totally convinced that he had just caught a glimpse of the last white angel, fleeing the apartment. There was still evidence everywhere as small, white feathers fluttered in the cool winter's breeze from the open window.

Balazs had never been the recipient of so many wonderful gifts, and much-needed "new" clothes. His thoughts went back to his grandparents' home and their small Christmas tree, sparsely adorned with homemade things and gifts "from the angels." This evening in Fuzfo, Eugene and Paula sat alone by their Christmas tree in the small room, while the howling bitter winter wind blew off the frozen lake, rattling the villa's shutters.

Among the many gifts he received from Kati and Sandor was a pair of ice skates. It could be fashioned and adjusted to his boots with a key as he grew. He tried them out right away at the nearby City Park, which had a skating rink and a frozen pond surrounding the small faux-castle that was a museum of history. A hooded monk, sculpted out of dark bronze and holding a quill pen sat near the entry on guard on a massive granite block. With his face mysteriously hidden inside the cowl of his hood, this was "Anonymous," the unknown author of the *Gesta Hungarorum*, which chronicled early Hungarian history. Later studies supported the suggestion that he was most likely Peter Posa, who served as a notary for King Bela III, and who finally became the bishop of Bosnia.

Nearby was Heroes' Square, which was erected in 1896 for the Magyar Millennium, marking the 1,000[th] anniversary of the arrival of the Hungarian tribes in the Carpathian basin. Actually a circle, it is occupied by gigantic bronze sculptures of the conquering *Magyar* ancestors riding on powerful steeds. The figures, 15 in all, of the House of Árpád, the original Hungarian line of kings, surrounded the centerpiece.

Next to the square was the famous *Art Nouveau* zoo, with its elegant architecture. History and culture surrounded Balazs wherever he went in this ancient land. He found it demeaning that, with a grand history and past, the

Hungarians were overrun by such "low lives" as the Bolsheviks of the violent Soviet system.

Balazs, like many of his generation, had become knowledgeable about politics early in life. They felt the pain of their country and lived with the deep desire to be free of political persecution. They wanted the Russians and their system out of their country.

The schools were broken down and the heavy scent of the urine and methane gas from the unkempt toilets lingered in the classrooms. The wooden desks were old and worn, carved with names from generations long before his. He had to bring bread to school, not for lunch, but to make an eraser by pressing it tightly and molding it with some spit.

There were continued shortages of thousands of items under the endless five-year plans. The communists decided to produce things by alternating industry every five years. They would manufacture items of heavy industry, then turn to light industry the following five years. So, for five years they manufactured shoes, then in the next five, tractors, etc. There were many such "ingenious" economic solutions with which they were to compete with the Western economies and the hated capitalists. Everyone always wondered why it was, if the West was so awful, that the Communists always wanted to catch up with it?

****

There was much to do in one corner of the dark school hallway one lunch break. Balazs was eating the lunch Eugena had packed for him—two generous slices of fresh Hungarian bread (bought at the baker's every morning) with a scrumptiously light, honey-brown crust. The oval-shaped loaf was about three kilos. Two slices of this bread, smothered with a thick layer of pork fat, sliced raw onion rings sprinkled with Hungarian red paprika and salt, were quite filling.

He continued to eat his lunch as he approached the commotion with reserved curiosity. One of the kids had a great treasure in his possession, American chewing gum! Coming from the country, he didn't have the slightest idea what they were talking about. What was chewing gum? But when he heard

American, he tuned in. He had never seen anything American—let alone dare to utter the word in public. These streetwise city kids were braver and savvier than he was.

Secretly, they passed the black market treasure around for everyone to smell. All carefully took the little shiny yellow package, pulled out the silver wrapping and its thin, light-gray contents.

When it was Balazs' turn to smell the gum, he almost dropped it in his excitement and fear of touching something so illegal, something from the enemy, from capitalist America. What consequences could come to him or his family if they found out? He quickly turned and scanned the hall, which appeared safe and free of adults. He lifted the gum carefully to his nose and deeply inhaled the fresh scent of Wrigley's mint gum. He felt a rush of excitement: this was Balazs' first encounter with the free West. As he inhaled, he wondered if all of America smelled like this.

A deal was struck—whoever took the gum home and chewed on it for one day had to pay one Forint, then, overnight, he had to soak the chewed gum in water, sugar and toothpaste to renew its taste for the next fortunate chewer.

He had a hard time understanding the concept—why would Americans chew something without swallowing it and still pay for it? He was so nervous that he might accidentally swallow it that he passed on the chewing. Besides they had no toothpaste. He opted to just smell the wrapper all evening and left the pre-chewed gum sitting on his night table.

In the following weeks, the school was hit by an epidemic of influenza, no doubt in part caused by the germ-infested gum passed through 200 kids. The school nearly shut down and the school officials had no clue what caused it. Only the kids knew. The real irony of this whole experience was even subtler. It was one of the Communist Party members' children who had access to such an item and brought it to school. With a dose of healthy capitalistic incentive, and a natural instinct for profit, he duplicated his money and gained capital. This was an enterprising kid, who practiced supply and demand. One was made to wonder how the Communists could succeed in suppressing this natural human drive.

TWENTY EIGHT

BATTERED

THE CITY BECAME more and more a part of Balazs' soul as the seasons passed. He discovered all the parks, all the indoor and outdoor swimming pools, which were more numerous in Budapest than in any other city in Europe.

One of his favorite swimming pools was the Olympic competition pool on Margit Island, situated in the middle of the Danube. The entire island had been dedicated to leisure activities some centuries ago. An old Roman hot-geyser bath was modernized in the 19th century with six major pools, including a wave pool. Thousands of the city dwellers would soak through the cold winter months in the hot, shallow geyser pools, some playing chess and turning into prunes while snowcaps formed on their heads.

Balazs enjoyed the ancient Turkish baths, with pools of varying temperatures and colorful glass-studded domes. The dim ancient steamy pools were alight with the colors of the rainbow, as the band of rays cut through the steam, inspiring his soul with magic.

He took many unauthorized visits to his father's house. He relished the times spent with Kati and Sandor, who always made a point of doing something meaningful with him, such as going to art museums. They were very impressed with his talent for sketching and wanted to expose him to the great Hungarian artists. By this time, Kati and Sandor were in great demand by the public, which meant many film engagements, radio, and dubbing of foreign films, though, naturally, none from the West. Balazs was encouraged to catch up with his brother's education, and was signed up for all kinds of lessons, including dance. Shy as he was, he hated it, and managed to attend only three sessions. Sandor didn't realize how introverted Balazs was. He rushed too fast to make up all the time lost in their relationship and Balazs' development in the arts. When he was taken to a film studio to join his brother in a reading for film dubbing one winter's day, he was so overcome with stage fright that he hid himself in a large garbage can outside the building. He nearly froze to death before the stagehands discovered him. His parents decided he should take piano lessons instead.

Dorotya Geczy, a beautiful, young and talented actress friend of Kati's, offered her mother's services. The winter was bitter cold and the central heating in Dorli's mother's building did not work. She compensated by having a tiny electric heater behind her in the ice-cold apartment where their breath could be seen. If she had the heater behind her thin frail bones, Balazs froze; when it was the other way around she caught cold. It was miserable even to hit the cold keyboards with frozen fingertips. In short, the teacher lost her student, but Balazs gained Dorli as a lifelong, loyal friend.

Sandor's last attempt before giving up on his son ever becoming an actor was in a film where the two boys played brothers. Balazs made it absolutely clear to the family that he hated all this and never wanted to do it again. However, in their living room hung a beautiful pastel portrait of Kati, which Balazs much admired. He asked his father if he could take art lessons from the man who had signed the work, Pal Fried. To his dismay Sandor told him that his friend Pal, who lived in Paris in 1941, had been forced to flee for the US before the war. He was a Jew.

Sandor and Kati lived a very rich cultural life. Like many of their colleagues, they enjoyed city living. Cities were the nucleus of culture and the energy of nations, naturally attracting people, especially artists, actors, filmmakers, poets, musicians and sculptors. They congregated in coffeehouses and art clubs, inspiring each other. Balazs was totally immersed in this kind of life as his parents included the boys in all their activities. Just being behind the stage whenever Sandor or Kati performed was an incredible experience for him. He loved everything—the stage sets, the colorful costumes, the rushing about of the actors, beautiful actresses leaving trails of powder and perfume in their wake. It was a magical world, very different from the depressing life outside. It was a great escape for everyone, actors and audience alike. Going home to the little apartment was an anticlimax, even though he came to love Eugena very much.

He still passed the time doing watercolors with her. They played with the funny green parakeet she had given him as a gift the previous year. They delighted in the little feathered friend's ability to learn and memorize countless words.

Balazs also had gotten a small pet leaf turtle from his godfather, Lajos. He and godmother Margit had been chosen for the honored appointment because of their devotion to the boy. In early 1943, Budapest was under siege while Jadda was pregnant with Balazs. The family often hid in dark, unventilated bunkers with other city dwellers, existing on meager rations of food and water. Between raids, they got out of the bunkers in search of something to eat. Sometimes they were able to find food in blown-out stores and houses. Everyone was near starvation; peasants were not able to make it to the city and sell their goods. These were difficult, desperate times.

Fortunately, Jadda made it to a nearby hospital in Buda and gave birth to Balazs, almost a month late. He was a tiny, three-pound baby and his mother was unable to nurse him. She had no milk. A young physician friend of Eugene offered to take care of the infant. He and his wife had no children, so they were able to devote all their time caring for him—totally removing him from Jadda for the time being. The two concocted a healthy diet for Balazs and he began to develop quickly. In fact, when it was time for him to walk, he was too fat to do more than just crawl. Out of gratitude, his parents asked the pair, Lajos and Margit, to become his godparents.

Balazs sometimes wondered in his moments of pain and anger (after his mother's outbursts resulting in beatings) that perhaps the early separation from her caused this rift and distance between them. Whenever there was an opportunity, she exhibited her preference for her first born, often in the presence of Balazs.

****

Sandor and Kati led an exciting but hectic life. There were many after theater parties and other social obligations, but they always found time to spend with the boys. Balazs observed with great pleasure their romantic, loving relationship and the genuine affection they had for each other. Balazs' frequent unauthorized visits infuriated Jadda. However, her jealousy did not result in more love and attention to win him. Instead, she fabricated the usual stories about "the Jewish whore" who began her career with topless displays in public and in circuses. His mother claimed that Kati viciously disrupted the marriage and stole Sandor and Jadda's "favorite child" from her.

Balazs was sick of listening to these fabrications. He knew the truth, that Kati and Sandor met after they were already divorced, and how Kati's career began with the help of her stepfather who was the theater director in the city of Gyor. He listened to her ranting about Jew this and Jew that, Gypsy this and Gypsy that, and became ever more disgusted. Did Eugene and Paula not raise her? They not only raised Balazs without prejudices, but they set good examples with their open-mindedness and their respect for other people's beliefs and values. Their example did not prevent the bitterness that engulfed their daughter after the divorce, as her permanent anger struck out against the world around her.

****

The sun shined radiantly on a clear autumn afternoon. With his spirits raised he hurried home. After a small injury at the gym that earned him his early release, Balazs was looking forward to the extra time to himself. After jumping off the electric trolley he rushed into the building, mounted the stairs by threes and burst through the hallway to Eugena's room. In his hurry he took a giant step into the room. Suddenly, he tripped and was hurled across two entangled naked bodies on the floor in embarrassing and compromising positions. Jadda was there naked with a man.

The boy's books flew in all directions, as did his mind, which he seemed unable to collect.

He heard Jadda scream at the top of her lungs, "What the hell are you doing here? You are supposed to be in school," as she awkwardly tried to disengage herself from him and her even angrier partner. She reached out in her fury toward Balazs, caught him by his pant leg and flung him towards the door. He fell across them again, so she rained down a fury of blows on his face. He was terrified and attempted to break away, but suddenly, he felt a heavy fist in his stomach and then in his groin. The pain struck him down, immobilizing him. Balazs saw the angry man's hateful face while he was exposed to Jadda's repeated blows. He closed his eyes and when he opened his mouth to scream for Eugena's help, he felt his lips split and blood squirt in every direction.

Tiny Eugena, with God's speed, rushed into this impossible scene, dropping the groceries all over the floor. "Oh my God, Oh my God," she screamed as she tore the child from the grips of the rabid, enraged couple. Balazs was shaking and held onto Eugena's small frame while spitting blood, and was overcome with a nervous hiccup attack. He could not breathe for a moment almost losing consciousness. Sometime after regaining his senses, he heard the entry door to the apartment slam. Eugena's loving hands tended his wounds with a cold compress. He kept crying, as did Eugena. She muttered, "This can't go on any longer." Balazs knew it was the truth.

He slowly got to his feet. Without looking into the mirror to examine his battered face, he took some necessary garments out of the 300-year-old colorfully painted Hungarian folk armoire. Eugena followed behind with a small suitcase which she laid on the couch. Traumatized and distressed, she did not help with the packing, but, knowing this was what had to happen, went to her room and fell face down on the couch crying. He threw his few belongings into the suitcase; then slammed the lid closed.

He went to Eugena's side. He felt a hundred years old as he gently kissed the back of her head. Before leaving he heard his little parakeet shout out some obscenities, which he had recently taught the bird. He swept up the small cage, grabbed the leaf turtle and headed for the streets.

Across the street was the No. 5 blue bus, which would stop a few blocks from his father and Kati's street. The brakes of the large bus squealed as it came to an abrupt stop. Balazs stood at the open door with a cage and a suitcase in hand, the blood still trickling down his swollen cheeks and split lips. He was definitely the sight of a severely abused child. The driver and the passengers stared in shock and instinctively got out of their seats to help him up. The passengers were quiet as Balazs announced that he forgot his money. The driver said, "Never mind, where to?"

"To my dad's home," said Balazs, through his swollen lips with much pride and a newfound sense of belonging. "He is the famous actor Sandor Szabo, the Maestro. My mother beat me and I want to go to my dad!" Balazs noticed the instant respect the mention of his father's name brought to the passengers and the driver. There were no voices raised in argument when the driver announced that the bus was being re-routed and would go to the Maestro's house and that anyone who wished to get off should do so now. No one got off, so the bus proceeded to the address. Some peasant ladies removed their scarves and with the help of some caring spit, began to tend to Balazs' wounds. He could smell their onion and garlic breath from sausages, but he had experienced much worse recently.

Within a few minutes, the bus found its way to the apartment building. The elevator did not work again, as usual, and as Balazs took to the stairs with the birdcage in hand, the driver was behind him with the suitcase. The remainder of the 40 or so entourage of passengers, followed in tight formation. Balazs rang the doorbell with their family code of three short and two long rings.

Kati answered the door, wondering why Balazs would be visiting at this time of the day.

Sandor, on his way to the kitchen, stopped behind her too, quite unprepared for the scene. Balazs stood in the doorway, with his face horribly swollen, one eye nearly shut and his bleeding lips double their normal size. The little mob behind him filled two flights of stairs as the uniformed bus driver, suitcase in hand, made this theatrical event utterly surreal and comical. Balazs broke the silence and even he was surprised at what he said, looking up at Kati's loving face, framed in her blond locks, "Mother, if you take me in I will be grateful to you forever."

Her knees gave way in an instant in a wave of emotions, as she embraced the battered Balazs in her arms. He held on and wept too. Kati could not help thinking that fate had replaced the two sons she once lost as a young mother. The bus driver wiped his tears, as did the entourage behind, not knowing whether to laugh or cry. Sandor was thankful to everyone and, in his sweet, endearing way, went down the stairs and hugged everyone.

Late that night, the phone rang and Balazs felt Jadda's evil presence as Sandor picked up the receiver. "Is my son there?" Came Jadda's demanding voice on the other end. "Yes, he is," said Sandor calmly. "Well, slap him across the face and send him home immediately," was her angry demand. Sandor deliberately and slowly replied, "Under the circumstances I don't think so." He hung up and disconnected the phone from the wall to prevent her further abusive calls. It was difficult for the family to rest that night—only Balazs slept, one of the best sleeps he had in a long time. The trauma left him exhausted and being with his father finally, even though not legally, made him relax. The next morning, since his father and Kati always slept late, he dressed himself but did not wash off any more of the evidence of the beating. He had a definite purpose and knew what to do. He knew the city's main courthouse was near the "secret" underground torture chambers. It was well guarded with machinegun toting soldiers. Balazs put on the bloody clothes he was wearing the day before. The second day of his ordeal, he looked much worse. He was more swollen and blue from the blows. One eye was totally shut and his lips were purple with coagulated blood. He approached a somewhat surprised guard and begged to be taken in to any judge because his mother had nearly beaten him to death! The effect must have been powerful because, without a word, the soldier said, "Wait here," and motioned to another guard. They spoke, and Balazs was taken up several marble floors to the judge's chambers. Without hesitation, he practically told his life story to an old judge, who listened patiently. Soon after, the judge called the guard and requested some files to be brought in. They waited a while and he asked some questions about his father. He added that he had seen his father many times in the theater and admired his great talent. Too bad, the judge remarked, your father has not yet joined the Party.

When he arrived back at the apartment, he realized that everyone thought he had gone back to Jadda. Balazs was beaming as he held out the signed legal papers his father had not been able to obtain for many years from the court. The papers, signed by the presiding head judge, gave permanent right for Balazs to live with his father.

TWENTY NINE

THE APPARITION

IN THE BEGINNING of spring 1956, as they waited to hear whether their trip to Austria would be allowed, Sandor and Kati were kept extremely busy fulfilling their many commitments. They often got home exhausted to the bone. One night, they were rudely awoken from their deep sleep at around 3am by the ringing of the phone—a device so loud that everyone in the entire apartment was woken. The dog barked into the darkness and the boys heard Sandor muttering something as he tripped over his shoes in his haste to reach the irritating and insistent ring. He picked up the phone and, after a moment of silence, heard his mother's panicked voice on the other end begging him to please come over immediately. He said he would be there right away and hung up.

****

As old Kati and Erno were sleeping lightly, they had heard the rattle of their triple lock on the outside door. A moment later they heard it creak open and close again. The frightened couple, suspecting burglars, sat up and held each other's hand and listened intently. They even thought perhaps it was their time to be taken, but without the "knock." The room was pitch dark with the blinds and curtains tightly drawn, and they could see absolutely nothing. Frozen with fear, they kept their eyes closed.

Methodical, heavy steps approached through the hallway toward their bedroom. Finally opening their eyes, their vision slowly improved as they strained into the darkness, still totally petrified. The wings of the three-meter high doors were unlocked from the outside and opened slowly toward them as they waited for some horrible fate. There was eerie silence. They could finally make out the shapes of the furniture in the darkness, but saw nothing moving. Again they heard the slow, heavy steps approaching the foot of their brass bed, where they stopped. The bed shook firmly. Old Kati let out a sharp terrified yelp at the invisible something standing at the end of the bed. They both felt a presence of something beyond fear, something heavy and painful, though they could see nothing physical. By now, Erno was frightened beyond his wits and yelled at the top of his lungs, "Get out of my house, whatever you are right now. NOW," he demanded.

There was no response and the persistent silence heightened their fear, yet the entity that filled the darkness somehow reached Kati in a warm, mysterious way. Catching her breath, she carefully leaned forward and with a cracked, loving voice, whispered into the dark, "Bobby, is that you, my dear son?" There was no reply, but the bed moved again slightly several times.

Silently, they waited in the darkness, as the beat of their hearts calmed. The heavy steps slowly withdrew from the bed and headed back toward the tall bedroom door. It closed gently. The key turned back to the locked position. The steps continued down the hallway toward the outside door, which opened and closed with the three safety locks locking.

The couple found themselves drenched in tears. Old Kati was unable to move, paralyzed by her thoughts and suspicions. Erno finally turned on the nightlight, looked at his wife in disbelief, got out of the bed and walked to the locked bedroom door. He carefully unlocked it and cautiously walked down the hall leading to the outside double doors. He pressed down on the brass handle and tried the door. It was locked. Then he checked the three locks, but also found them secure, as he left them the night before. He examined the entire apartment, but everything was in order, there was no evidence of anyone or anything. He wondered about his wife's intuition, addressing the unknown as Bobby, who had not been seen since his arrest after the war. He dialed Sandor's number and handed the receiver to his wife.

The next day everyone in the Szabo family heard about the event and no one could come up with any sane explanation. Some even dismissed old Kati's notion regarding her son, but Erno was not so cynical: they had shared this nightmare together and, in 50 years of marriage, this was the first time anything like this happened.

****

Nikita Khrushchev was now in power and people were under the illusion that things were getting better, perhaps simply because Stalin was so horrible in comparison. But Khrushchev had opened Stalin's gulags, and many of the survivors began to show up in Hungary. They might as well have been dead people, as they looked like wretched, walking skeletons in rags.

They were starved down to their very bones. Their eyes were sunken deep into their skulls without the slightest glimmer in them. They remained silent and unapproachable. Some were seen at the shores of the Danube sitting for days on end simply staring at the passing water. Their faces were ashen gray with deep grooves, weighed down by gravity and the scars of their suffering.

Sometime after the night visit, one such apparition rang Kati and Erno's doorbell, and simply stood there for a time before uttering a word. He stared into nothingness facing them, then almost inaudibly said, "I am Zsolt. Bobby and I were in Siberia together after they took us off the Chinese rice fields. We were there for years. He was very weak and could not get used to the bitter cold and caught pneumonia. We had no medicine, no food but a small daily ration of bread. Bobby developed gangrene, too, but he traded his last ration of bread for a cigarette from me. I am sorry, but he is gone now. He did not suffer in his death."

They stood there for a moment—old Kati suddenly lost her footing and leaned back pale against the wall then slunk onto the floor. Shortly after the initial shock, she regained her composure and inquired about the time of his death. Zsolt said it was recent, just before the news of amnesty and their release. She thanked him as she cried with grief that shook her entire body. When Erno looked up, the man was gone. They felt cheated and miserable. There were so many things they wanted to know which now had vanished with this broken man. The visit on that unusual night was no longer a mystery, at least to the old couple; they understood now and it comforted them to know Bobby had come to say goodbye.

THIRTY

TASTE OF THE WEST

THE SCHOOL HE attended was just a few blocks from the Parliament building. It was also two blocks away from the office where Jadda worked. Before the ugly incident that had caused him to run away to his father, he used to visit her there after school. Now, he feared that she would try to nab him at the gate to reprimand him or inflict whatever abuse she might have in store for him. He feared her, but he was obliged to see her because it was the law. These were the most uncomfortable days for him. To ease the situation, it was decided that his brother would accompany him on these visits. Balazs entered the apartment, and rushed to Eugena's arms in order to avoid any physical contact with his mother. Jadda planned to play her "emotional pain game" again; giving special, thoughtful gifts to, and doting on, Barna. She made sure that Balazs heard all the comments about his brother being her favorite. Eugena's loving attention made up for the emotional abuse from his mother. Balazs ran to visit a group of little friends as Eugena pointed out some good news.

Directly under their window was an acacia tree whose topmost limb was home to a pair of gray, ringed-neck doves. In the spring of every year they would lay two little eggs. Balazs and Eugena, spent hours watching at the windowsill awaiting the new hatchlings. Two new eggs appeared again on schedule. Within two weeks, little gray, fuzzy doves would fill the nest. It always seemed a miracle that, during the wind and rain they never fell out of their flimsy built nest onto the busy street below.

He felt relieved and energized after departing. In a few days the exams would be over and they were going to spend the entire summer at the lake. Some member's of his father's family were still not his favorite people, but he knew that a 15 kilometers ride on the new bicycle which he got for Christmas would take him to his grandparents.

Summer by the lake would be fun, he thought. As the train raced through the towns toward the lake, he could reach out the window and grab the cherries off the trees by the tracks. As the cherries ripened in the warm, summer sun, the plum and apple trees bloomed in pink and white to catch up. Balazs had seen a striking painting from a Dutch painter in the art museum, which captured exactly what he felt seeing this scene. The painting was not as well done as some of others in the museum, but it had strength and heart, and it even conveyed the smell of the flowers.

The Szabo clan of the six boy cousins was at the lake town of Akarattya. Sandor's father, Erno, had helped to establish a workers summer spa before the war. (Sandor did not know that his father was secretly a Communist, nor did anyone in the family.) The madness began with all the shouting, laughing and fighting of six wild city boys. They could not get enough of the lake, the cherry trees or of the blackberry tree that was laden faithfully every year. They would spend so much time in the shade of the weeping blackberry tree, eating the fruit, that they all had the runs at the same time.

They would ride to different towns at the lake and see the sights. On clear, starry nights they would build campfires and roast bacon. Now that Balazs lived among the affluent, he had pocket money and was able to go to the town's movie theatre. He could not get enough of seeing his father in films. Balazs biked over to spend time with Eugene and Paula as often as he could. Frequently he stayed the night cuddling with them. They could not understand why he had left his mother's home, and as he tried to explain it, a rift came between them. They could not imagine anything negative about their daughter, so Balazs dropped the subject. This time he came with great news to share with them. His father and stepmother were invited to play at the state theatre of Vienna, outside of the Iron Curtain, for the summer!

No civilians before had been allowed out to the West, as tourist or under any other circumstances, except for the athletes. The government agreed that, as long as the children stayed behind in Hungary as hostages, the pair of actors would be allowed.

Sandor and Kati left for a short stay of stage production in Vienna, then returned to the lake.

They related stories about the freedom and happiness of the people there. The recent departure of the Soviets, from the occupied portions of Austria, had totally changed the spirit of the nation. Balazs clearly remembered the day of their liberation. The church bells in Austria rang in jubilation. The winds carried the tolling of bells that rang out for freedom across no-man's land and across the border towns to occupied Hungary. The hearts of the Hungarian people sank, believing that their time of freedom would never come. Nevertheless, they took to their churches too and rang their bells. They rang them for Austria's freedom, and in protest at their own bondage and hopelessness. Like a domino effect, the bells had been answered across the nation in every town.

As Sandor talked about the freedoms and the wealth of the Austrians, he and Kati unpacked a suitcase of treasures. They were able to bring back things of what the boys had only heard about. Balazs got two bananas and a brown liquid in a beautiful bottle that said Coca-Cola on it. He almost dropped it as he read the embossed glass label. He was taught in school that the imperialist capitalist pigs in America gave this drink to the people because it was a barbiturate with which they could get more work out of the masses. Yet his father now looked at him and said, "Come on, open it and try it." Balazs, in truth, was not very impressed; it tasted kind of bittersweet, so he passed it to his brother. He hid the bananas and the orange in a sack.

After the chewing gum experience at school, this was his second exposure to items from the West. Kati said that Sandor took an incredible chance with their lives by smuggling wristwatches across the border. He bought a vest in Vienna and purchased 100 watches that he had sewn into the lining. As they drove back, the border police thoroughly searched them. The guard kept giving the Maestro familiar slaps on the back. Sandor and Kati were sweating bullets, and, quite possibly, would have taken some right between the eyes if the guard had touched him any lower.

As Kati cut open the seams of the vest, beautiful, sparkling new watches poured out onto the bed cover. Plastic was not yet a common material in Hungary. These watches floated in clear plastic, so one could see the mechanism on the back, and more clear plastic embraced the face of the watches, too. They were in many colors, and Sandor was hoping to get a great deal for them on the black market. All this worried Balazs, because if Sandor got caught, he would most likely be sent to Siberia like his brother before him. Kati and Sandor bid goodbye to everyone and departed again for Vienna for a longer stay of stage appearances.

Balazs went to his hiding place and he took out the banana. Before he lifted it to his nose he could already smell its unique aroma. He ran his fingers on its smooth yellow skin and admired it, but, as he was going to take a bite of it, he thought of his grandparents.

He put the banana back into the sack and took out the orange. As with the banana, he smelled the citric aroma so alien to him. He ran his fingers on the bumpy skin and as he did so, he accidentally scraped it with his nails. The oils of the skin seeped out with a wonderful scent. He could not get enough of this, so he kept scratching the surface over, and over and inhaled deeply. When he arrived at the villa to rattle off all the news about his father, Vienna, bananas and oranges he spread out his valuable stash on the vinyl tablecloth. His grandparents had not seen tropical fruits since the war began. Neither of them wanted to deprive their grandson of the experience and declined to join in on the tasting. Balazs finally grabbed the banana, making sure to bite into the top end, not where the stem was. But Paula stopped him, and with a smile began to peel the fruit first to expose its soft white inner meat.

"Now you can begin to taste it," she said to him awaiting his reaction. He took his first bite and exclaimed, "It's like eating flowers, Grandma." Eugene began to peel the orange for him as well. Balazs would only continue if they joined him. He was delighted as the three of them huddled together over the tasty fruits of the tropics, a place they may never, ever get to see.

A month later, Sandor and Kati's second trip to Vienna was cut short by the death of Sandor's father. Erno fell asleep in the yard, sitting on his favorite bench, under the apricot tree, during his afternoon snooze, never to wake again.

THIRTY ONE

A NATION RISES

WHILE BALAZS enjoyed the elitist lifestyle of his father, he felt guilty knowing that the rest of the country was getting desperately poor. No matter how many hints or direct requests he was given through the theater director's office, Sandor had still not joined the Party. He was at the zenith of his career. He had the main role of Rostand's *Cyrano de Bergerac*; the greatest hit ever to be in the theaters of Budapest. It brought incredible revenue to the government coffers. Tickets sold out for many months ahead, and people went multiple times to see it.

Sandor was nominated several times for the country's highest artistic award, the Kossuth prize, but in retaliation for not becoming a Communist, he was repeatedly denied this honor. This was, perhaps, the only disadvantage he now experienced under this regime. Balazs had seen the play a dozen times and every time found himself crying at the death scene his father played so well.

On his second trip to Vienna, Sandor was fortunate, for he earned so much income from his appearances that he was able to purchase a beautiful, brand-new Austrian Opel Cadet. It was a large, beautiful cream colored convertible with rich, red leather interior.

Only the Communist Party members were running about Hungary with cars (the rest of the vehicles were trucks, public transportation and bicycles) under government license plates.

All were somber black. This bright symbol of capitalism was a sensation, which drew crowds around it every time he parked on the street. While onlookers stroked it and smelled the new shiny leather, Balazs felt ashamed to get into it in public. Incredibly enough, when people recognized Maestro Sandor, they smiled with approval. It was nice to see a non-Party member having a piece of the good life.

Despite Communist efforts to raise previously poor, working class children into devout Marxists and give them extensive education with powerful positions in the government, the truth began to appear. Many of them began to realize the tremendous gaps between the promises the Communists made to the people when they were trying to get into power, and what they actually delivered once they had it. Eugene had often remarked, "The way these Communists educate the masses will eventually backfire on them. These new and fresh intellects will go beyond the brainwashing process, independently asking questions of the Party. Then the system will be unveiled as a lie and it will collapse."

The process began. The workers received nothing but propaganda and promises. But, they noticed who got hold of the goods, the food, and the luxuries. Hungarian culture was attacked on every level: Hungarians had to learn Russian, read Russian books, and attend Russian plays, and Russian movies. They were taught how capitalism humiliates the people, and that Communism exalts the workers. But, these same workers began to see that Hungary was being used as a tool to strengthen Russia. They could not remember a single decision that was made for the good of Hungary, as everything benefited the great leach, the Soviet Union. Even the secret police, the AVO, had multiple levels in their organization, each checking the other. The supreme AVO group checked on the whole setup, and, in turn, was checked on by the Russians.

The culture of suspicion and mistrust was built into every level of life to control people with an invisible leash. Finally, people began to see the truth; life under communism was bleak and meaningless, without hope, without future. Wages were so meager that no one could make ends meet, and all worked and lived under conditions of poverty. Communism was a big fat lie.

****

On October 23, 1956, the days were already short and darkness fell quickly on Balazs' last class. Their literature teacher was a former nun deposed by the Communists. As she read one of her favorite poems to her pupils, the class was disturbed by noises from outside. The disturbance grew louder with the sound of thousands of marching boots. The roar of a shouting mob was heard, "Russians go home. Down with the Soviets!" Everyone looked at each other, first in horror, then, as if given permission—they all sprang to their feet, totally forgetting their usual discipline and respect for their teacher. But then, she too was already at the window, opening it wide into the cool October night. The air was fresh with the scent of autumn leaves and the open windows instantly chilled the room. As they all hung out to better see the commotion, the crowd of thousands, young people and workers alike, marched and chanted anti-Soviet slogans. Many of them were waving the Hungarian tricolor flag of horizontal red, white and green, but, curiously, a circular hole had been cut into the center, where the hated Russian sickle and hammer in a wreath of wheat used to be. Such daring was suicide! How could any of this be possible? The children expected to hear the rattle of machine guns, and see armored cars running down the protesters. There had never been a protest against the Russians or the Communist government anywhere! No one would dare risk their life and those of their families. Yet, as the hundreds grew into thousands, Balazs and his entire school abandoned their books, and joined the brave people in the streets. Balazs knew where they were headed as the procession faced the direction of the great Parliament building. The Gothic towers loomed into the dark sky with sharp points, no longer symbols of beauty and freedom with its present tyrannical occupants. They looked menacing and evil. The spirited crowd brought with them a list of demands drawn up by a group of young Communist intellectuals (as Balazs's grandfather had predicted). They demanded that the Soviets cease the occupation of Hungary, open the borders to the West, and allow trade as well as other reforms.

They arrived at the gates of Parliament, and the people began to shout the name of Imre Nagy, a moderate Communist who, like Khrushchev, was of peasant birth. As he was not a puppet of the Soviets, he held no great power in the Party. The people were aware of his loyalty to the Hungarians. They wanted him as Prime Minister, believing he would not sell them out. The chanting of his name lasted at least a half-hour, when finally Balazs saw a side door open slowly on a balcony above him. A portly figure stepped out, and after great cheering; he addressed the people, "Dear Comrades!" Immediately, echoes of enormous groans and boos came from the disapproving crowd below. He paused, cleared his throat, and then began again, this time shouting, "Dear Friends!" The crowd approvingly cheered, and cried out his name over and over again. Balazs could not hear any of the remaining words that were spoken.

Nagy began to sing the Hungarian Anthem as the entire assembly of people resoundingly and freely joined him for the first time in public since the Russian occupation. They sang together the Anthem when it would have meant death to do so before. Balazs had as much patriotism as the next person, and sang with passion the hymn he knew well, tears running down his cheeks and those of the people around him.

Then the cry came, "To Radio Budapest! Let's go to the Radio." They wanted their demands read out on the air, so everyone could hear them. The dark mass of humans with flags waving marched with high spirits, and grew like an avalanche. The radio station was the main horn of the Communist propaganda machine in Hungary, and heavily guarded by the AVO. With the crowd moving like a swift river current, Balazs was swept along and deposited a few buildings from the radio station. The shouting crowd was loud as the reflector lights of the AVO began to sweep into them. Everyone knew that they were being photographed for later prosecutions. The students demanded to read the 17 points of reform, and were permitted to enter the building by the secret police that immediately arrested them, and closed the gates behind them. The mob went berserk at the trickery of the AVO. Balazs did not know from where, but he heard the sharp echo of a single gunshot that reverberated off the surrounding buildings.

Balazs saw missiles of rocks now being hurled at the bright lights without success. Behind him the people were yelling, "Make way, make way." Some trucks were arriving with government soldiers who, surprisingly, began handing arms and ammunition to the people. Men from Csepel arrived with trucks loaded with weapons. Balazs could not believe his eyes. The workers from Csepel Island were the very pride of the Communist Paradise. Csepel was the main industrial center of Budapest and its workers were presented with all the glory of Soviet propaganda. Yet they were living in poverty, awaiting the fruits of their labor somewhere in the distant Communist heaven. The AVO began firing their machine guns from the radio station into the crowd. People fell to the cold concrete, and cried out in pain. There was blood everywhere. Balazs was horrified as he realized that the situation has become serious. The Csepel workers immediately began to shoot out the lights, and fired at the AVO on the rooftops. People ran for cover trampling each other. A car was burning in front of the gate. An ambulance came crushing through the crowd indiscriminately without care, injuring many. The Csepel workers stopped it near the gate. Balazs, standing in a nearby doorway, watched as the driver was dragged out from the ambulance. He did not comprehend why the crowd began to stomp and beat the driver until the men opened the ambulance and exposed the cache of weapons the driver, an AVO man, was trying to smuggle to his cohorts into the Radio building. The AVO driver was shot a few minutes later.

The battle for the radio station began in earnest with the people now equally armed. Suddenly, Balazs remembered his father was inside the studio scheduled for some poetry recital. He became terrified at the thought that his father would get caught in the crossfire. The strong doors were blown open, and armed fighters rushed the building. He stayed and waited for what seemed an hour but actually ran into dawn until the ensuing battle was won.

A rumor spread through the crowd that the fighters discovered an old tunnel leading from under another building into the studio. Finally, the men of Csepel were able to attack the AVO from within and took the building; but not before a grenade brought down one of the studio's front walls. The abandoned broadcast equipment was left dangling from wires between floors. A reinforcement group of young men with more weapons and supplies set up positions across from the station and opened fire continuously and in earnest.

Grenades were hurled into the studio building; the white dust of plaster and smoke was flying everywhere, covering everyone's clothes below. As the building was taken and things got quieter, the crowd dispersed, joining other groups headed for the hated eight-meter high iron statue of Stalin in the park. Balazs ran up to one of the men coming out of the blown-out doors of the radio station and asked if they had seen his father. The man said they had only found the AVO. He was relieved and now feeling the freezing cold without the jacket he had left at school, he ran home as fast as he could.

THIRTY TWO

GLIMMER OF HOPE

THE WARMTH and safety of the apartment felt good on his frozen ears and fingers. His step-grandmother, Eta, a jovial, slim lady in her late 50s, was making her daily visit from across the street. She was excited about all the news circulating concerning the revolt. As she hovered over some tasty Hungarian chicken soup, Balazs inquired about his father. She said he was still working at the radio station. He was bewildered and told her that was impossible. There wasn't a radio building. She said, "You are crazy, the station is airing right now. I am waiting for the news, since there was some trouble on the streets."

She reached out and turned up the volume. Sure enough the hated Gero, Rakosi's criminal partner, was making a statement to the Hungarian people about how some "fascist groups and reactionaries had attacked our great nation. They are being dealt with as we speak, and the country is safe. The Radio Station is safe, and will continue to broadcast to the people." Balazs was disgusted to hear the usual lies when he had seen with his very own eyes the occupation of the building, and some AVO men shot.

189

As he explained to Eta what he just witnessed and shared his concerns over his father, Sandor and Kati burst into the apartment. Both were covered with the same white dust as Balazs. Kati looked at Balazs with mixed emotions of fear and elated excitement and asked, "Were you outside the Radio Station?"

"Yes, Mother, I was there from the very beginning, I was so worried knowing that Dad was inside, I didn't know you were there too." His brother came running into the apartment now with news of people marching on the streets, and running to Stalin's statue.

Sandor interrupted to tell them what happened to him. He was to recite poems on air, and Kati had joined him because later there was a meeting scheduled by a group of artists and intellectuals regarding their lack of freedom of speech at the exclusive artist club called "Feszek," the nest. As Sandor prepared to review his work, got his espresso and lit his cigarette, there was a hard jolt and vibration right through the building. Everyone thought it must have been an earthquake. No one inside had a clue of what was happening outside on the streets of Budapest. The AVO, who was always stationed in the building, suddenly came to life, running throughout the building and gathering extra arms. Minutes later, the regular government guards were doing the same and ushered the artists and technicians into alternate studios and rooms.

There was pandemonium. Everyone was assured that there had just been a small disturbance outside, but it had been handled without incident. The programs could go on in the next studio. As preparations were made to refit the studio for change of operations an enormous blast shook everything. Sandor was hit by a wave of pressurized air as he was reaching for his mike. He found himself back in the opposite end of the room next to his wife. Everything in the studio went dark. As the cloud of dust settled and the light filtered in from outside, they saw a great gapping hole where the wall used to be facing the street. They saw occasional streams of lights and herd the rattle of machine-gun fire. Before they knew what happened, Kati and Sandor were lifted to their feet and whisked off through dark hallways.

The State Guards held flashlights, and guided them through all sorts of underground tunnels into the open, onto the streets a block away. They were told to go into the safety of their homes. Sandor wanted to find out what was going on, and grabbed a young man running by him. "We are taking over the radio station and there is fighting with machine guns and grenades." Before coming to their senses, they were swept along by a mass of people rushing toward City Park, where the Soviets had razed the much loved Regnum Marianum Church to the ground. In its place the huge monstrosity of Stalin's statue had been erected. They were now caught up with the revolutionary spirit, along with the rest of the country. They learned from demonstrators about a meeting that began at Bem Statue, which led to Parliament and continued to the radio station.

By the time they reached the park, there was a sea of people chanting, "Down with the Stalin statue," "Out with the Ruszki!" A rope, which was tied about the statue's neck, was being tugged, and some welders were busy with their equipment at the back of the knees. The behemoth came down, with a big thud, face first into the concrete, almost injuring those gathered around. People, men, women and children, cheered, spat on and kicked the wreckage. The falling of this hated symbol of oppression brought great satisfaction and a sense of relief to everyone. Balazs and his family could not believe the coincidence that he was outside the radio station just as the wall went down. Sandor was laughing as he said that one-minute he was holding the microphone, and the next he was holding his butt, which hurt so much from being blown clear back across the room.

Soon they were gathered around the table eating hot soup and excitedly discussing the future. They knew that the Russians and the AVO would retaliate. Many people would die, and others would be sent to Siberia. The phone rang all through the morning as excited friends and colleagues kept calling. By the time they fell into their beds, exhausted, Sandor had been convinced to stand the following day on the steps of Parliament. He was to recite the revolutionary poem of 1848, written by the poet Sandor Petofi at the time of the Hungarian revolution and war of independence. (Petofi was one of Hungary's foremost poets and revolutionaries who perished in the war against Austrian oppression before the age of 27.) There was to be a major non-violent demonstration the next morning to present the demands of the people to the government. This was drawn up by the Communist youth of the "Petofi Club" the night before. These were the same demands they had been attempting to read over the air on Radio Budapest.

THIRTY THREE

MASSACRE AT THE PARLIAMENT

AS THE EXCITED family entered the streets on a gray winter morning, they did not notice the chill in the air. The city was in a buzz, unparalleled in their memory. The buses were filled. The packed yellow streetcars had people hanging off outside of the open doors and on the iron bumpers. Everyone headed in the direction of Parliament.

When they arrived, they could not believe the mass of people already there. The mood was electric, so positive that Balazs felt everyone's heart was connected by their desire for freedom. He saw thousands of children, as complete families turned out, even with infants. It was the happiest and most encouraging sight to behold. He felt very proud to be a Hungarian, and to be taking part in such an historic event that just might be the beginning of a free Hungary; no Russians, no terror of the hated secret police. Sandor was concentrated and focused. He reviewed the poem of 1848, which began as the young poet called to the nation, with the famous words "Talpra Magyar." It began with the verse;

Magyars, rise, your country calls you!
Meet this hour, whate'r befalls you!
Shall we free men be, or slaves?
Choose the lot your spirit craves!
By Hungary's holy God
Do we swear?
Do we swear, that servile chains
We'll no more bear?

The significance of the moment gave him chills. He felt it his utmost duty to deliver these sacred lines to further lift and direct the people to their destiny and freedom. He pressed on, with his family tightly behind him, through thousands towards the steps of the grand Parliament building. As the public recognized the handsome six-foot-three frame of their favorite star, they parted and cheered him as he passed. The people were proud of Sandor's resistance in not giving in to the Communist pressure to join them. The noise increased and the size of the crowd gave everyone a sense of security and strength. When the family finally passed through the gates, Balazs reached out to steady himself and avoid being crushed against it. As he got hold of the gate he felt one of the ornaments give way under his grip. He withdrew his hand, but not before he clenched his fist to recover the black-metal flower decoration, which had rusted off the gate. He felt this was an historical piece given the circumstances. He pocketed it.

On either side of the stairs were two high walls; on top of each sat a menacing black bronze lion. On this side, with its wide stair entrance, the building faced the city, not the Danube. Balazs looked up. Next to the giant lion stood a young man above them, waving a large Hungarian flag with the now common hole cut in the middle. The tricolor gently lifted into the cool breeze on its long pole. He was a handsome, muscular young man in his early 20s, wearing the heavy boots of the working class. His shirt was undone despite the chilling breeze, which caught his long hair along with the flag.

Kati froze suddenly. "Sandor, something is wrong! I don't like this. This can't be!" Sandor, turning to his wife, who looked very pale, said, "What's wrong?"

"I don't know, but it's too perfect, I don't want you to go up there yet!" A few people about them began to chant Sandor's name. Then more joined, and soon thousands were calling upon him to deliver the revolutionary words. He turned, encouraged by the crowd, and extended his arm toward the young man holding the flag. He would need to be pushed from below and hoisted from above to get to a position where everyone could see and hear him.

Suddenly, like thunder from the sky, a deafening burst of machine-gun fire rained down upon the unarmed people. It came so unexpectedly that people stood frozen. Sandor fell back, still holding onto the severed arm of the young man who was no longer standing above him. He had become a mass of warm, bloody flesh torn asunder, and spread all over Balazs, and Kati, and everyone below; and the now blood-covered lion. Horrified, Sandor lay on the ground, not knowing whether it was his own blood that covered him. Balazs saw him separate his fingers from the man's, and drop the arm. The blood-soiled flag slowly slid off the lion to the ground, covering the remains of the young hero like a pall. The terrifying scream of bullets rained down, penetrating through layers of people. They fell all about them, dead and wounded. The AVO had set up machine-gun stations across the rooftops of the government building to deliver death upon the unarmed, defenseless people. There was no shelter in the open park for anyone, save behind the person in front. Sandor was grabbed by someone, and dragged to the left side of the wall as his family crawled and scrambled amid the flying bullets behind. Balazs could see the missiles that missed their mark, hitting the pavement with sparks. He was sure he would get hit, too. It seemed there could be no chance of survival from the rain of bullets. All about him people were falling. They fell in front of him as he stepped on their bodies. He and his brother were shoved into the corner of the building where two walls converged. Five or six layers of people collected there, following behind them, pressing backwards for shelter to avoid the onslaught. He heard Barna scream from pain as the pressing mob shoved him into a wrought-iron frame that was covering a basement window. Balazs, with his years helping Eugene, was stronger and more fit than his older brother, and was able to free himself enough to stand up. His father and Kati were somewhere on his right. He could sense but not see them in the maddening chaos.

The firepower increased and he saw the front row fall dead to the ground. Balazs was facing out and the pressure of the frightened, people pushing backward actually pressed his body upward, so he could see the whole park. It was filled with thousands of screaming and yelling people running in all directions. There were fallen bodies everywhere. He saw parents who were still clutching their children's dead bodies in their arms and children who held tightly to their dead parents, soaked in their blood. It was incomprehensible! A white ambulance with a large Red Cross sign pulled up. White-robed medical emergency people with stretchers rushed to pick up the wounded. As they ran, they were mowed down, and dropped dead to join those they were trying to save. The spray of machine-gun fire came toward them again with deliberate, deadly accuracy, as the metal ricocheted off both walls. The plaster and the sharp stone splinters added to the hail of bullets. Again, another layer of people in front of him doubled over dead. There were only three rows left as a buffer in front of Balazs and his family. There really was no escape; it was only a matter of time. They wondered how long it would take. Kati turned to the left from the tight squeeze, and saw Balazs just standing and staring expressionless, observing every detail: she wondered if this were the last time they would ever see each other.

While Balazs was looking at the carnage and the devastation, he noticed a man running at great speed; following behind him the bullets were tearing up the ground. For a moment, he seemed to be winning, but then a string of bullets caught up with him, and in an instant separated him from one of his legs. His inertia continued to carry his body forward, causing him to roll many times with one limp leg flopping with him. The horror hit Balazs even more when he noticed that the severed leg kept kicking and moving in an apparent running motion, bending at the knee, jerking at least five or six times in the dirt in a reflex, as if attempting to reunite with its owner.

Again, the inevitable wave of bullets returned to seek out the small crowd. This time he saw a woman tightly close her eyes, waiting for the bullets as she was the next in row to die. The shouting stopped, the guns went silent. Then she opened her eyes, wondering if she was already dead. Incredibly a Russian tank had pulled up the side street. Its cannon aimed at the AVO rooftop position and, with a single, perfect shot, blew out the miserable murderers. A loud creaking came from the right side of the group as Sandor and some of the other men began trying to break a door down to escape into the cover of the building.

Another group of AVO men began to fire from where the first ones left off. But several more Russian tanks joined in, and a small battle ensued between them. Miraculously, the Russians had decided to take sides and protect the unarmed, innocent people. Another Russian soldier guarding the Parliament opened the door from within. Quickly the group poured into the stairway. Some were wounded and bleeding badly. Sandor gathered his family. The soldier smiled and kept pulling the people inside. This was the first time they ever saw a Russian do something good for the Hungarians. Almost two hours passed before the Russians overcame the AVO with their cannons and machine guns. There was permanent silence from the guns; smoke lingered over the brown grassy knoll like fog. Bodies were lying all over the steps and grounds; piled over each other in every direction and position. Red blood splattered and flowed everywhere, from the stones and the steps of the Parliament. It soaked the brown blades of the dead winter grass in the park. Hundreds of people were coming in from everywhere to help the wounded, and to care for the dead. Doubtless, this was one of the most horrible unprovoked mass murders in the history of Hungary. The city was shocked into mourning, and now thirsted for revenge.

THIRTY FOUR

PEOPLE UNITE
FOR FREEDOM

THE CITY WAS armed overnight. Now it didn't matter that civilians were not allowed to own weapons of any sort: previously, being found in possession was punishable by death or the gulag. Yet Hungary was manufacturing much of the arms and munitions for the Soviets. Naturally, the workers at Csepel and elsewhere in the city opened the warehouses to the resistance fighters. The streets were filled with multitudes of youths—girls and boys, from 12 and up, armed to the teeth. Katica, Sandor's older sister, her husband and two teenage sons. Csaba and Attila, lived in Pest, across the street from the Killian Army Barracks.

The government called upon the Killian commander, Pal Maleter, to crush the revolution and join their "Soviet brothers." Maleter met with his men of 400 well-trained, but not so well-armed young officers. Normally, the fortified barracks held more than 2,000 in its four-foot thick walls. But it was not so now. The decision was unanimous to support and protect the people, against their orders to stand by the Russian army. This was despite the fact that the consequences of their actions, – should they end in defeat, would result in death.

Not long after their decision, preparations were made for the battle. The information about the officers' "defection" was passed to the authorities, and the Russians responded immediately. The first Russian armored car appeared from the Petofi Bridge, across from Buda, and headed for the Killian Barracks. The reconnaissance car approached from Ulloi Street. The officers nervously waited until it crept into range. Within seconds it was set ablaze by "Molotov" cocktails hurled from soldiers stationed on the roof.

Ironically, it was the Russians who had taught this tactic to them. A simple homemade device of a gasoline-filled bottle and an eight-inch fuse was lit and thrown at the intended target. Several other armored cars followed the first. But, seeing its destruction, they were more cautious, and began to fire on the barracks from a safer distance. This time the Russians were surprised by attacks from all sides of the street by young civilian fighters.

The vehicles were destroyed at the front and at the back of the convoy, trapping the remaining Russians inside the barricades created by the burning wrecks. The fighters, recognizing the situation, put 15 armored cars out of commission, killing their occupants within a few hours. The attack was effective and thorough, despite the gunfire from the armored cars, which killed and injured many. This became the first real battle of the revolution in Budapest.

One ingenious civilian, who had joined the officers, realized that one of the big guns on a Russian vehicle was still usable. It was quickly dismantled and dragged-off to be restored, and then placed in a strategic position at the corner courtyard in front of the Corvin Cinema, below the apartments where Sandor's sister lived with her family. This was an excellent position, with views of three boulevards; yet, the gun itself was undetected. As the next armored car came in sight of the barracks, a civilian carefully aimed, hoping that the gun wouldn't blow up in his own face. He fired and blew up the Russian armored car with perfect accuracy. Maleter knew that from then on the Russians would return with tanks. No one at this point in history had ever challenged the Soviet army in the occupied countries.

The soldier was correct. The following battle was against tanks, which were now fast approaching the barracks from every direction. From better positions and with better guns, shooting from greater range, the Russian tanks began methodically to pound the building. Huge parts of the thick corner wall fell tumbling down in the first barrage, along with the bodies of dead and wounded Hungarian soldiers and civilians. With the continued attacks, the casualties steadily grew. The defeat of the Killian Barracks, which had instantly become a significant symbol to the resistance, meant the lights of freedom would be extinguished swiftly by the tanks.

The Russians felt the same way and the tanks' drivers, emboldened by the results of their cannon fire, began rolling closer toward their targets.

No sooner had they made this fatal move than children appeared from buildings with buckets of soap and water and with cooking oils from their kitchens. They ran beneath the sights of the guns and splashed the pavement ahead of the approaching tanks. The massive iron treads began to slip and slide on the slippery road, heaving the heavy machinery in every direction.

Another group, brave and fearless girls of about 13, ran to roll grenades between the treads which then blew asunder in every direction. Unfortunately shards of shrapnel injured many young attackers, too. The tanks thus disabled and anchored, the Russians were forced to open the hatches to escape. In that instant, a barrage of Molotov cocktails flew through the air from windows above. Some hit directly into the opening and some over the tank. The Russians were scrambling in all directions trying to get out of their vehicles, screaming and running like living torches. Some were shot and some were allowed to continue burning.

The city was filled with similar episodes, everywhere that day. Many children and fighters died from the guns of the tanks. However, all the tanks that were dispatched by the Russians were destroyed and their occupants killed.

Sandor picked up the ringing phone as the family returned from the nearby streets. Katica told him about the incredible fight the Killian Barracks had put up against the Russians and that their apartment was totally destroyed by a tank's cannon shot. They had lost everything, yet felt fortunate in being spared.

Although many of the fighters' positions were spotted by the tank commanders and simply destroyed by well-aimed cannon shots–killing hundreds at a time–the battle went well. Many Russians were killed and much of the hated AVO flushed out too. Sandor and his family had just returned from a gruesome exhibit of desperation and suffering. Down the street from Madacs Square, where their apartment was located, stood the building housed the AVO headquarters.

Throughout the night they heard the heavy fighting that took place as the people attacked the building, killing most of the defending secret police. In pursuit of the escaping scoundrels through underground tunnels, the fighters came upon the torture chambers which Budapesters had long suspected were hidden beneath the city. No one who survived and later released knew where they had been taken. Constructed many levels below the street, and filled with hundreds of political prisoners, men and women, this was where the torture (the Communists called it "rehabilitation") took place. The conditions and the suffering that the liberators beheld were sickening beyond imagination. The cells were opened and the captives released. The cornered AVO men who surrendered begged for mercy. They were dragged above ground to a small peaceful park with benches. This was always kept well manicured, with flowers and trees, in total contrast to the horrors that took place below.

It was October; the trees and bushes lay barren of leaves. The angry, revenge-thirsty fighters tied the legs of 12 or so kicking, squealing AVO men and strung them upside down from the trees.

On this cold morning the people looked on, remembering all their loved ones and fellow Hungarians who had been murdered and tortured by these sick, vicious dogs. The crowd was quiet at first. They had never seen these monsters so exposed and out in the open. These murderers were helpless and vulnerable, dangling from trees with torn clothes; their white flesh looking tender. "They don't look so tough now," remarked a bystander. "What the hell," said another as he approached to spit into the face of one of the frightened AVO.

Then the crowd ignited and lost control, closing in on the victims to pay their homage, too. In a very short time they were kicked and punched, spit upon, defiled with urine and shot many times. The bodies writhed in pain as they tried to free themselves, knowing that the inevitable was approaching. They screamed the screams of their past victims, echoing the years of suffering which they had dealt out to the innocent and the helpless.

By the time Balazs and his family were able to push through the crowd and fill their curiosity; most of the AVO men were dead or nearly so. Some were being used as knife-throwing targets. As awful and inhumane as the sight was, the boy's family felt no compassion or sorrow in their hearts as they looked at the fate of these killers.

As Balazs stared at the bloody, hairy white body dangling in front of him, he wondered if this could have been the one that hurt his uncle. Eugene's older son, Eugene Jr., was shoved into a cold underground cell. He could tell by the smell of mildew and the dampness of the wall, which his naked body was thrown against. The humiliation began with the stripping of his clothes and, while tightly secured, he was forced to face an incredibly bright light. He could not see his assailants. Someone held his eyes open by pulling on his sparse hair. The lights made his eyes tear so much that he could feel them streaking down his cold skin.

Someone kicked him in the stomach and the thrust brought vomit into his mouth. The AVO could see that his delicate frame could not take much. "This one is not going to be much fun," said one, while another landed a heavy fist into Eugene Jr.'s mouth breaking some of his front teeth. Before he could even taste the blood pouring out of his loosened jaw and remaining teeth, he felt an enormous buzzing sensation in his head and loss of hearing.

He came to, not knowing when. He felt his lips swollen and split. One of his eyes was stuck shut with blood. The AVO method of breaking people in was first to deny them the knowledge of time. The intolerable bright lights were always directed into the face of their victims. The very small meals were irregular; to further confuse them, sleep was deprived and interrupted. He felt the pangs of hunger and thirst. He dared not ask for anything, knowing that a beating would be the only answer.

Somehow he understood, even without previous experiences of captivity or torture, the sense of evil. After what seemed an eternity he could smell the food before he heard the tin plate hit the ground. Eugene Jr. knew they would keep him alive with food in order to continue the torture.

As he reached with chained hands toward the perimeter of the light, where he recalled the plate being dropped, a stream of warm urine hit his face, body and hands. His plate was contaminated; the AVO men laughed. He was given nothing more for what seemed like days in the silent solitary room. Endlessly he heard excruciating screams of suffering through the walls all around him as he tried to prepare his mind for his turn. He knew he was innocent of "collaboration with the fascists and the imperialistic capitalists of America," and he also knew that his captors were aware of his innocence as well.

While delirious, from the beatings and tortures, he recalled faintly, voices from some lost time informing him of his crimes. He knew this was going to be one of the mock trials and the "softening" process which he must endure. He also knew that the trial would end in a guilty verdict no matter what. As thousands before him, who were tortured, he would sign a confession to end the pain.

As the cruel AVO men knew from practice, the survival drive would take over Eugene Jr. He had been living in his urine and excrement for so long he could not smell the rotten food that he ate. His humiliation began on his genitals and rectum. The team alternated the methods by gender. The female AVO officers were feared the most because they caused the greatest pain and humiliations to the prisoners. Some burned and scorched the scrotums of their helpless victims or probed an object into their rectum, breaking it inside.

These despicable creatures would force them to perform cunnilingus on them while their vaginas were unclean and then defecate into their faces. They often ended their so-called "fun" by inserting thin glass tubes up into the urinary track—smashing the penis to break the glass into smithereens. There were no doctors or any care for these poor victims. If they did not die from shock or infection, their broken unset bones would mend into contorted, monstrous shapes.

Only the Nazi female prison guards paralleled the female AVOs' creative methods. In the eternal inferno of time, Eugene Jr. suffered from bucket drowning, standing for hours on one leg and not being allowed to urinate. Beyond the unimaginable and inhuman pain, he was forced to drink his own urine and eat his own excrement. His captures were not done with him yet.

One of the AVO men relished the act of fingernail pulling after he beat his victims senseless.

Eugene Jr. prayed for his death after surviving each torture, despite his thoughts of his family. He thought of how much he wanted to care for them and love them, if he survived this hell, but he wanted no hope. Having hope was a trap to suffer further. It hurt so severely that death was more beckoning than life. When his time came for trial, he signed many sheets of confessions of guilt and collaboration against the good working class of Hungary, making him also a traitor to the Soviet Union. Guilty as charged, he waited for the firing squad.

But with Stalin's death, many surviving prisoners were released. One day the doorbell rang and Elizabeth, his wife, opened the door. An emaciated figure of an old man stood there, hardly able to hold himself up. He stood, unable to speak as he stared through tear-filled eyes at his wife who did not recognize him. His abused body could not embrace the powerful emotions, and he lost consciousness.

She screamed upon realizing that this was her lost husband. Her sorrow was mixed with incredible happiness. Quickly, she dragged his listless, frail, and light body inside the apartment before fate would rob her of him again. He survived, silent and speechless for years.

Balazs searched his heart for sympathy for the AVO man hanging before him, but found nothing. The bruised body was turning blue in the cold air and the blood brown. A large, gaping wound dripped clear liquid and dark blood into the dirt below. As he stood there deep in his thoughts, he was engulfed with feelings of hatred and dread. A man in work clothes, with a blood-soaked band on his wounded arm, walked up to the body. He took a long, deep drag on his cigarette and adjusted the strap of the machine-gun slung over his shoulder. With an expressionless face and a deliberate move, he stuck the still burning butt into one of the gaping wounds.

The flame sizzled against the moisture and extinguished itself with a small puff of smoke. The smell of burning human flesh nauseated him. He quietly turned toward the man and said, "He deserved worse." But, the man had already disappeared, and melted into the crowd.

THIRTY FIVE

THE STORM CLEARS

THE MOOD WAS jubilant at the seemingly complete victory over the AVO and the Russian occupying forces. The farmers from all over the countryside poured into the city. They came on horse-drawn carts, on horseback and in trucks from collective farms laden with supplies.

People showed their gratitude with gifts of abundant and free food for everyone in the city, especially for the families of the fighters.

People everywhere joined to help those who had lost or wounded relatives. On every street corner were posted empty, unguarded donation boxes inscribed "For the Families of the Fighters." In the evening, children collected the revenue to distribute among the needy. No one ever touched the collection boxes and they were full by the end of each day. Hundreds of stores were wide open, either with their storefronts broken or their walls demolished by tanks and cannon fire, with the goods thrown everywhere. People restrained from looting despite their needs and actually put the often-precious items back into the stores; no one was going to taint this revolution. The still-operating government radio broadcast from some hideout the expected propaganda:

"Dear comrades and faithful citizenry of the Communist Revolution—we have been attacked by underground fascist and reactionary forces supported by American Imperialists. We will prevail and protect you with the support of our faithful Soviet brothers so be patient as this is a temporary situation."

Everyone chuckled at this predictable Communist propaganda and the usual spinning of the truth. The revolution was fought by the disillusioned proletariat and youth Communists "pampered" by the system and by ordinary citizens who were fed up with the tyranny of the Soviets and the Hungarian puppet regime. There were no foreign imperialist forces, as much as the people hoped that the UN would get involved.

There were many overtures to that end from the Hungarians to the West, and Vice President Richard Nixon of the United States pushed for an intervention by recognizing Hungary as a free republic. Gen. Dwight Eisenhower, the President of United States, refused to send any military divisions to be stationed in Hungary or even to recognize the new government as "legitimate."

The Hungarian Revolution, which caused a terrible blow to Russian international politics, was totally undermined by Eisenhower's decision. It sent a message to the world that, indeed, the Russians were right and this was not an uprising of the people in Hungary, but rather what the Russians called a Fascist movement undermining the "legitimate Communist government."

The people of Hungary still hoped that the West and the USA would come to their aid before the Russians returned in force, and return they did.

Sandor took his family again through the streets of the city. The damage was tremendous; many buildings and stores were destroyed. Hundreds of Russian soldiers and AVO men were lying dead everywhere, covered with white powder of lime to prevent them decomposing and the spread of disease.

On October 24, with Rakosi, Gero slipped out to Russia. Imre Nagy was appointed by an emergency committee as Premier of Hungary with Janos Kadar, who assumed temporary leadership. Hungarians agreed that many social services, if reformed, would benefit the nation and should be kept. They were hoping to build a new government modeled after the Swiss and Swedish systems.

The new revolutionary Workers' Council and local committee prepared lists of demands, including the removal of the Soviet Union and its troops from all of Hungary. They called for the dismantling of the secret police, and demanded the withdrawal of Hungary from the Warsaw Pact. They wanted free elections, freedom of speech, of the press, free assembly and free worship. They wanted Hungary's neutrality. Cardinal Jozsef Mindszenty's years of imprisonment by the Communists symbolized religious oppression, was now liberated from captivity. This marked the highest point of the revolution along with the seeming withdrawal of the remaining Soviet army.

Western chronicles wrote, "It appears that little Hungary, in an incredible feat of national heroism, had liberated herself from the shackles of the Soviet tyranny without outside help. Admiration for Hungary is boundless all over the free world and hundreds of millions hold their breaths over the news coming from Budapest. Within a few days, the volcanic eruption of the indomitable Hungarian spirit had shaken the world in a way almost unexpected. Amid torrents of Hungarian blood, a new Phoenix of Liberty emerged from beneath the Hungarian soil."

Many free newspapers, now able to report the truth, were hand-distributed to the population. The victories of the freedom fighters and the aspirations of the nation to be freed from bondage were reported. As people read the lines out loud they were overcome with emotions. Only Hungarians at that time of history could have understood what it meant to be free of Russian imperialism. There was not a soul in Hungary that doubted the eventual helping hand of the Western Allies to preserve the hard-earned victory, especially with the constant reports of Radio Free Europe on the progress of the revolution. There were rumors that the borders to the West had opened. The idea of no longer living in a political concentration camp they called "Russian democracy behind the Iron Curtain" sent an indescribable emotion through everyone.

The large, spontaneous march through the streets of Budapest was such a historical scene that one only sees on paintings in the museums. The city's two million people, Sandor's family included, jammed the sidewalks as they applauded thousands and thousands of victorious freedom fighters marching together arm-in-arm through the avenues of Budapest. The fighters were an incredible mix of young and old. Men, women and children were solidly outfitted with "Russian guitars" (as the distinctive Tommy Guns were known) and grenades. Many who were injured proudly wore blood-soaked bandages, long overdue for a change. His heart skipped a beat on seeing several of his classmates, dirty and bloodied from fighting. They were carrying arms and proudly grinning from ear to ear, many of them girls of 13 and 14.

He tore free of the crowd, shouting their names. As they embraced, he joined them to proudly march in their company. Large groups began singing the outlawed Hungarian anthem and it seemed that the cheering would never stop. As they marched past many destroyed tanks, guns and piles of the dead enemy, his classmates pointed out where they had fought victorious battles and where they had lost companions to bullets. Balazs climbed onto many disabled and captured Russian tanks to get the feeling of victory. He could not believe how shy girls who sat in class next to him had became fighters overnight, handling machine guns and actually killing Russian soldiers and AVO men.

They became giants in his eyes, and deep inside he envied them. He found out from the girls that there were many others from his school who had fought and died in the first few days of the revolution, learning to take tanks out with Molotov Cocktails. For hours the march continued until the early darkness of winter set over the city. However, the lights were lit in all the homes as everyone celebrated with their friends and families.

THIRTY SIX

THE RETURN OF
EVIL IN FORCE

THE GRAY LIGHT of winter's morning gradually separated the contours of rooftops from the sky. Slow streams of white smoke rose from thousands of chimneys in a straight line into the sky like ribbons connecting heaven and earth. Everything else was still in the usually loud, bustling city of streetcars, trucks, buses and multitudes rushing to work. The streets were empty. A nation drunk with the taste of newfound freedom had a hangover and was in its slumber.

Suddenly, and without warning, Budapest shook into sobriety with incredibly loud explosions. Each loud thud shook the ground and the buildings. Lightning flashes lit the gray sky and black smoke rose in every direction, as buildings trembled and vibrated under their quake. Windows cracked if they were not already blown out from the rattle, and the air pressure from the blast of explosives.

Sandor and his family jumped to their feet. In an instant, they had realized the truth: the Russians were back. Sandor tuned in to one of the new, free radio stations called "The Fox." The anxious voice of the reporter warned citizens to stay in their dwellings or, better yet, if they had access to bunkers to go there and prepare for a major bombardment. They should take food, water and kerosene lights with them. More than 2,000 newly designed tanks were sighted the night before on the perimeter of Budapest. These tanks were unlike the earlier models that the freedom fighters had been able to destroy with Molotov Cocktails. These new models had no blind spots at the gunner's station. They had additional guns mounted on them. They were faster, larger and more powerful. They approached from Czechoslovakia, whose residents did not warn the Hungarians.

There were rumors that hundreds of young fighters, mostly schoolgirls, had rushed to the main boulevard leading to the city. Naively, they lay across the pavement holding white flags of peace to prevent the Russian force from entering the city. The appeal had zero effect on the Mongol divisions that the Russian Communists now dispatched to crush the Hungarian revolution.

They were ordered to kill anyone they saw and blow up anything that looked like a fortification for resistance. Most of these soldiers were not even told which country they had been sent to annihilate. Some, driving their tanks on the shores of the Danube, thought they were in Egypt by the Nile.

As if the youth lying across the pavement with white flags of surrender were not human, but only so much debris, the Russian tanks kept rolling forward without hesitation. Proceeding slowly, crushing bodies under their massive treads, tearing and separating flesh from bone as the martyrs stood their ground to face their inevitable fate of dying, one by one.

By the time the city woke, it was totally surrounded by tanks. The heavy artillery was set up on the highest point at the Citadel of Buda. Initially built by the Austrian Habsburgs as evidence of their dominion over the city, a Russian monument was now erected there. Ironically it commemorated the "liberation" of the Hungarian people by the Russian army in 1945.

Balazs dressed hurriedly and put on his coat. This time he would not be left out; he would join his friends. Sandor, knowing his son well enough and realizing what Balazs was up to, got physical with him for the first time. He was unable to contain him, and in his panic he called for Kati to get some belts. Sandor struggled to hold his son down despite his large frame. He found it impossible to manage the determined teenager. With Kati's help, they tied him to one of the heavy antique dining room chairs with three of Sandor's leather belts.

Almost frothing at the mouth with frustration and rage, Balazs protested vehemently. He wanted to be with his classmates. He had a feeling of complete selflessness—not caring whether he lived or died. He wanted justice and freedom for his country. The same emotion for the cause that had swept much of the rest of the Hungarian youth to the streets to fight also boiled in his blood. He loved his country and the people in it with a passion and he hated the Russians. Balazs realized that whatever was accomplished by the sacrifices and heroics of thousands up to this point was now in jeopardy. He simply did not care what happened to him, he felt totally at one with the fighters. He cursed his father rudely and insolently for being a coward. He insisted that his father and brother Barna should join him. They should seek out a group to get armed, and fight with the resistance.

Just a few days ago Sandor was asked to drive a truck loaded with arms for the freedom fighters. His refusal caused Balazs to feel dismay and shame. Now, Sandor had a chance to redeem himself in his son's eyes.

The explosions kept coming closer and with more frequency. They became so loud that they could hardly hear each other. As Balazs was yelling at the top of his lungs trying to dislodge himself by rocking his body to tip the chair, Kati calmly walked over to him. She looked him lovingly in the eyes and with one swift motion slapped Balazs across the face so hard that he thought his head would spin off his shoulders. The sudden shock of her blow certainly drowned out the explosions outside and sobered him into reality. Kati was not a sentimental type. She had great and deep love for Balazs, but she always seemed to know when and how to act to meet any situation. She looked at his stunned expression, rubbing her aching hand as she explored Balazs's face to see if her action had accomplished the desired effect. Then Kati embraced and kissed him. She said, "God help us all now, Hungary is abandoned by the Americans and the Allies. We are facing the Russians alone. Whoever fights them now will surely die as a sacrifice to a lost cause! I am not going to lose any of you to that!"

Early in the morning, not long after the invasion of the city, they heard fighter jets rip the skies above. They flew so low that people were convinced that missiles were being hurled at them. Everyone scrambled to basements and bomb shelters in panic, trampling one another as they rushed down through dark stairs and corridors.

In their deep cellar, the smell of coal and dampness chilled the bones of the Szabo family and nauseated the occupants. It felt more foreboding than safe. Balazs had the feeling that he'd rather be above on the fourth floor, seeing what fate would befall him, than be caught down below under the rubble of thousands of tons of concrete debris, to be crushed or worse, die a suffocating slow death.

Hundreds of tenants huddled together as they gathered with frightened faces around a pair of lit kerosene lamps. Children cried and women prayed aloud. It had been only 11 years since the war and the memories of the bombing of Budapest were still fresh for many. They remembered the Russian soldiers who descended on the Hungarian population—raping, pillaging and murdering innocent citizens indiscriminately, and feared this would surely come to pass again. The question was not if, but when. How long could the freedom fighters, with their limited arms and numbers, hold out against the most numerous and powerful army of the world? The Russians dispatched 2,000 tanks, the same size of force against the Hungarians that Hitler used to invade France in 1940.

Finally someone connected a wire from a radio to an electrical outlet. The light was also turned on, revealing age-old dirt and spider webs. Though it was a little easier breathing without the kerosene, the flickering of the lights frightened the children even more.

****

Sandor looked at his nearly grown sons as he remembered the war. They spent many months down in the bunkers then. There were no provisions left and the bombardment lasted long periods of time, not allowing people to ascend to find food and comfort.

Everyone had become sick from the cold and dampness. People had to relieve themselves in the cramped bunker in the presence of all. The stench was horrible. It was winter then, too, and once the sirens went off, indicating a lull in the raids, Sandor rushed out to forage in the city.

He was lucky one day. Within two hours of searching, he came upon a dead horse half cooked by the explosion of a bomb. Already several men were carving at the carcass and since he did not have a knife, the others carved a sizable hunk from the rump for him, too.

They were all starving from the meager rations of potatoes, salt and water. The horsemeat, more pungent than beef, tasted good to all. He had relished being the provider of the bunker's population that day.

****

Every one was quite perturbed as they listened to the free radio stations still in existence, broadcasting the gloomy events taking place above ground.

On November 3, the day before the new invasion, a Russian delegation was sent to Budapest, asking for a Hungarian committee with whom they could work out the "details of the Soviet military's evacuation of Hungary." A short time afterwards, the committee was hastily formed and headed by the newly appointed Minister of Defense, General Maleter, who was driven to the island of Csepel. After a while, Maleter called his delegation in Budapest and told them that he was safe and everything was in order.

When he related some of the discussions of the meeting, the Hungarians were appalled at some of the Soviet officers' request that a "rain of flowers" be showered upon the departing Russian soldiers at their withdrawal by the Hungarian population.

Their hopes were crushed soon after they realized that it was simply a ruse to lure the newly formed government leaders into a trap. Maleter was arrested shortly after. The day following the treachery, on November 4, Nag, the newly appointed Hungarian leader, announced the Soviet attack to the Hungarians and to the world. He appealed to the United Nations for help. The Russian forces quickly occupied the bridges, highways, industrial centers, and the main prize for Russia, which they had been robbing since 1945, the Hungarian uranium mines. These mines were the third largest in the world, situated in the southern city of Pecs.

Soviet paratroopers landed in the city of Gyor and at Budapest's four airports. Heavy fighting broke out across the nation as the armed Hungarians—civilians, men, women, and children alike—were joined by the local Hungarian military to defend the country. Until November 9th many of the free radio stations informed the residents of the defeats the freedom fighters suffered, despite the heroic defense of the earlier gained freedoms. The bloodiest battles were taking place at Csepel, where almost every one of the workers turned against the Soviets. They even succeeded in destroying one of the attacking jets. They accessed fuel lines and oil to create homemade flame-throwers and destroyed many more tanks.

Meanwhile, the Killian Barracks, which had remained a fortress after the first attacks, suffered near total destruction. But outside of the severely wounded and the dead, the Russians could find very few fighters, as many of the survivors escaped through the sewer system. Above the city on top of the Buda hills, both sides sustained heavy losses in a long battle. When a group of young freedom fighters ran out of ammunition and appeared with a white flag, the Russians mowed them down on sight.

This practice was prevalent throughout Hungary as the Russian tanks destroyed entire building blocks if they suspected one fighter was taking refuge in the buildings. If no one was found, they rooted out the surviving residents instead, and executed them on the spot. They killed anyone they saw on the streets, men, women, or children. It made no difference to them.

From time to time Sandor and his family quietly made their way up to the apartment for water, food and bathroom facilities. When they could, they crawled to the phone on the floor to avoid being seen and shot at through the windows. Sometimes they were able to contact other family members, but most of the time there was no service. When they realized that one of the windows was blown out, Balazs and Sandor crawled to the window to spy on an approaching tank which they had heard entering their street. As they raised their heads slightly above the windowsill, they saw from the right a huge tank speeding toward a telephone booth. It was across from an empty building site used for dumping rubble.

A lone freedom fighter was running as fast as he could a few meters in front of the screeching, clanking tank treads. They saw the young man, his machinegun in hand, turn and take refuge in the open booth, then close the door. Sandor and Balazs could not believe their eyes. What an idiotic decision: all he had to do was take a short sprint to enter a building with an arcade leading through to the adjacent street and then to his freedom. He was obviously not from their neighborhood and was unfamiliar with the terrain.

Father and son were petrified as they watched the Russian tank slow down to a crawl, and then stop completely. As if it were some live, intelligent metal creature, it seemed to look at the booth. It backed up, then turned again and continued slowly. Its large gun was lowered, inch by inch, pointing into the young man's face. He was trapped. He looked down the barrel of the tank as the black diesel smoke blew from its backside in rapid succession. Sandor and Balazs feared that the next moment would bring the awaited, fateful blast of the cannon, as there was no machine gunner atop the tank.

It was an eternity before the tank's sadistic commander engaged his forward gear and began to crush, inch by inch, the glass and metal kiosk. The front of the booth cracked, warped, then the glass burst splintering into millions of pieces. The entire booth was ripped off of its concrete base and backed against the stone wall of a courtyard. The young man, realizing that his death was going to be slow and agonizing, tried to escape in panic through the broken side glass, slicing his already pierced flesh, but to no avail. Trapped, his gray garments soaked with blood, hung heavily on his young body. The tank, like a cat with its victim already injured beyond redemption, stopped for an ever so slight moment, as if to lend its victim false hope of escape. But, as the man's arm struggled to extend through one side of the already tight, flattened wreckage of the booth, the tank came forth relentlessly and methodically crushed the metal box against his body. Pinned and totally trapped him.

Despite what must have been excruciating pain, the young man held his "Russian guitar" in his free hand as best he could. He raised it slightly and began to fire at the tank aimlessly. His body vibrated with the rattle of the machine-gun rounds. The tank stopped to enjoy its invincibility, allowing the sparks to fly harmlessly off the armor while the empty metal jackets fell impotently to the ground.

Again, the tank renewed its slow torturous maneuver toward its victim. More glass popped and broke and fell onto the pavement. The booth became imbedded, one with the fighter's body. Only then did they hear his horrible screams of agony and pain. They could almost feel his ribcage being crushed into his lung and heart as the gurgling sound of blood-filled lungs finally drowned out his scream to a silent gasp.

Balazs and Sandor were in such a tight embrace that they might have broken each other's ribs. The tears streamed down their cheeks as the terrifying scene penetrated their psyche. The sound of the tank's sudden move made them alert again. It reversed and began to back up to the open park where the rubble was. But it could not rid itself of the booth. The cannon had somehow got stuck to the carnage. It charged forward and rammed the wall to knock the irritating wreckage off, but to no avail. It went sideways and tried to scrape it off. All the while they saw the limp body bounce and hang within the crushed booth, like some gruesome circus puppet show. The frustrated tank finally turned back toward its original destination of the open boulevard then quickly rolled out of sight with its unwanted trophy. A few minutes later they heard an enormous blast. They knew the tank commander had found his solution.

THIRTY SEVEN

ELUSIVE LOVE

THE FAMILY SPENT less than a fortnight below ground. Despite their fierce resistance, the fighting civilians and the Hungarian military that joined them were no match for the power of 20 divisions and fighter jets. All who fought now knew they would die, and die they did by the thousands. More than 25,000, including hundreds of children fighters, perished. By November 14, most of the major fighting was over, the resistance extinguished by the ruthless Soviet army. Only the echoes of lone maverick, machineguns were heard here and there sporadically throughout the city. Everyone knew that they would be silenced soon. The explosions of cannon fire roared, and then an entire building would fall, followed by a dust cloud and silence. Only an occasional, painful scream could be heard from the injured and trapped survivors. Budapest lay in dust and rubble again as it suffered major physical damage.

There was much politicizing and philosophizing among the bunker residents during their 10-day stay underground. The country's free radio stations faded out like their hope as the broadcasters were methodically routed out, caught and executed by the Russians. The dark shadow of Russian

Communism began again to eclipse the short-lived blue skies of freedom over Hungary.

Millions of Hungarians and millions of free people in the West listened to the last pleading broadcast of a rebel radio station to the world, before it was silenced:

"Civilized people of the world: On the watchtower of 1,000-year-old Hungary, the last flames begin to go out. The Soviet army is attempting to crush our troubled hearts, their tanks and guns are roaring over Hungarian soil. Please do not forget that this wild attack of Bolshevism will not stop. You may be the next victim. Save us, SOS, SOS...Show that the United Nations can carry out its will and by its resolutions declare that our country shall again be free. We appeal to your conscience and call on you to act immediately...

"People of Europe, whom we defended once against the attacks of Asiatic barbarians, listen now to the alarm bells ringing from Hungary. Civilized people of the world, in the name of liberty and solidarity, we are asking you to help. Our ship is sinking. The light vanishes. The shadows grow darker from hour to hour. Listen to our cry. Start moving. Extend to us brotherly hands....

"God be with you and with us."

The plea for help fell on deaf ears in the western democracies. To the many captured, punishments were administered swiftly. More than 20,000 Hungarians were deported to the Soviet Gulags. Thousands were sent to the usual Hungarian torture chambers and political jails. Janos Kadar, a Communist puppet to the Russians, slipped across to the Soviets during the revolution and returned to Hungary at the helm of the Russian army that placed him in full power. The population was devastated at the thought that Communism was not defeated. The West gave only lip service to freedom in support of democracy. Hungarians felt betrayed. Sandor, who was very intuitive when it came to politics, spoke to the group huddling now in despair of the news of gloom. "Listen friends, the United States and the United Nations missed one of history's best opportunities to free Hungary after the Russians were beaten and the local puppet government dismantled. Ours was an open, independent land for Western democracies to recognize as a legitimate nation. Our country was free for them simply to walk across the reopened borders with a few divisions. With the world's opinion on our side, after our heroic bloodshed and victory, the Russians would not have dared challenge the entire world. "The remaining satellite countries would have followed suit. I think now that the opportunity to stop the spread of Communism was missed, there will be more triumphs for them in spreading to economically poor, gullible nations. I predict that there will, in the future, be more Stalins, and there will be more revolutions like ours where the statues of dictators will be toppled and their heads dragged through the streets of the cities by the oppressed. The world stopped Hitler; therefore there will never be another one like him. But because they did not stop Khrushchev and his disciples there will be many similar repeats. "

The talk went on about the defection of thousands across the temporarily reopened borders to the West, to Austria. Ironically just before the revolution, one of the Communist members of the government ordered the minefields to be cleared at the Austrian border. As the government did everything sloppily, much of it was not cleared. A considerable number of them injured and killed people on their escape.

There seemed to be three waves of mass exodus out of Hungary. The first consisted of opportunistic, selfish young adventurers, and many criminals who were freed along with the political prisoners. The second wave was a large group of people who were fed up with the system and the economic situation. This group was comprised of the elite workforce much prized by the Communists, including doctors, engineers, other professionals, and highly skilled workers with their families. The last wave had the most difficulty in escaping, because the borders were by then shut down by the Russians and the Hungarian AVO, who awaited them. A great number of this group were freedom fighters that fought to the bitter end and knew if they remained, they would eventually be rounded up and executed.

Others, like Sandor, who now contemplated escape, were patriots who might be used as symbols of the "enemy" and executed to set an example of fear into the hearts of the population. This was the price that a Hungarian paid for straying from Communism and being disloyal to the Soviets.

The news of the many horrors spread quickly through the land. A brilliant young (White) Russian actor, Ivan Darvas, a good friend and colleague of Sandor, had already been arrested, and was being tortured.

The new president, Kadar, had the young freedom fighting girls and boys who were under 18 rounded up. He jailed them and waited for them to reach adulthood. They were to be executed on their 18th birthdays. All those above 18 were executed immediately without trial.

Once above ground, Balazs took to the streets and inhaled the fresh November air. He did this several times to flush out the stale underground air that he had been inhaling for days. The city was quiet of traffic save for the Russian tanks that polluted the city.

Suddenly he remembered Eugena. Almost before he had realized what he was doing, he had run more than halfway to her apartment, which was within a three-kilometer range. As he ran he had to climb over high piles of rubble that were once buildings filled with hundreds of people. Occasionally, he saw piles of frozen bodies of Hungarians and Russians alike. He stopped to spit at the dead Russians. It made him feel good, even if it was but a small way of getting even and contributing to a failed cause. He finally reached the apartment and ran up three flights of stairs. Eugena lit up with joy as Balazs embraced her. Both were jubilant in finding the other unharmed and alive. Despite much destruction to the neighborhood, her building was intact. They hurriedly shared information, uninterrupted by Jadda who was out visiting her siblings. Balazs, who had been guarding the secret of the family's plan to defect, decided to tell Eugena about it. As if the walls had ears, he whispered the secret to Eugena, who went pale from the gravity of the news. Her first thought was that she would never see her beloved nephew again, but it was overcome by thoughts of Paula and Eugene. "Balazs, your grandparents will die of broken hearts if you leave them at their age." Soon after she said that, she felt guilty at burdening Balazs with the thought. She corrected it right away with the suggestion that they should have an opportunity to say goodbye to him.

Balazs's thoughts immediately turned to his grandparents. He could clearly imagine the two frail figures of Paula and Eugene huddled day after day by the radio. The few revolutionary radio stations, mainly *The Fox*, situated underground somewhere beneath the citadel inside Gellert Hill, gave detailed accounts of the developments. The initial victory of the revolution was an unbelievable accomplishment in their minds, but knowing full well the nature of the Russians, Eugene fully expected that it would be followed by ruthless revenge. Eugene and Paula had no communication with the family. They had no idea if any of them were injured or lost. The news of mass defections across the open and later closing borders of the "Iron Curtain" was of great concern to them. Had any of the family defected? What about Balazs, had he joined the thousands of young freedom fighters? Was he one of the ones caught, executed or fleeing across the border? All these were painful questions without answers. The maddening uncertainties persisted for weeks before they heard from anyone in Budapest.

There was only one phone in town, located in the Party member's office where no one in his or her right mind would discuss anything like the revolution or defection. The trains were not running since there was a general protest strike throughout the land. This was also a first in Soviet occupied countries. Balazs realized that there was absolutely no way to see the most precious people of his life ever again. There was an eerie silence between them as their thoughts consumed them. Eugena's expression changed suddenly to a joyous smile. Balazs thought she had a solution to his dilemma, but no, that was not it.

"You will not believe that the other day my phone, which had been dead for over a week, rang and, as I picked it up, I hoped it was you calling. There was too much static on the line for me to hear properly, but an excited, older voice with a familiar accent kept calling my name: 'Eugena, Eugena, my love, can you hear me?' It was a good thing I was already sitting on the couch, because it was no other than the voice of my love, Imaoka! Can you believe it?

He said he was not in Tokyo, but was standing across a small bridge in Austria that connected with the border towns of Hungary, and that he was coming to get me. My heart leaped into my throat and I could not find words to even respond. He said that he attempted several times to pay people that brought others back across the border for money. No one would risk taking him at his age, because he was too much of a risk."

Imaoka, after a life of unfulfilled romance, stood at the border in desperation, unable to claim his denied love. The one thing that occupied his mind secretly throughout his entire life was to be with Eugena. He had crossed continents to come this far at the news of Hungary's liberation, just to be cheated again by fate and politics. The frail, old Japanese man tried in vain to conjure up all his traditional masculine posture of honor by not showing his emotions in public. Finally, he realized that his mission was impossible; he was fatigued and felt his age. He stood there weak, frozen in time, feeling a tremble from within his chest that overwhelmed his entire body. The anguish, which he felt long ago the first time he left Eugena, returned anew. Imaoka collapsed forward onto his knees in defeat and wept uncontrollably at his own tragedy.

Despite the gravity of the news that he was not able to come for her, Eugena, an ultimate optimist, held on to her belief that Imaoka would try somehow. Unbeknownst to her, after his call to Budapest, Imaoka re-gathered his strength and indeed made several attempts. On the first, at great expense Imaoka hired a guide to take him to Hungary. The two managed to cross the Hungarian border and the guide, before departing, gave Imaoka specific instructions that would easily lead him to Budapest.

The next day, to the guide's amazement, a disheveled Imaoka was back in Austria. Imaoka, ironically, successfully defected from Hungary on his own instead of ending up in Budapest. He had become a disoriented Oriental and unwittingly returned. At the final attempt the guide and Imaoka nearly ended up in an AVO trap. He finally gave up, lonely and broken, and returned to spend his remaining unfulfilled years in Japan. He continued to express his love for her through letters and beautiful poetry written all in Hungarian.

Balazs was so excited by all this unexpected news that he forgot his dilemma concerning his grandparents. As they continued to discuss Imaoka's plight she led him with a somber expression to the window below which his favorite ringed-neck dove family lived. She opened it to the cold winter air with tears in her eyes. Balazs beheld the most heart-wrenching vision of the entire revolution. He did not understand why this seemed to be more painful for him than all the human suffering he witnessed.

The bare branches of the tree below the window were black and appeared to be petrified into onyx. The thicker ones reached upwards like a modern metal sculpture in a desperate gesture for help. He noticed in the wedge of a Y-shaped branch, two small, charred, little objects, melted into what may have been the remnants of the poorly constructed doves' nest. His heart sank as he imagined the two little souls tightly huddled in terror together in their last moment of life. This minimalist art of horror represented his entire nation's scorched annihilation by the Russians.

THIRTY EIGHT

UNINVITED HOUSEGUESTS

BALAZS WAS increasingly frustrated. He heard news of many friends who had left the city to defect. He could not get America out of his mind and he did not want to live under this hateful system any longer. He could not imagine returning to school to further study the compulsory Russian language, an ugly language that now openly stood for these murderous barbarians in his mind. His cousin, Kati Szoke, a beautiful girl who competed in the 1956 Melbourne Olympics in Australia for swimming, "forgot" to come back to Hungary after slipping away from the watchful eyes of her AVO guards. Her family later received a letter from her with a colorful card, showing palm trees from an exotic place called Honolulu. Balazs's heart leaped at the sight.

Days passed amid horror stories and news of much suffering under the hands of the Russian soldiers. Despite their defeat, the country folks held out and refused to bring goods into the city, though they continued to feed the fighters and their families secretly. People stopped going to work in an attempt to shut down the economy. All systems failed as the trains and buses and every facet of transportation came to a halt. The Russian army began again to attack villages and plunder for food and provisions.

Sandor went over the arguments back and forth daily, trying to decide whether he'd attempt to take his family to freedom or not. Though he was a successful star, he was concerned about a future career elsewhere. His actress-wife was in the same predicament. His mother, too, was alone after her husband's death. Kati thought of her mother, who was her only close living relative. Then there was their country that they loved so much: they really didn't want to leave this beautiful land, this nation, with 1,000 years of such proud, heroic history. As artists, they thrived on its beautiful poetry and literature, which ran through every ounce of their blood.

Just the thought of separation from that tore their hearts to pieces.

Yet, what of their children's future if they remained in this terror-run hellhole? Perhaps, they would have to sacrifice everything in the end for them. Sandor Schwartz, a good friend in Vienna, had made a promise to the maestro in the summer, which echoed in his mind persistently, "My friend, if ever you are able to defect, I will help your family get to the American embassy."

Yet, they waited. Balazs nagged daily as to when they were going to defect. He heard that the borders were getting tighter everywhere. Soon it would be next to impossible to escape without being captured.

Russians and the resurfaced AVO were already capturing thousands of families en route to their escape, shaving their heads and loading them onto cattle carts bound for Mother Russia. If they happened to escape, their shaved heads would identify them. Balazs thought it was a good thing they did not circumcise them as the Egyptians had done to their slaves as permanent identification.

With Sandor's constant vacillation bringing him no closer to any decision, fate came knocking on his door on November 19, dressed as two plain clothes armed AVO officers. After Sandor responded to the heavy rap on the door, the whole family stood in the hallway and felt the blood draining from them in fear. The one who spoke had the typical unhealthy, pockmarked face as was often found among the choice recruits of the AVO. The organization searched out people who hated the rest of humanity for the injustice done to them by their very birth, and who now wanted to get even on the more fortunate through their evil power.

They needed no introduction. The family and Kati's mother, who had moved in with them during the revolution, stood in tight formation as Sandor automatically, like a protective hen, stood with arms spread backwards, as if trying to shield his family from the danger lurking within these two evil entities. They were stunned when the man informed Sandor that they were assigned by the government to "protect him." Sandor and his family understood the double meaning of those words, and that his appearance at Parliament had not gone unnoticed. Balazs felt ashamed and guilty for calling his father a coward and insisting on his involvement. Now all hopes of defection were sealed.

Before they realized what was happening, the two bullies herded them like cattle around the apartment. One pushed Kati into the kitchen and commanded her to prepare a meal. He said he knew she would be hiding food that the rest of the proletariat would not have access. The other creep ordered Sandor to open his roll-top desk so that he might examine his correspondences, prying for incriminating evidence. Balazs felt sickened, knowing that the more than 400-year-old antique desk held a secret drawer built into it by the clever Renaissance craftsmen. In that drawer his father kept his important correspondence, which didn't pass through regular mail. Many had been arrested as the result of letters they wrote and trusted in the privacy of closed envelopes. When the smaller fellow saw Balazs and Barna idly standing by, he barked at them to get their Russian language textbooks out because he would test them later.

Despite the wonderful smells Kati created with the fried onions, potatoes, sour cream, and sliced hard-boiled eggs layered with delicious smoked sausage, none of them had an appetite for eating. The two seated themselves at each end of the large table. One of them shouted at the family, who had no further than holding their utensils from lack of appetite. "Eat!" he yelled so loudly that Kati nearly jumped out of her chair.

Balazs was looking down at his feet, afraid to give away his thoughts. He was in a quiet rage contemplating murder. Secretly, he sized up the weaker one and realized that if he quickly jumped up; he could easily strike and stab the one sitting to his left, who was now busy gorging himself. He imagined turning the knife deep in his throat, so that the sausage would be regurgitated through his trachea onto his lap as his eyes bulged. He could not imagine his father fighting for the man's gun because that was too dangerous. But then he thought Sandor had a huge fist, and if he would strike out at the man's temple, Balazs would move in to stab him. They could shoot the unconscious AVO officer with his own gun, and be free. They would keep the gun, take the identification papers, pack, get into the new Opel Cadet, and show the papers at the border check-point. Or, if all failed, they would smash through the border patrol barricades. He had it all worked out in a flash, and there was no time to waste as the pigs were eating fast. He looked askew at his dad from the corner of his eye, making certain that he was not noticed. Sandor saw it immediately and Balazs noticed panic in his face. He tried to understand why Balazs kept shifting his eyes from right to left toward the man next to him. Balazs slowly grabbed the sharp knife to get the point across and pretended to use it for eating.

Balazs looked him straight in the eyes to guide his father's glance toward the other man, near Sandor. Before Sandor had the opportunity to catch on, a powerful blow of a strong fist came crashing down onto the wooden table making the silverware lift high into the air. The AVO man barked right into Balazs's face, screaming while spitting food toward the shocked kid, "Don't you get any funny ideas you little twerp, or I'll beat the daylights out of you!"

Balazs coiled back like a snake, as he felt venom flood his brain. He sat back and his mind went into overdrive thinking about overcoming these two criminals who certainly would be taking his father to the gallows. He did not for a moment think that anyone else in his family would be working on the same equation.

THIRTY NINE

BOLTED

SANDOR AND HIS family was left mute in the presence of the men who seemed to be everywhere at all times. They had no opportunity to communicate. They were in a limbo. No one dared to ask how long they were staying, because the time of their departure probably meant the time of Sandor's arrest. These two strangers were their enemies by the true definition, yet in an instant, they settled into their lives.

After dinner, one of them closed the door of the family's main bathroom and relieved himself loudly as if he were at his own home. This symbolic "marking" of their territory nauseated them. This very act sent a message to everyone that the AVO men were staying the night. They thought it was time to do something.

The family realized that desperate measures were necessary; Sandor's life was at stake and his end imminent. The man who was calling the shots demanded to see Sandor's wine collection. They knew that Sandor had excellent wines given to him by fans and admirers. Balazs and Sandor felt alarmed by the request, knowing that violent minds don't mix well with alcohol.

Now there was the possibility for physical violence, too.

Balazs had already noticed the shifty looks they gave his desirable stepmother. Yet to Sandor and Balazs's surprise, Kati volunteered to satisfy their demand for wine. Not only did she become pleasant and talkative, but she patiently went through the entire wine list with them. She told them where the wine came from and chatted endlessly, totally out of character.

Shortly after, they decided which wines to sample. Kati moved about smiling with ever so much grace and pleasantry, making the creeps feel like her special guests. The family was flabbergasted at her behavior, but soon realized that she must be up to something. The strangers, unaware that she was acting out of character, suspected nothing and mellowed. She picked up the first bottle and disappeared into the kitchen, then came back for four more, explaining that these wines had to breathe a long time before serving. She emerged not with crystal, but with their finest silver chalices to distract them with the fineries. The drinking began.

Everyone now, including Balazs, thought this was a very good idea. Perhaps she was going to use her charm and smarts to convince them into letting Sandor go. The night seemed endless and the two gradually became quite friendly. Now everyone in the household joined in the act. The comrades mentioned the plays in which had seen Sandor and Kati, and which ones they liked more than others. They began to brag and cozy up to the point of gossiping about the private lives of other stars on whom they had been assigned to spy. They even revealed to them the times when Sandor and Kati had been under AVO surveillance in the past and what intimate things they knew about them. This bizarre behavior clearly showed that, if they revealed so much to them, Sandor and his family were truly doomed. They obviously did not care what inside information they knew, since the outcome would be their end anyway.

Late in the night, the two were drunk out of their minds, but still in some ways with the awareness of guard dogs. Several times one fidgeted with his gun under his leather jacket. At one point, the aggressive one sat on the floor, his legs spread across the open doorway leading to the hall. The other one posted himself against the front door, barricading the only available exit out of the apartment.

Kati and Sandor kissed the boys goodnight in their bedroom and quietly assured them not to worry. Everything would be all right. The boys felt frustrated by not having the opportunity to whisper with their parents in the dark. Kati's mother, Eta, retired with the boys, three into one bed. All was dark, but Balazs remained totally awake. He began to whisper to Eta and wanted to know if she had any plan of action. She tried to calm him, and told him to sleep. Tomorrow may bring better news. Balazs was totally unconvinced. His brother was either in shock or did not weigh the seriousness of the situation, because he was already fast asleep.

Staring at the ceiling, Balazs' eyes slowly grew accustomed to the darkness. All the while his mind was churning furiously. Should he sneak up to the one with the gun in his jacket and finish them both off in their sleep? Were Sandor and Kati planning something? What if he attempted something and the guy was just pretending to sleep. Maybe he was actually waiting for an excuse to shoot somebody? If he made a blunder then the men would have an excuse to kill Sandor. As he was evaluating the odds, he drifted off into sleep.

****

Not realizing the short duration of his sleep he woke in total panic. Balazs worried that he missed out on something. But all was as he left it, still and dark. No one stirred. An enormous urgency came over him. He must act now! Nothing would change unless he did something. Quietly, he rolled out of the bed after he freed his body from the tightly tangled limbs of the other sleepers. He looked through the old-fashioned gaping keyhole as the outside city lights diluted the darkness in the hallway.

The man against the door snored. It was real, not pretend. He could tell because when Sandor had too much to drink, his snore was considerable and his breathing long. He slowly opened the door just a crack. It creaked, but nobody seemed to notice. The snoring went on. Great guards, he thought to himself.

"Eta, wake up! Wake up," he shook her several times gently so as not to frighten her. She came out of a light sleep and focused on his silhouette created by the white wall behind him. "What is it? Did something happen?" she whispered in a worried tone. She could feel that he was fully dressed and had on his sweater and shoes.

"What are you doing?" "I am going to defect and get some help for Dad. Do you have any money you could give me?" "You are delirious and out of your mind. Go back to sleep, they told you everything will be all right."

"Do you have any money you can give me?" he insisted, but got no reply this time. He gave up on her and woke his brother. Annoyed at Balazs's "moronic" requests; Barna vehemently refused to join him in his plan to get some help for the family. He also suggested sleep as a remedy, and burrowed deeper into his pillow.

But Balazs' mind was made up. The key to the lock for the two new bicycles was in Barna's pants pocket. He removed it without a jingle and approached the already opened bedroom door.

He stood there a long time watching the sleeping men. As his eyes got clearer in the dark, he realized to his relief that the man at the entry door was hunched forward over his left leg, his head dangling. He was leaning away from the door. He saw that there was at least a 30 centimeters crack left of the front door if he opened it, through which to slide.

He took several careful steps forward, toward the door. As if on cue, the guard stirred, frightening Balazs out of his wits, almost making him jump. With his heart pounding, he retreated into the darkness of the bedroom and removed his shoes, all the while watching the man. He held them in one hand. Luckily, nothing happened, and the man settled back into the same position.

Balazs went into action. Like a shadow he stole back to the door, and saw to his amazement that it had been left unlocked the night before when the AVO entered the apartment. The keys were left on top of Sandor's shoeshine box next to the door. He hardly could believe his good fortune. Before he knew it, he was outside the front door, which he closed again carefully, easing back the handle without a click. He kept his shoes off, and quietly went down the staircase until he reached the bottom floor.

Once in the lobby he saw the two bicycles leaning as usual against the radiator, chained together securely. He unlocked the chain as quietly as possible, and took his bike. After he cleared the heavy glass, wrought-iron door and stood in the street, he glanced up toward the apartment windows. Everything was dark as he left it. He felt an enormous rush. Hurriedly, he put on his shoes, mounted his bike and flew beneath the large archway of the building into the open boulevard. He was familiar with the road that led to Austria. Most people had that road etched into their minds in Russian-occupied Hungary. It was the road to freedom, where no Hungarian was allowed to travel beyond the border.

His plan, first and foremost, was to get the city behind him. He pedaled furiously with the seemingly infinite energy that only teenagers possess. He didn't notice the bitter cold that froze his uncovered ears and fingers. His favorite brown beret, which he wore almost always through the cold months, did not reach below his ears, leaving them exposed to the bitter-cold wind created by his speed. In his hurry to dress, he had neglected to bring gloves. He thought finding his jacket would create noise anyway and wake up the guards, so he left without it. He gained distance on the deserted streets. In the dull light of the city, a dark mass appeared on the horizon approaching him. He jumped off the bike instinctively, and hid beneath a gate. The object moved slowly and without the rumble of tanks. Just to be certain, he waited patiently for it to draw near.

Catching his thoughts, he realized how unprepared he really was for the 200 kilometer trek ahead of him. No money, no clothes, and worst of all, no identification papers if he was stopped. He knew, surely, that was going to happen. Just then, he saw a man driving a cart laden with supplies and directing two frisky horses toward him. The cartwheels were made of auto tires, which were often used by the country folks to keep their ride smoother and quieter on the city's cobble streets. It also made an easier pull for the horses. Close up, Balazs could see the friendly face of a peasant. Feeling safe, he ventured out into the open to inquire, just to be sure, that he was on the right road to Vienna.

He waved the man down. "Whoa… whoa…" the peasant gently called out as he restrained his steeds. White steam came rushing from their wide-open nostrils toward Balazs's face as he approached. The familiar smell of the horses felt comforting to him.

"Sure you are on the right road, son, but that's a long way, and you sure don't look to be properly dressed for it," the man responded good-naturedly as he wiped the hard frost from his long trailing mustache.

"Yeah, I know, but I left in rather hurried circumstances," said Balazs, avoiding wasting time now on long explanations.

"Well, good luck then wherever you are headed," said the man.

As he was about to lift the reins and move his cart, Balazs quickly reached up and put his hand on the man's arm. "Just a minute, sir, please, would you do me a simple favor?" "Well that depends on what that is, son."

"You see, I left in a bit of a hurry from home so my parents might be worried. Could you let them know that I am all right and that you saw me on the road?"

"Sure, I can do that. What's your father's name?" the man asked.

With pride Balazs said, "He is the famous actor, Sandor Szabo, and lives on Madacs ter #3."

"No problem, son, I know who he is and I am heading in that direction anyway. But, before you go, let me give you this."

He tied the loose reins on the side of his bench and reached behind his seat. He pulled out a short-handled shovel and handed it to Balazs, "Take this with you, son. If anyone in authority asks you where you are headed, you tell them you are going to work in the next town, or the one beyond. So be sure you always ask, and find out the names of families before you go. This may slow you a bit, but you have better chances of getting there. Too many kids like you end up in Russia. Now we don't want that to happen, do we?" He smiled affectionately at the skinny boy and, as he bid him goodbye, he wondered how far the child would get before his capture.

Balazs mounted his bike again, crossed the shovel across his handlebars, and pushed off on the most decisive journey of his life. He wondered if the kind man would really talk to his father.

FORTY

ON THE ROAD

THE THOUGHTS flooding his mind prevented him from noticing November's bitter cold. Putting the shovel across the bar proved not to be such a good idea, because his hands were not large enough to maintain a grip for long. He stopped for a moment, and stuck the handle through his sweater at the back of his neck, and lowered it through to hang out at his trousers. The cold air rushed up his shirt, but he did not feel it. The hard, wooden handle rested between his shoulder blades as the plate of the shovel formed a peculiar shield against the back of his head. Since neither the peasant nor he thought about a method to tie it securely, this was the only solution until he could get something with which to secure the shovel.

He kept pushing ahead, passing through the ruins of the city, then the outskirts of Budapest with its industrial and ugly parts. People began to stir and move about in the early morning light. They went about their chores, unaware of a determined 13-year-old speeding by on a shiny green bicycle, forging his destiny.

Once he was clear of the city, the buildings became houses, and then the houses began to have gardens and larger spaces between them. The main thoroughfare of Hungarian towns was always lined on each side with acacia trees, which were trimmed to their knuckles in the fall. The stumps looked like fists or the congealed faces of monsters from some Grimm fairy tale. An occasional, rusty iron well pump between the trees broke the rhythm of their planting pattern here and there. As the houses became spars, and open fields more prevalent, the teenager felt comforted by this familiar environment from his childhood. He passed through currents of warm air mixed with the smells of farm animals and freshly burning wood. Sometimes the lonely call of a magpie pierced the empty silence of winter. As he listened to his own heaving chest, far in the grooves of plowed, brown fields, hundreds of black crows picked at the frozen ground with their powerful beaks.

As distance and time stretched between him and the city, the reality of what he had done rose slowly to the surface of his psyche. The road ahead seemed so far when he searched the empty horizon. Where was the border? What could he expect to find? Would all the Russian tanks be lined up, facing in his direction while the AVO looked down from their watchtowers, searching for easy targets like him?

He began to entertain doubts and fears. His concern for his family became acute. Did the AVO men carry his father away when they discovered his escape? Were they on the road in a speeding car in hot pursuit to capture him? Why was he attempting to escape when the borders were once more secured and shut down by the military? What kind of a coward might he appear to everyone for abandoning his family as they dragged him back in shame? Worse, he saw himself being loaded onto a Russian train, baldheaded, destined to Russia, never to see his family again.

He felt strongly about being Hungarian. He remembered his proud heritage of the Huns. He thought of his great ancestors, conquerors of the past, who fought for this beautiful land. What good custodians they became, defending Europe's culture and territories from the Tartars for more than 150 years against the Turks? The small nation of 10 million souls had contributed so much to the world's culture and betterment. He thought of the artists and composers, including Liszt, Lehar, Bartok and Kodaly. There were also the great Hungarian mathematicians who helped create the atomic bomb for the US that helped bring an end to World War II. The Hungarian genius Edward Teller, the father of the H bomb for America balanced the Cold War. Dr. Ignatius Semmelweis, who discovered the cause of mortality in childbirth, saved women from the epidemic. There was Joseph Pulitzer, in whose memory the U.S.A. hands out the annual awards for achievement in literature and who, before his death, bequeathed money to fund the eternal floodlights on the Statue of Liberty in New York Harbor.

How proud he was when his people won 16 gold, 10 silver and 17 bronze medals while competing in the 1952 Olympics in Helsinki, against nations with populations of 200 million (USSR) and 180 million (U.S.A.) and numerous other larger nations. In 1956 they performed equally as well. In soccer the Hungarian "golden team" was undefeated between 1950 and 1954. The team that dominated the international water polo for more than a quarter of a century was Hungarian. They had a bloody encounter with the Russians team at the 1956 Olympics. The Hungarians, as all of the other satellite nations, were "encouraged" to lose against the teams of great Mother Russia, to save face for them in the global arena of propaganda. The Hungarians, inherently proud and rebellious people, refused to give up their well-earned victory to politics. So the Soviets committed all the foul underwater violence they could think of to assert their will. To the horror of the audience, the water of the Olympic pool ran red with the blood of the athletes. With these thoughts of passionate patriotism, he ran up against an invisible wall. He felt the pangs of homesickness before ever leaving the land he loved.

He stopped his bike and stood at the edge of a small village, listening as he contemplated his next move. Puzzled, he looked ahead onto the straight, long, paved road. At the end of it lay the horizon in a veil of soft fog and mystery. He looked back the way he had come, and observed a similar view. The veil of fog camouflaged an uncertain future if he returned. Beckoning smells of the small village filled the cold air about him.

As he stood lost in thought and time, the silence was slowly, almost imperceptibly, eroded by a low rumble and vibration beneath him. He turned in both directions and saw nothing, but the still and undisturbed fog in the horizon. The sound became louder, more defined when he finally recognized the grinding and clanking of the heavy metal treads of Russian tanks. Suddenly, from beyond a row of yellow farmhouses, large armored vehicles appeared, dwarfing the homes.

Balazs turned and darted toward the nearest house for cover. The shovel slipped off to one side, scraping the back of his head. Instinctively, he twisted the opposite way and lost his balance, tumbling, bike and all, into the ditch. He panicked realizing how vulnerable he was. Images of the young freedom fighter in the phone booth flashed before him. He tore himself loose of the bike. Then, with the shovel still sticking out of the back of his shirt, Balazs dived through the already open farmhouse door. Someone pulled him through. Immediately, the door slammed behind him, as he was dragged through several dark rooms into a pantry. Yet, another door slammed on him. He could still hear the tanks outside, but the rumble gradually dimmed. Did they notice him and stop? Were they still waiting outside to ambush him? He had no idea. All he could do was wait patiently in the dark. God, he thought, I hope these people will not get killed for harboring me.

He heard small noises like wooden shutters being slammed or opened, he could not tell. As the nervous sweat dripped from his forehead, he could smell the dry corn stored in the burlap bag on which he had learned. The small room was filled with enticing smells of dried fruits, smoked sausages and walnuts, these aromas reminded him of his grandparents. The door opened slowly, and a busty little peasant woman greeted him, "You had a close call, young man, but don't worry. They didn't see you." His heart was still pounding loudly in his ears, but the first thing he thought of was his bike. Before he had time to ask, she was ready to calm him down. "Yes, I saw your trapeze act into the ditch. After the Ruszki drove off, I went and got your bicycle and leaned it next to the hen house. You must be some rich kid to have such a thing at your age," she observed; Balazs did not respond to her remark, but embraced her, and thanked her for her help.

With the shutters now opened, the little house was filled with light inside. Colorful country embroidery covered the cot against the wall and hand-painted plates hung on every wall of the little room. It had a dirt floor. The tall, domed stucco stove, with a traditional bench hugging it was a welcome sight. He put his open hands and body against it and it felt great. When she helped him get free of the shovel she remarked with a cunning little grin, "Identification papers?" They both laughed and felt better with the danger gone.

"Jancsi, my husband, is out with the sheep, and will be back momentarily." Shortly after, Jancsi entered the room from the back courtyard of the house, and put his smoldering pipe down on the old wooden table to greet Balazs. They turned out to be a chatty bunch. In a short time, Balazs had told them of his plans. Hungarian peasants like this couple were known to survive the harshest political times through occupations and wars. They always fared better than city folk. Though they labored on the collective farms, they tended to their own animals and had a small garden with vegetables and fruit trees.

Balazs was fed a wonderful hot meal, but was urged to continue on his road and not to turn back. They told him of the rumors about retaliations, and insisted he must be gone. Besides, the chances of escaping and making it through the border were diminishing by the hour. The farmer gave Balazs a reversible, lamb fur-lined jacket. It was old and well worn, with two enormous pockets. The couple opened a small cupboard by the kitchen and removed three Ft100 paper bills and shoved them into the protesting hands: it was a lot of money at the time. "You have a long journey ahead of you, son, with many turns, and no doubt you will be in need of this."

He fashioned a leather sling on the shovel's handle so Balazs could comfortably swing it over his shoulder. For safety measure, the generous couple sent him off with the names of families, three villages away. Now determined to face the border, and without a doubt in his mind, he mounted his bike. The jacket felt nice and warm, and had the smell of sheep. When he reached into the inside pocket to stash his money, he found a pair of two fingered knitted gloves. Balazs felt ready to brave whatever was ahead.

FORTY ONE

OUTFOXING THE FOX

SANDOR AND KATI returned to their bedroom after saying goodnight to the boys and Eta. They quietly closed the door between them and the room where the first AVO man with the revolver was lying across the entry. Kati had been given no opportunity to look at Sandor throughout the night's ordeal, and she had avoided it too, lest she somehow raise suspicion.

In the past few weeks, Kati had been experiencing difficulty in sleeping, which she attributed to their hectic lifestyle. Her doctor had prescribed a very strong sleeping potion in powder form. Also, cautioned her to use it sparingly, only when absolutely necessary. She was also given strict instructions as to the amount. For her convenience, the doctor gave her ample supply, her future refill. Little did Kati suspect that one day this powder (kept in a jar out of reach of everyone) would play a vital role in saving their lives'.

When the AVO demanded wine, Kati reeled into action. She acted like a charming hostess, talking of the special wines, which she started lacing with her sleeping powder. After the first four glasses of wine consumed by the "guests," she felt confident that their taste buds would be numb. She poured the contents of her entire prescription into a bottle of a fine red cabernet from Lake Balaton. Shaking it slightly, Kati held the bottle to the light to examine it.

The powder dissolved easily, and only slight dark grape sediments were visible at the bottom of the bottle. She was actually hoping to do away with them for good, but putting them into a deep coma would work just fine, she thought.

The two houseguests began snoring. Kati confessed to Sandor what she had done, and told him there was no time to waste or to hesitate about their next move if they were to survive. They all knew the returning government had sealed his fate, and they understood what that meant. They hurriedly discussed the plans to escape using their car. Kati began to pack the very essentials in the dark—money, some small valuable jewelry and identification papers. Sandor packed the leftover watches from their last trip in Vienna and rolled up two very valuable oil paintings, one painted by the great 16th century master, Bassano. What to do with everything else they would be leaving behind was a big dilemma. How to communicate with the rest of the family to come as fast as possible and clear out the apartment before the government did?

Parting from their loyal Cocker Spaniel, Haver (meaning friend), was heart breaking and painful. They decided that Eta might be a problem. Crossing swamps and mountains or other rough terrain in mid-winter was not for the frail. Many elderly and weak died at the border or caused the capture of others. Eta would have to deal with the two bodies of the AVO, the dog and the remaining property. Their hearts felt heavy with these decisions, but there was no other choice.

Kati was afraid to check the results of her poison. So, they lay in bed talking the rest of the night about their fears and hopes. They eventually fell asleep, and remained thus far into the afternoon, as was their habit.

The phone rang and Sandor flew out of bed to silence it. He swept it off the receiver, and with a hoarse voice answered, "Hello?"

It was a longtime friend on the other end. "Sandor, we must leave the country. We are all in danger. It's all over for us!" Before Sandor was able to respond the voice informed him that he and an actress colleague of Sandor were joining them. He had known the man for more than 25 years, although their relationship was very odd and mostly one-sided. Sandor always felt used.

The "friend" was from a wealthy family before the war. Interestingly, he had known both of Sandor's wives before the maestro ever met them, and had, indeed, pursued both relentlessly, but unsuccessfully. Balazs was always suspicious of the man, because it seemed he did very well whatever the political regime. Yet, no one really knew what he did for a living, and was convinced that the man was an informant.

"Sandor, go and see how the AVO are doing," Kati urged her husband. She opened the door and peered through the crack. The man closest to them slid all the way down to the floor and was sprawled out like a corpse, motionless, apparently not breathing. Sandor reached for one of his shoes on the floor and tested the waters by throwing the shoe at the seemingly lifeless body. The shoe hit its mark hard, right on the shoulders; nothing followed.

The couple crawled up to the AVO man and watched him closely for a moment. They saw no breathing. Sandor, though petrified, reached out and shook the man gently. There was no response. He got braver and shook him more vehemently, but with the same result. They looked at each other and smiled with relief. More confident this time around, they repeated the tactics with the other man, ending with the same result. Sandor grabbed the man who was blocking the front door, curled up like a dead fish, and deposited him on top of the other.

Kati quickly gathered some winter clothes and entered the room where the children and her mother Eta lay fast asleep. Kati shook the sleeping bodies in the bed and realized that, amid the lumps of blankets and pillows, something was not right.

"Where is Balazs?" she asked the sleepy faces of her mother and Barna. They looked bewildered and not yet awake from their deep sleep. Suddenly, Eta came to life and screamed, "Oh my God, he defected!"

"What nonsense, don't be absurd," Kati screamed back at her. "What are you saying, Mother?" The panic swept the family as everything came to a halt. Sandor was beside himself, extremely upset. Eta was hysterical. Why she hadn't thought of waking her daughter and Sandor was beyond her. She didn't act on it because she did not take Balazs' plans seriously. When she then learned of the incredible and immediate changes of her life she felt discarded, worthless, abandoned. She and the dog were to be left behind, but Kati, loving and firm, remained with her decision.

Sandor realized that if Balazs really was on the way, he could only be on the one road, which they had to drive on until the border. If he left eight hours ago, it now being 2 p.m., he could not possibly have gotten far on a bike. As they ran about the apartment in a panic, there came a knock on the door. Sandor ran to open it, expecting his friend, but to his surprise a stranger with a droopy mustache stood in the doorway, humbly apologizing for the disturbance.

"Maestro, I have news from your son, Balazs." The weight of the unknown lifted from everyone with the knowledge that he was well, and on the same road they would take. Now, more than ever, they must be off immediately to find him, and take him with them.

The good-byes with Eta and Haver were terrible and quick. They flew out the door. Once out on the street, they heard tanks rumble through the avenue. Kati and Barna slipped back into the vestibule of the gate. Sandor was careful not to awaken suspicion, and strolled slowly to the nearby garage where his car was parked. The gas tank was full, since it had not been used since the beginning of the revolution. By the time he pulled up to the gate, the two extra passengers were already there, waiting for their ride. The haste and chaos of their departure from the apartment, and their lives as they knew it, was surreal. In an instant it was all behind them. All Kati could think about was Balazs. Her heart was heavy with worry. She felt her love for Balazs deeper than his birth mother Jadda could ever feel for him. Balazs and Kati were mystically linked. She saw him as her "soul mate child." Her fear that their party might be stopped on the road concerned her less than the thought of Balazs being stopped and captured if they did not catch up with him on time.

Before too long, they encountered their first road block miles out of the city. Fortunately, Sandor cleared himself and the group by claiming that they were going to Gyor, a city of theaters, to guest star. Since the AVO recognized him, his famous wife and their colleague in the back seat, they let them go. But, they reminded them that if they were contemplating other programs like defecting, all their families left behind would suffer the consequences. This threat filled Kati yet again with guilt for leaving her mother behind, a target and victim for their retaliation. She was miserable in every way, but found some solace by pulling Barna closer into her protective arms.

FORTY TWO

PLOTTING FINAL ESCAPE

JUST AS BALAZS was preparing to continue his journey, and as the peasant couple helped adjust the shovel on the back of his warm sheepskin coat, a neighbor, by the main road was drawing water from the community well. He noticed a shiny, spanking-new sedan with a private license plate speed by. It was a rare sight on the Hungarian roads. He admired the stylish cream-colored Opel, and released a deep, long sigh, knowing that he would never own such a vehicle. He painstakingly lifted the full bucket and walked back towards his house.

Balazs did not have to go through many towns before the first barricade appeared. He had taken the advice of all his guides and spent time remembering the names of people in the towns he had to use as alibis. The shovel acted as a very good passport for him and his worn peasant sheepskin added to his peasant boy look. His successes made him feel confident and positively happy. He was also enjoying this extended ride on his new bike. From time to time he couldn't help looking at the shiny, green metallic bar between his legs. Ever since he was a little boy, colors always had given him unusual sensations of pleasure.

He traveled through Gyor, with a few stops from the Russian uniformed soldiers. Here they did not care about names from the next towns, and his get-up seemed sufficient to get him by. With no belongings, he did not appear to be a defector. It was defectors the Soviets were looking to capture. He had to reach the ancient city of Sopron. Ironically, Balazs could have been in Austria already, because there was a finger of landmass reaching from Austria, into Hungary. This heavily guarded stretch had to be traversed in order to reach the city. Sopron was the last city near the Austrian border and Balazs, like most of the 200,000 defectors, was headed in that general direction. He stopped for a loaf of hot, freshly baked bread at the city's outer edge and fashioned a deep groove into the bottom of the crust, then placed it securely on the bar of the bike. This availed him to eat and ride without losing precious time. He pressed on to reach Sopron by night fall and find shelter.

He had no plans or information on where and how to escape. So, Balazs began to attach himself to other bikers on the road asking questions. His concerns were different now that he was nearing the border. The incriminating questions had to be well camouflaged, so as not to raise suspicions. He never knew if the person he was addressing was an informant or an AVO.

He was getting anxious as darkness fell early on winter days and the cold became a major obstacle. Balazs knew he had to find shelter where he was invisible, yet remain warm. The roads were filled with people going to and from the city. He entered an industrial area with many smoky factories where thousands were changing shifts. If people chose not to use the public transportation system, their only option was a motorcycle or a bicycle. People often chose the latter for privacy.

He attached himself to a young group on bikes to see if he could get some information. Through the short, veiled and less-than friendly exchange, he realized that they were also in the process of defecting. But they did not trust him for fear that he was an informant. Finally, as a great number of workers poured out of a factory gate, Balazs changed his tactic and pulled next to a single factory worker, who looked like the genuine article. He was exhausted and ashen gray. Like a ghost, the typical victim of Workers' Paradise always appearing to be from some graveyard. They worked six days a week under slave conditions. The man appeared to be in his forties, but most likely he was ten years younger. He seemed the quiet type, but not unpleasant or unfriendly. After a while, in the conversation, he dropped a clue that it was okay for Balazs to reveal his mission. They pedaled ahead of several other bikers, so as not to risk being overheard.

"You know," the man said, "there is a train at dawn, preparing to run the border?" The boy nearly jumped off his seat. He looked carefully at the man, whose face was visible now by the dim streetlights. Balazs was reluctant to give himself away so readily by responding.

"I don't know what you are talking about." He responded casually.

"Right," said the man, and looked straight ahead, pushed down on his pedals.

But, he continued with his narrative, as if he were talking to himself. "Just the same, there is a train leaving from the main station at dawn and we could get you a ticket on it. It does not stop, if you know what I mean? I noticed you have a new bike. Perhaps we could make a trade? You are not going to need it on the train. So, here is my offer."

Phrased that way, Balazs realized the man was genuine. "What's the deal?" Balazs asked. "Though I really don't know what you are talking about, because I am going to work in the next town." He still did not trust the man completely, and he was not going to jeopardize his plans and get arrested before he had an opportunity to escape.

The plan laid out for him seemed perfect. The man offered him room and board for the night and said he would even purchase the "two-way ticket" at the train station while Balazs washed up and had a hot meal. The man would give him two small aluminum flasks of strong Hungarian plum brandy, in case Russian soldiers captured Balazs. Alcohol, everyone knew, was like gold to a Ruszki. Also, he would transport Balazs to the train station in the morning.

Balazs's heart sank when the man mentioned his last ride on his own bike. It was hard to think of parting with it and someone else riding it. And Balazs a passenger, no less!

"So, what do you think?" the man posed the question twice, as Balazs's thoughts were stuck on giving up his precious bike. Finally he returned to reality and his choice was bittersweet.

Reluctantly, he muttered, "Okay." Frightened, he looked at the man, half expecting to be arrested on the spot. The man's ashen gray face, with the premature wrinkles, lit up with an incredible joy. In Balazs's mind, it was the expression of a horse thief who just ripped off an unaware customer. Balazs didn't know what to feel. His problem of how to escape had just been solved by a total stranger. Why did this happy moment have to be spoiled with giving up his bike? As he continued to push down on the pedals next to the man, he worked on getting used to the idea. The man, who had known nothing but poverty, hard labor, living a life deprived of possession, could not believe his good fortune meeting up with this kid.

They continued by each other silently, each with his private thoughts, until they arrived at a typical Communist "prefab concrete heaven." Hundreds of gray buildings stood atop each other, without a tree or a blade of grass between them, appearing like overgrown cemetery headstones.

They mounted five flights of dimly lit stairs in a ten-story building that had no elevator even on its original blueprints. Balazs could smell every dinner menu from the apartments they passed, so by the time the man ushered him in to his own, he would have eaten anything.

Balazs could not believe how young and attractive the man's wife was. She, like all women under Communism, had a job. Part of the real reason for full employment under the system: ten people shared the job of one. The genius of Communism was to split that one salary among the ten "employed" persons.

The man quickly told his story to his wife, who made no protest. Balazs noticed immediately that there was no demonstration of affection between them. The man had a cold, remote personality.

He quickly grabbed a bite and left Balazs behind while he flew off toward the train station, naturally already on Balazs's bike.

The small size of the rooms baffled Balazs. How could anyone keep their sanity living in such a small space? The twin bed nearly took up the whole bedroom. Besides two small night tables, there was only space for a metal washbasin on the floor at the foot of the bed.

The tiny kitchen held a small table which could only accommodate two. She called to him to come and eat. He sat across from her and, as she dished out the soup from the pot, Balazs noticed her smooth skin and well-shaped arms. His eyes traveled to her neck and pretty face. Like most Hungarian girls, she wore no bra and her full breasts heaved with her breathing.

His inquisitive glances satisfied her female ego. To increase his heartbeat, she stretched her arm out to lift the soup ladle over Balazs's bowl, leaning forward just enough for him to get a glimpse of her firm breasts. He may have been young, but was an astute observer of human behavior, growing up in a small town surrounded by nature. He observed that animals and humans were totally alike in all their mating games. The language was always clear. All one had to do was simply pay attention.

She smiled like a Cheshire cat; a smile which echoed off his face. When she caught it, she realized he was not a virgin. She spoke to him softly and asked things about him without expecting any return questions. He noticed that she wanted to remain mysterious. He did not push it. He felt his fatigue. After dinner, she said with emphasis, "The train station is at the far end of the city, so we don't have to wait up. Why don't we bathe, and then go to bed?"

She filled the large metal basin, at the foot of the bed, with hot water. She placed two clean towels and a bar of soap next to it. The room was lit by a solitary, bare light bulb, which hung on a wire from the center of the ceiling exposing the prison-cell like barren walls. The warm steam from the water rose invitingly. "You go first," Balazs said, realizing that she had made no attempt to leave the room. "Okay," she said.

He expected she would turn off the light, but with ease and natural candor, she took off her blouse and the rest of her clothes, revealing a beautiful and youthful body. She stepped in the middle of the water, caressingly running her soapy fingers all over her velvety skin. Suddenly, his fatigue vanished and his insides tensed. When she was done, Balazs knew it was his turn to do the same. He had never undressed in front of a girl before, but he did not want to appear a greenhorn. After she brought fresh water, he quickly undressed. She now wore a light nightgown, and lay down on the bed watching him.

He turned his back to her to hide her effect on him. She relished his discomfort and stared approvingly at his tight muscular behind, the result of his soccer playing. He hurriedly finished bathing and wanted to get into bed before the man returned and, quite possibly kill him. Balazs slipped his underwear back on, shut off the light and slid under the covers. She got up, turned the light back on to empty the water basin. Shutting the light off again, she returned to join him in bed, close.

The street lamps of the city outside cast a soft glow into the room, so he was able to see her beautiful face. She placed one arm under her cheek and the other hand on the pillow next to it while she studied him. She could not see him clearly, but was fully aware of his condition. She enjoyed her power, and continued to toy with him.

His heart was beating so wildly in his throat; he thought he was going to choke. Her eyes reflected the light coming in from outside the window. Like a mouse, he knew by instinct, that the cat was about to strike, but felt immobilized by her stare. She moved her hand off the pillow and like a snake it slithered down to his hip and then on to her real target. His mind went blank and numb with the sense of pleasure flooding him. The outside door slammed hard and her hand withdrew in an instant as she turned her back to face the other wall. She pretended to sleep. Then the bedroom door opened, followed by some fumbling noises in the dark. Her husband dropped his tired body next to his wife, and instantly fell asleep. Slowly she reached back for Balazs under the sheets, and pulled him tightly into the valley of her soft warm buttocks. She sighed and shivered with the release of his pleasure. They drifted off into a deep sleep which seemed only to last a few moments before the loud alarm went off.

FORTY THREE

"THAT IS FREEDOM, IT'S AUSTRIA"

ETA STOOD IN the door way; dumbfounded and disoriented. Up to this moment, her life had revolved around her only daughter Kati. Now that life had been yanked out from under her, she did not have the slightest idea what to do next.

As she hesitantly closed the door behind her departing family, she realized the tragedy of the moment. Her entire life became meaningless. She heard the fat little dog scurrying across the wooden parquet behind her. It sniffed at the unfamiliar scent of the lifeless bodies lying on the floor. One of them twitched. Fear hit Eta like lightning. My God, she thought, they are not dead!

She bolted behind one of the tall chairs, as if to barricade herself. She stared at the bodies, still piled one on top of the other, as Sandor had left them for dead. In her panic she totally forgot her own woes and went into survival mode.

Eta observed them for a moment. The dog kept nudging at the face of one of them, but there was no further response. She got some of her courage up.

She slithered like a snake next to them, to determine their exact condition. She detected a slight movement of their chests, but not their mouths. She gently reached for one of the wrists to check for a pulse.

After a while, she was able to sense a slight beat, and her fingertips registered some body heat.

For a moment she was relieved that they were not dead, but then became frightened that they were not! Her family had left her in quite a jam. She was confident that the drug would last a long time and would give her opportunity to accomplish things. She took an empty suitcase out of the closet, and began stuffing it with as many valuables and memorabilia as possible. She emptied the secret drawer of the antique furniture and, seeing the phone on the desk, quickly called one of Sandor's sisters. She told her there was no time to waste, but that she must come immediately to remove anything she could carry before the AVO men sobered up.

Eta could hardly lift the heavy suitcase, so she dragged it toward the door as the dog followed pulling on the leash close behind her. She pressed the elevator button, not expecting anything, and was startled when she heard the gears engage in the shaft above her. As the superintendent's half-witted son opened the old folding doors, she stepped into the elevator and made her final getaway, never to return.

****

It wasn't until the next morning that the AVO men began to stir with an incredible hangover, the like of which they had never before experienced. Finally, they came to their senses. The apartment was totally empty around them, save for a few nick knacks here and there. They knew the dire consequences they would pay for their mistakes. It would certainly be execution or deportation to the Gulag. Their only alternative was to face the border too, and attach themselves to the rest of the refugees as many other communist spies have done.

Kati was in hysterics, to the point of demanding they stop, return to Budapest, and find her son. Not surprisingly, no one listened or supported her idea. As they drove, they saw truckloads of people of all ages heading back toward the city. As the drivers were all Russian soldiers, they knew what unfortunate human cargo they contained. Was her son among them she wondered with her aching, miserable heart?

Near the border, they stopped in a small village. Sandor spoke with several peasants who knew the border well. He offered them money to take them across. The men suggested avoiding the bridge at Andau. It had been so popular in the beginning of the exodus that it was now swarming with AVO and Russians. They were to select a path only known to those who lived there.

Sandor made his decision, and paid large sums of money to buy their freedom. Naturally, not a penny of contribution came from his "friend." Sandor gave one of the men the equivalent of $1,000 to go back to Budapest and seek Eta out, because if Balazs failed in his escape attempt, he would surely return to her. The man was to fetch Balazs and bring him across the border.

Kati felt better for the moment. Somehow, her feminine instincts and sixth sense began to kick in, and told her that Balazs was probably all right and had succeeded in crossing the border. She did not know why, but, all of a sudden, she felt an inner peace. Then she fell asleep under the puffy goose-down covers the peasant's wife had offered them. The couple had been helping hundreds of people cross to the other side, but this was their first celebrity. They felt honored to help, and even gave up their own bedroom to the actors.

Sandor fell into the same dilemma his son had faced in giving up his bike, but decided to part with the car. Unknown to Kati and Sandor, Balazs was asleep only a few kilometers away.

****

Balazs and his hosts jumped to the sound of the alarm clock. Without delay, omitting the usual morning preparations, they scurried out the door of the apartment to run down the staircase.

Only after reaching the bottom did Balazs realize he had not even said goodbye to the young woman. Her scent was all over him still, as he mounted the bar on his bike. As the man pushed off, he let the boy know that he was taking the back streets to avoid the authorities. Government spies now swarmed at all hours in the border city. Hundreds who weren't careful or knowledgeable about the city were captured daily.

Now that Balazs was near the border, for the first time he began to feel serious fear. The streets were dark as they left the man's apartment, but unusually busy for such predawn hour. Every shadowy figure posed danger, increasing his heartbeat. What seemed to take forever was probably only a 25-minute journey to the station. As he took in the familiar smells of burning coal and steam, he realized the train, his friend was near.

He thought it ironic that the train, which had become such an integral part of his life, would now complete his final journey, delivering him to freedom.

They jumped off the bike and rushed under the arched gates of the train station. Several tracks were laid under the protective dome, occupied by steam engines warming up, ready to break out of their corral like giant, angry black bulls. Balazs looked up at the closest locomotive and noticed, to his delight, that the hated red Russian star had been ripped from the front of the engine. A pale, faded gray image was all that remained.

The whistles, the huffing and puffing from the locomotives echoed off the walls, adding to the colorful noise of the gangway. No one had ever before seen such a mob at this station. All types of people were there. Peasants, who proudly wore their traditional hand embroidered clothes, which the Russians had forbidden them in their effort to wipe out their national identity. There were elegantly dressed city people, and ladies with old fox stoles from before the war.

Many young and old fighters still proudly carried their "Russian guitars" machine guns slung over their shoulders. A young warrior walked passed him with several grenades attached to his belt. Balazs felt envious and sad that he still had played no part in contributing to the revolution of his people, even if it had ended in defeat.

People were calling out for friends and family. Children cried, and in the general commotion there was much shoving and pushing. Balazs began really fearing for his life. What he originally believed would be some clandestine train escape now unfolded into a frenzied free for all. This for certain, must become a target of the authorities. He could not help looking around, expecting the thunder of heavy boots. He imagined armed Russian soldiers descending upon these naïve people and mowing them down.

He had no time for further worry as his guide lifted him into the air, depositing him on the top steps of the train bound for freedom.

The man shouted above the noise, "Balazs, God be with you, good luck. I will take good care of your bike!" His last words almost meant more to Balazs's comfort than his genuine wish of farewell. He turned and attempted to wave back to the man, but was pushed forward by the pressing mob from below.

The tumult forced him into the already crammed wagon. He was pressed so tightly he could hardly breathe in the already exhausted oxygen of the stifling compartment. Some desperate woman pleaded in protest of being crushed. She met with no response. Everyone had their own concerns. Children screamed and men yelled for the windows to be opened for air. Irritated voices replied, complaining that they did not want to catch pneumonia. The circus continued. Finally, Balazs felt the jolt of the train. On masse bodies hurled in both directions, causing people to fall and trample one another. Eventually the wheels eased into their continuous forward motion. They were off!

"This is going to be a short, hard ride and you better hold on," said a tall muscular man towering over him. Balazs could tell he was a coal miner by the permanent coal-dust filled wrinkles on the back of his neck and hands. He smelled strongly of deep earth and sweat.

In contrast, Balazs still sensed the pleasant lingering scent of the young woman on him. The locomotive began to gain speed rapidly. The floor of the cabin shook more than usual from bearing three times the original weight designed by the train's engineers.

Balazs felt the planks bending and rising under his feet. It occurred to him that the floor might give way, and they could fall through and under the razor-sharp iron wheels. Finally, someone opened a window. The fresh icy blast rushed through the hot cabin, replenishing the oxygen depleted lungs. The passengers inhaled like fish released to water after being snared. At each end of the car, the doors remained open with people hanging for dear life off them.

No one wanted to be left behind by the train that was to break through the border. Many who arrived late could not get on, and with frustrated tears, watched their train, their salvation, pass out of sight.

****

Sandor and Kati were also awakened by their hosts in the middle of the night. It was time to go. Sandor arranged one more thing regarding his beloved car. Before grudgingly handing over his keys, he made the man promise that they would donate it to a hospital of his own choice. This made him feel better than just abandoning it somewhere in the forest.

The five of them were ushered through hills and a leafless forest, whose sharp branches cut their faces relentlessly. In a short time, the feeling of unbearable cold was gone as they ran up and down the hills.

Not being able to see properly because of the dark, they often fell on the hard frozen ground and were soon bruised all over. None of this mattered, of course, as Sandor thought of the AVO and the Russians who were probably following not far behind them. But he felt safe in the company of these good people. They were honest, helpful and, most of all, knowledgeable about the border area.

Kati held Barna's hand tightly throughout the ordeal, not taking any chances on losing her only remaining son.

They were impressed at how expertly their guides operated, avoiding all the guards positioned throughout the border, delivering them through a frozen swamp to freedom.

One of the men came to a sudden halt, and crouched. He waited a moment, motioning for everyone to do the same. He ventured forward and passed a small hill to scout out the conditions. The reeds were undisturbed, nothing moved. He was satisfied. He ran down the hill to test the soil for its hardness and it was good, too. He gave a short scout's whistle for them to follow. When they reached him, he pointed in the direction of a distant, blue glow in the horizon. "That is freedom. It's Austria," he told them.

As they stared, catching their breaths, their hearts filled with hope. On both sides, not too far in the distance, they saw flares go up into the sky. Reaching their zenith, they hung there for a moment, illuminating the sky and land bellow. The hard rattle of machinegun fire followed. They looked at the men, frightened. Had they been brought to a trap, or had their guides lost their way? Were they surrounded? Would they be captured?

One of the men sensed their doubt and whispered, "Don't worry, as long as they are busy killing the people escaping on both sides of the swamp, you are safe to go. Just stay facing the lights at all times, and you will get there." The thought of people being shot and killed all around them made them feel sick with guilt. Still, they felt fortunate to have the advantage. They bid farewell to their guides, who disappeared into the dark night. They stood there, frightened and insecure for a moment. Kati broke the silence and urged, "Let's hurry!"

Everyone in the group crouched to avoid being seen by possible stray guards. Cautiously and quickly they started their escape. A meandering path took them through the reeds, across the frozen swamps, towards the faint, blue lights of freedom.

****

Penetrating screams surrounded Balazs. To avoid detection, the train's engineer had earlier turned off the lights, leaving everyone insecure in the dark. Only the sounds gave hints as to what was happening. The people hanging outside in cold and those near the windows had the advantage of visual information.

The border was nearing as the train sped confidently ahead with its full cargo to freedom. Unfortunately, the earlier fears of Balazs came to pass. The Russians had heard from informants about the intended breakout. Instead of preventing its departure, they cruelly waited in ambush to destroy it just before it reached freedom. Several tanks blocked the train tracks with floodlights to stop the speeding train, knowing full well that the drivers were not going to chance derailing and having everyone's death on their hands. The Russian commander, luckily for the passengers, was incompetent, and lined his soldiers up for the ambush on one side only.

When the engineers of the train saw what was in store for them, they did as the Russians were expecting. They did not risk the lives of the people. When the madly speeding train finally came to a screeching halt, the engineers hoped their passengers could take advantage of the commander's obvious blunder in the positioning of his men.

With the sudden stop, the bodies flew forward on top of each other. Many were severely injured, and some were crushed, dying instantly. An explosion was followed with machine-gun fire. Bullets flew everywhere, and splinters of train particles filled the air. Balazs's legs were trapped under lifeless bodies. He could not wriggle free. He struggled to push his body toward the opposite side, away from where the shattered glass shards and the spray of victims' blood were coming.

He felt like he had at the Parliament with his parents, but perhaps this time his fate was sealed. Balazs was convinced this was his end. He would die here. His parents would know nothing of his fate, and may never find his dead body. As the images of his life went before him, his thoughts were interrupted. Windows were opening fast on the opposite side from which the machine-gun fire was coming. People piled out as fast as they could, pulling others with them. The panic became incredible, as people tried to flee from the carnage.

Suddenly, Balazs became airborne. Huge, powerful hands grabbed the scruff of his neck and crotch and heaved him forward, right through one of the closed windows, his head breaking the glass. Flying through the air, Balazs landed on top of people who had fallen into the ditch before him. His thick, sheepskin coat softened his fall. When he quickly examined his body for injuries, he discovered the two flask of brandy still intact.

A large figure climbed through the broken window after him and landed loudly, feet first on the gravel by the tracks. He recognized the shape of the miner, who wasted no time taking two large flying leaps over the scrambling bodies. Like a black puma, he disappeared into the night, toward the direction of the distant blue lights. Balazs got to his feet. Following the blue lights, he, too, melted into the darkness.

AFTERWORD

AFTER SUCCESSFULLY CROSSING the border on Nov 21, 1956, I was moved through several refugee camps and ended up at Eisenstadt Castle, outside of Vienna, Austria. The castle had been converted into a refugee camp, where the Austrian people were most generous in helping. My parents searched via the radio for me, and received an anonymous call reporting that I had been seen alive. After spending several days sleeping in piles of hay among hundreds of other homeless refugees and wondering about our future, Kati, my relentless "mother," and my father, Sandor, found me at 3am after tireless and intensive searches through many camps.

Because of my father's fame, our family was granted special status with immediate asylum to the United States. Our flight was on a four-engine old military prop plane. After surviving a bumpy emergency crash landing at Ireland's Shannon Airport, we flew to the USA and arrived at Camp Kilmer in New Jersey.

We spent a short time there as my father was awarded "honorary citizenship" to the state of Rhode Island by the governor with the stipulation that, if we should settle there permanently, we would receive a home and an automobile.

After spending our first Christmas with the generous John Sweeney family in Hope Valley RI., my father decided to take our family to New York. On the way, he was invited to visit a distant relative who was living in Connecticut, Jolie Gabor.

She was an earlier refugee who escaped the Nazis 10 years before. We brought along father's long-time friend from Budapest, Mr. Odon Szigeti, whom we had discovered at Camp Kilmer. Jolie and Odon fell in love at first sight and were married three months later in March 1957.

As years passed, Jolie Gabor became a life-long friend and mentor to me. Zsa Zsa Gabor, her beautiful and witty daughter, continued the same kindness toward my family after Jolie's death.

After settling in NYC, father received The Rockefeller Foundation Scholarship to study English. Having a brilliant mind, he excelled quickly. Within one year, he was not only fluent in English, but also appeared Off-Broadway. His first role, ironically, was in Chekhov's play the *Three Sisters*. He played the Russian general.

Soon, he was on Broadway as well, and performing in many TV series including *Mission Impossible, It Takes a Thief, The Defenders, Bonanza*, and *Sea Hunt*. He played a major role with Gregory Peck at the NYC Lincoln Center *in The Matter of Oppenheimer*. In Los Angeles, he appeared with Jack Lemon in *Idiot's Delight*, and on Broadway in New York in *Barefoot in the Park* with Myrna Loy and Robert Redford. He appeared with Charles Loughton, Celeste Holm, Hermina Gingold, Robert Wagner, and Hugh O'Brian among others. His major film roles in the US included Hitchcock's *Topaz* and *The Sunshine Patriot*.

My parents lived in New York City until 1967. They then moved to Minneapolis, where he acted in the plays of the dissident Russian playwright Aleksandr Solzhenitsyn at the Guthrie Theater. They also lived for several years in Chicago and in Hollywood, California.

Meanwhile, Mr. and Mrs. Robert P. Morningstar, the owners of the Paisley Chemical factory in NYC, lovingly provided Barna and me with the finest private school education from schools, such as Storm King School on Cornwall on The Hudson, Peddie School in Hightstown NJ, and Eron Preparatory in NYC. I was awarded a scholarship to Pratt Institute in NYC, but, to the dismay of the Morningstars, I chose instead to attend the Fine Arts Academy in Vienna, Austria. Later, I switched to the applied arts school, the Bauhaus, and the Angevandte Kunst school in Vienna. Before returning to the USA, I took a risk, and legally crossed the Hungarian border to visit Paula and Eugene, whom I found in good health. They continued to live into their early 90s.

In time, the Hungarian government realized that if all the refugees would return to visit with US dollars to spend, it would benefit. Therefore, they passed an amnesty to all the 1956 refugees.

In 1967, I convinced my parents to visit Hungary, despite their grave fears. Thousands awaited their return with cheers and flowers at the train arriving from Vienna. In 1976, father permanently returned with mother to Budapest, after spending 20 colorful years in the US, to reclaim their successful positions in the arts. This was the result of several visiting delegations dispatched to the States by the Hungarian Communist government, aiming to convince them of their safety.

In the following 20 years of working in Budapest, my father received all the awards an artist possibly could, many of which were denied him before the revolution. Sadly, Hungary still lingered under the same cruel political and economic system. Kati did not pursue her field in the US or in Budapest, because she was left disabled by a malpractice hip operation in NYC in 1961.

Despite her constant struggle with pain, she remained a positive, loving mother and an inspiring wife. She did not live to see Hungary's liberation from the Russian occupation, as she passed away in 1989 at the early age of 67 from cancer. With the Soviet system's collapse in 1991, the Russians finally left Hungary.

With his re-established success, my father regained his wealth. Unfortunately, shortly after my mother's death, he married a "gold digger." The marriage lasted just two years. After a financially draining divorce, his ex-wife's girlfriend, a mediocre opera singer, decades junior, befriended him. While dating her and under her "expert" care, my father fell into a mysterious five-week coma. Many people, including my brother and our spouses, observed her on several occasions administering Sandor's heart medication in Scotch. After surviving his first coma, he left the hospital to discover that he was miraculously married to this new girlfriend.

Somehow, his entire will had also been re-written with little mention of Barna or me. While in the "care" of this "loyal wife", he soon entered into another four-week coma.

This time, she did not contact any family members regarding his condition. He never regained consciousness and passed away at the age of 83. Only after his death and her invitation to us to attend his funeral were we made aware of his last hospital stay.

Since 1956, excluding the time I spent in Europe for my studies, I've lived six years in New York State, three in Chicago, five in Los Angeles, four in Connecticut and 20 years in Hawaii. In 1993, my family and I moved to Raleigh, N.C., where I live and work today as an artist. I have two wonderful grown-up sons.

The risk I took crossing the border in 1956 was not in vain as ever since then I have had the privilege to live in freedom and to be protected by a republic. This land still inspires the world with its ideas of freedom and liberty.

To view my works of art, please visit the website at www.balazsart.com.

Because information seeped through the "Iron Curtain" regarding the advantages of freedom under Democracy and Capitalism, Communism collapsed in the imperialist Soviet Union, and its occupied territories. Russians and their subjects experienced first hand the terrors of Communism, and the inefficiency of Socialism.

Because of complacency and the lack of information regarding their inherited freedoms and privileges, people in the United States will bring about the collapse of their system. They will lose private ownership, and the freedom to excel. Through ignorance, the American masses and the "intelligensia" are slowly seduced by the empty promises and lies of Socialism. Perhaps we will wake up before it's too late.

Listening to our media and our politicians in the USA, I hear the echoes of the same double talk and rhetoric I heard six decades ago in Communist Soviet occupied Hungary. Because of my past experiences, I recognize the direction we are heading.